Baby Names For Boys & Girls That Really Rock (2014)

Louise Nolan

Paperback and electronic versions published by:
Magnificent Milestones, Inc.

ISBN: 9781933819747

Disclaimer:

Table of Contents

Chapter 1. Introduction: The Challenges of Choosing the Perfect Name

Few things are more exciting - or complex - than choosing a child's name. The stakes are incredibly high: this beautiful little boy or girl, who has no say in the matter, must live with *your* decision for the rest of his/her life. Even worse, you must make that decision before you know your child's personality and temperament, which determines whether or not the name you have chosen will truly "fit" him/her.

Years ago, when I perused various books of baby names, I was intrigued by the authors' arbitrary "rules" for first, middle, and last names. Yet, in reality, the beauty of a name is subjective - and what one person considers an excellent choice, another person may not. Thus, I offer only one hard and fast rule in this book: the only opinions that matter are those of the *parents* who will love and raise the child they are naming. Other people may agree or disagree with your choice, but they don't have to live with it - and their input should be considered accordingly.

That being said, there are several factors to consider when choosing a name:

1. **Tradition / Modern.** Do you want a masculine/feminine name or something that is gender neutral? Likewise, do you favor traditional names or something modern or unisex? The difference:

Felicia, Savannah, Evangelina	vs.	Blake, Brett, Flynn
Alexander, Maximilian, Jonathan	vs.	Quinn, Rain, Tai

2. **The family's last name.** Ideally, the child's first, middle, and last names should have a pleasant flow. Ironically, what is "pleasing" to one family may seem harsh and abrupt to another.

For many parents, length and alliteration are also critical. Do you want your child to have a short name that is easy to write and spell - or do you believe that the beauty and flow of a longer name are worth the trade-off?

Patricia Paulina Post	vs.	Jane Lee Post
Maximilian Michael Miles	vs.	John Mark Miles

3. **The uniqueness of the name.** Most parents follow trends, rather than start them. As a result, there are usually five or six students with the same name in every classroom, simply because it was popular the year they were born. In contrast, there will inevitably be one or two students in the same school who have unique names that no one has heard before.

Which of these scenarios do you prefer? Do you want your child to have a popular name that is easy to spell and pronounce, but not particularly creative? Or, do you favor distinctive names that will garner your child (possibly unwanted) attention? The difference:

Sophia Ella White	vs.	Moonbeam Destiny White
Michael John Stanton	nvs.	Rebel Legend Stanton

Thankfully, there are thousands of names that fall between these two extremes that you can choose, depending upon your personal and familial preferences. When you consider your options, bear in mind: you are making this decision on behalf of a child whose personality may be very different from your own. Are you willing to take a risk - or would you prefer to play it safe?

4. **The longevity of the name**. That cute baby in your arms will eventually become a successful adult with dreams and aspirations of his/her own. Will the name you choose last a lifetime? In making this decision, consider the following questions - and whether the answers make a difference to you:

a. If given the choice between a physician named Sonia or Buffy, which would you choose?

b. Likewise, can you imagine a district attorney - or circuit court judge - named Bliss or Genesis?

The choice you make will affect how your child is perceived for her *entire life*. What seems "cute" now may not be nearly as desirable on a professional resume.

5. **Consider the initials** your child will have if you choose a particular name. If possible, avoid embarrassing combinations, such as IOU, LOL, PIG, FAG, and WTF. Many times, you can avoid bad combinations by choosing an alternative middle name.

6. If you choose a long or formal name, **consider the nickname** the child is likely to inherit. Some names, such as Katherine and Elizabeth, have multiple options, while others have only one. Even worse, once your child enrolls in school, you are unlikely to control whether or not an undesirable nickname "sticks." Bottom line: if you don't want your kids called Trish or Ginny, don't name them Patricia or Virginia.

7. **Consider the spelling and pronunciation** of the name, which can be a source of confusion and frustration for many children. If you name your child Epiphany or Xaviera, there is an excellent chance that she will spend her entire lifetime explaining to people how to spell and pronounce it. This isn't "bad," per se, but it may be annoying for your child.

8. **Consider the meaning of the name**, if that is important to you. Unfortunately, some popular names have truly awful meanings:

Cameron means "crooked nose"
Kennedy means "ugly head"

Granted, most people do not know - or care about - the meaning of a given name. They simply take it at face value. But if the translation of a name (and the underlying connotation) bothers you, an alternative choice may be best.

9. **Pressures from relatives to choose a "family" name**. There is nothing inherently right or wrong with naming children after beloved relatives. In many cases, it is a lovely way to honor and preserve the memory of someone important to your family. Nevertheless, problems arise when:

a. the name is question is not particularly pleasing
b. the relatives pushing it will not take no for an answer

In these cases, middle names can be an excellent solution. In my experience, a child's middle name is usually chosen for one of three reasons:

a. it is a short, pleasant, and generic "placeholder" between the first and last names:

Examples: Stephanie Ann Miller
                Alexander Lee Ruggerio

b. it is the "second choice" name that was vetoed at the last moment:

Examples:　　　Millicent Marianna Miller
　　　　　　　　Alexandra Augusta Ruggerio

c. it is the name of a beloved relative that the parents did not want to use as the first name:

Examples:　　　Jennifer Mildred Miller
　　　　　　　　Jada Esther Ruggerio

Rather than argue with your sister, mother and spouse about a particular choice, using it as a middle name can be a great solution.

10. **Following - or avoiding - trends**. In recent years, there have been several trends in baby names that have influenced parents' choices, including:

- unisex (gender neutral) names
- last names as first names
- naming children after famous places
- creating unique names by adding/deleting letters and changing consonants or vowels
- using names from different cultures or eras
- naming children after celebrities, fictional characters, or historical figures

As a result, baby names are more varied and exotic than ever before. Nevertheless, some parents have resisted these trends in favor of classic and traditional names that will stand the test of time. This book, which presents more than 5,000 names for boys and girls, offers extraordinary choices for *both* groups of parents- and for those who are still sitting on the fence. Use the lists as a starting point - and see what works best for you and your family. Experiment with different names that capture the sound and feel that you desire. Choose the name that perfectly reflects the baby you are carrying - and your hopes and dreams for her future.

How to Use this Book

By design, this book is arranged in a logical way:

1. the chapters are clearly labeled to guide your search

2. the names are presented in alphabetical order (unless noted otherwise)

3. the meaning of each name is clearly presented, although some names have multiple meanings, depending upon the original language and interpretation. Due to these variations, we encourage you to conduct additional research into the history and derivation of the names that you choose, both to learn more about them and to explore alternative spellings. By doing so, you can confirm that the name truly feels right and has no negative or unusual connotations.

4. in recent years, parents have expressed a preference for unisex, or gender neutral names that they can use for their babies, regardless of their sex. To honor this request - and to showcase the dozens of names that can be used for both boys and girls, this book presents an entire chapter of unisex names for you to consider.

5. finally, for readers who prefer a direct approach - or simply get tired or overwhelmed by the "themes" we have used, the final chapter of the book presents an alphabetical list of more than 5,000 names for boys and girls.

Why 5,000, rather than the 100,000 presented in other books? Because we have streamlined the approach by focusing on the names that you are most likely to use, rather than including odd and esoteric choices from 200 years ago that no one can spell or pronounce. We have also avoided the temptation to turn Katherine into 20 different names, simply by making a few spelling changes.

And, that, ultimately, is the final topic of this chapter: the emerging trend of creating unique and customized names by varying the spelling of a classic name. In most cases, **that** is how most baby name books manage to present 50,000 choices - they include every possible alternative way to spell every name they present. On one hand, that is valid, because many parents like the idea of a unique name. On the other hand, it is somewhat misleading - is the name Caryn really all that different from Karen? And do you really *want* to change the spelling of a classic name - knowing that your child will have to explain, correct, and re-spell it for the dozens of teachers, employers, and business contacts who get it wrong?

If the answer is yes, here is a quick summary of how to create a customized name:

1. **Change a consonant:**

C to K: Catherine/Katherine, Crystal/Krystal, Christine/Kristine
C to CH: Cris/Chris, Ciara/Chiara
C to S: Cheryl/Sheryl, Cynthia/Synthia
F to Ph: Filippa/Phillippa, Felicia/Phylicia
G to J: Gillian/Jillian
X to J: Xaviera/Javiera
Z to S: Inez/Ines
H to S: Janesha/Janessa

2. **Change a vowel:**

A to E: Megan/Meagan
A to Y   Megan/Megyn
CE to SS: Jocelyn/Josslyn
CI to SH: Lacrecia/Lacresha, Marcia/Marsha
E to Y: Karen/ Karyn, Hailee/Hailey
E to O: Conner/Connor, Ellery/Ellory
E to EI: Andre/Andrei, Keegan/Keigan
EO to E: Geoffrey/Jeffrey
I to Y: Nanci/ Nancy, Brandi/Brandy, Katherine/Kathryn
I to E: Austin/Austen
IE to Y: Debbie/Debby
O to EAU: Bo/Beau
U to EW: Drew/Dru
U to W: Laurence/Lawrence

3. **Add (or subtract) a letter or phrase:**

Add an O: Alphonso/Alphonse
Add an S: Apollo/Apollos
Add an E: Clancy/Clancey, Emil/Emile, Axl/Axel
Add an L: Alan/Allen, Chancellor/Chancelor
Add a "son:"   Anders/Anderson
Add a "ton:"   Fuller/Fullerton, Jack/Jackson
Add a "de:"   Wayne/Dewayne
Add a "mac:"   Kenzie/Mackenzie
Add a "lyn:"   Brooke/Brooklyn, Joss/Josslyn

4. **Combine two names into one:**

Ashlyn: (American): a combination of Ashley and Lynn
Deandra: (American): a combination of Dee and Andrea
Deangelo: (Italian): a combination of De and Angelo
Kaylin: (American): a combination of Kay and Lynn

5. **Use non-traditional words as names**, such as places, surnames, and personal ideals (such as honor, heaven, and bliss). The chapters in this book will provide the inspiration you need to find distinctive and creative names from unusual and unlikely places. For more traditional parents, we have also included quality choices from history, literature, and the Bible. Use the lists as guidance and inspiration for your search - and choose the name for your baby that truly works best for you.

Chapter 2. The Most Popular Names for Boys & Girls

For many prospective parents, this chapter is a logical place to start - with the most popular names for babies in the United States. Ironically, readers like this chapter for two very different reasons: some love the idea of giving their child a popular and trendy name, while others hate the concept - and immediately dismiss all top names from consideration.

Regardless of your own inclination, it's fun to explore the current trends in names on a national basis, if only to know what other parents consider trendy and desirable. As you read and consider each name, you can use this information to add (or subtract) various possibilities from your list.

Finally, a word about "popular" names in a nation as large and diverse as the United States: different names are popular in different regions, depending upon the cultural, spiritual and socioeconomic backgrounds of their residents. In an area with many Asian families, for example, names such as Ling and Ming will be more popular than those in other communities. Likewise, in regions that are predominantly Christian, Biblical names will be more popular than those in communities that are spiritually diverse.

On a practical basis, this information may not affect you (or the choices that you make). But it *does* explain why the variation among children's names is so broad in different parts of the country. In some cities, there will be five Emmas in every classroom, but no one named Ling or Carmella. In other places, there will be several Javieras, but no one named Cynthia or Kristen. Ultimately, the names in this chapter are the most popular in the US *on average*, which may (or may not) reflect the demographics in your own community.

Finally, a quick word about the source of this data, which is the U.S. Social Security Administration (SSA). Every child in the U.S. must have a Social Security number in order to be claimed on his/her parents' federal income tax forms (and to qualify for various benefit programs). Every year, the Social Security Administration records the popularity of names based on these applications and releases that information to the public. The SSA does not, however, break the data down by race or ethnicity - as a result, the rankings are averaged over all U.S. citizens who applied for a Social Security number in their child's name that year.

The names in this chapter are the most popular choices for babies who were born in the U.S. in 2012, which is the last year for which data is available. We have presented them in order of popularity, from 1 to 100.

The 100 Most Popular Names for Boys

1. Jacob: (Biblical): supplanter; (Hebrew): he grasps the heel

2. Mason: (French & English): stone worker

3. Ethan: (Hebrew & Biblical): firm, strong

4. Noah: (Biblical): rest, peace; (Hebrew): comfort, long-lived

5. William: (English, German & French): protector

6. Liam: (Irish & Gaelic): determined protector

7. Jayden: (American): God has heard

8. Michael: (Biblical & Hebrew): like God

9. Alexander: (Greek): protector of mankind

10. Aiden: (Irish, Celtic & Gaelic): fire, fiery

11. Daniel: (Hebrew & Biblical): God is my judge; (Irish & Welsh): attractive

12. Matthew: (Hebrew & Biblical): gift of the Lord

13. Elijah: (Biblical): the Lord is my God; (Hebrew): Jehovah is God

14. James: (English): supplant, replace; (Israel): supplanter

15. Anthony: (English & Biblical): worthy of praise

16. Benjamin: (English, Hebrew & Biblical): son of my right hand

17. Joshua: (Hebrew & Biblical): Jehovah saves

18. Andrew: (English, Scottish & Biblical): manly; brave

19. David: (Hebrew, Scottish & Welsh): beloved

20. Joseph: (Biblical): God will increase; (Hebrew): may Jehovah add/give

21. Logan: (Irish): small cove; (Scottish): Finnian's servant; (Gaelic): from the hollow

22. Jackson: (English): son of Jack; (Scottish): God has been gracious

23. Christopher: (Biblical): Christ-bearer; (English): he who holds Christ in his heart

24. Gabriel: (Israel): hero of God; (Hebrew): man of God; (Spanish): God is my strength

25. Samuel: (Israel): God hears; (Hebrew): name of God

26. Ryan: (Gaelic): little king; (Irish): kindly, young royalty

27. Lucas: (Gaelic, English & Latin America): light

28. John: (Israel): God is gracious; Jehovah has been gracious

29. Nathan: (Hebrew & Israel): gift of God

30. Isaac: (Biblical): he will laugh

31. Dylan: (English & Welsh): born from the ocean, son of the wave; (Gaelic): faithful

32. Caleb: (Hebrew): resembling an aggressive dog

33. Christian: (English & Irish): follower of Christ

34. Landon: (English): grassy plain; from the long hill

35. Jonathan: (Hebrew): Jehovah has given: (Israel): gift of God

36. Carter: (English): cart driver

37. Luke: (Greek & Latin America): light

38. Owen: (English, Welsh & Celtic); young warrior; (Irish): born to nobility

39. Brayden: (Irish & English): broad hillside; (Scottish): salmon

40. Gavin: (English): little hawk; (Welsh): hawk of the battle

41. Wyatt: (English): guide, wide, wood, famous bearer; (French): son of the forest guide

42. Isaiah: (Hebrew): the Lord is generous; (Israel): salvation by God

43. Henry: (English, German & French): rules his household

44. Eli: (Hebrew): ascended, uplifted, high; (Greek): defender of man

45. Hunter: (English): one who hunts

46. Jack: (English): God is gracious; (Hebrew): supplanter

47. Evan: (English): God is good; (Welsh): young; (Celtic): young fighter

48. Jordan: (Hebrew): to flow down; (Israel): descendant

49. Nicholas: (Greek): victorious people

50. Tyler: (English): maker of tiles

51. Aaron: (Jewish): enlightened; (Hebrew): lofty, exalted

52. Jeremiah: (Hebrew): may Jehovah exalt; (Israel): sent by God

53. Julian/Julius/Julio: (Spanish, French & Greek): youthful

54. Cameron: (Irish & Gaelic): crooked nose

55. Levi/Levin: (Hebrew & Israel): attached, united as one

56. Brandon: (Irish): little raven

57. Angel: (Spanish & Greek): angelic

58. Austin: (English): from the name Augustin, which means revered

59. Connor: (Irish): strong willed, much wanted

60. Adrian: (German, Spanish & Italian): dark; (Greek): rich

61. Robert: (English, French, German & Scottish): famed, bright, shining

62. Charles: (English): strong, manly

63. Thomas: (Hebrew, Greek & Dutch): twin

64. Sebastian: (Greek): the revered one

65. Colton: (English): coal town, from the dark town

66. **Jaxon**: (American): son of Jack

67. **Kevin:** (Irish & Gaelic): handsome, beautiful; (Celtic): gentle

68. **Zachary:** (Hebrew): Jehovah has remembered; (Israel): remembered by the Lord

69. **Aydan:** (Irish, Celtic & Gaelic): fire, fiery

70. **Dominic**: (Spanish): born on a Sunday

71. **Blake:** (English): pale, fair

72. **Jose**: (Spanish): God will add

73.**Oliver:** (French, English, Danish & Latin America): the olive tree; (German): elf army

74. **Justin:** (English & French): just, true; (Irish): judicious

75. **Bentley:** (English): from the bent grass meadow

76. **Jason:** (Greek): to heal

77. **Chase:** (English): hunter

78. **Ian:** (Scottish): gift from God

79. **Josiah:** (Hebrew): Jehovah has healed; (Israel): God has healed

80. **Parker:** (English): keeper of the park or forest

81. **Xavier**: (Spanish): owner of a new house

82. **Adam:** (Hebrew): red; (Israel): man of the earth; (English): of the red earth

83. **Cooper:** (English): barrel maker

84. **Nathaniel:** (Hebrew & Israel): gift of God

85. **Grayson:** (English): son of the bailiff

86. **Jace**: (American): God is my salvation

87. **Carson:** (English): son who lives in the swamp

88. **Nolan:** (Irish & Gaelic): famous; (Celtic): noble

89. **Tristan:** (English, Celtic & French): outcry, tumult; (Welsh): noisy; (Irish): bold

90. **Luis:** (Spanish): famous warrior

91. **Brody:** (Irish): brother, from the muddy place; (Scottish): second son

92. **Juan:** (Hebrew): gift from God; (Spanish): God is gracious

93. **Hudson:** (English): son of the hooded man

94. Bryson: (American): son of a nobleman

95. Carlos: (Spanish): a free man

96. Easton: (English): from east town

97. Damian: (Greek): one who tames others

98. Alex: (Greek): protector of mankind

99. Kayden: (American): fighter

100. Ryder: (English): knight

The 100 Most Popular Names for Girls

1. Sophia: (Greek & Biblical): wisdom

2. Emma: (English, Danish & German): whole, complete, universal

3. Isabella: (Hebrew): devoted to God; (Spanish): God is bountiful; (Biblical): consecrated to God

4. Olivia: (Spanish & Italian): olive; (Biblical): peace of the olive tree

5. Ava: (Latin America): like a bird

6. Emily: (Latin America): admiring

7. Abigail: (Hebrew): father rejoiced; (Biblical): source of joy

8. Mia: (Italian): my; (Biblical): mine

9. Madison: (English): son of Matthew

10. Elizabeth: (English): my God is bountiful; (Hebrew & Biblical): consecrated to God

11. Chloe: (Greek): verdant, blooming

12. Ella: (English); beautiful fairy; (Spanish): she

13. Avery: (English): counselor, sage, wise

14. Addison: (English): son of Adam

15. Aubrey: (English): one who rules with elf-wisdom

16. Lily/Lilly: (Hebrew, English & Latin America): lily, blossoming flower

17. Natalie: (French): to be born at Christmas; (Slovakian): to be born

18. Sofia: (Greek & Biblical): wisdom

19. Charlotte: (French): feminine

20. **Zoey:** (Greek): life, alive

21. **Grace/Gracie:** (Latin America): grace of God; (American): land of grace

22. **Hannah:** (English & Hebrew): favor, grace; (Biblical): grace of God

23. **Amelia:** (English & Latin America): industrious, striving

24. **Harper:** (English): musician, harp player

25. **Lillian**: (Latin): resembling the lily

26. **Samantha:** (Hebrew & Biblical): listener of God

27. **Evelyn:** (Celtic): light; (English & Hebrew): life, hazelnut

28. **Victoria:** (Latin America): winner

29. **Brooklyn:** (English): water, stream

30. **Zoe:** (Greek): life, alive

31. **Layla:** (Indian): born at night; (Arabian): dark beauty

32. **Hailey:** (English): hero, field of hay

33. **Leah:** (Hebrew): weary

34. **Kaylee:** (American): pure

35. **Anna:** (Hebrew): favor or grace; (Native American): mother; (Israel): gracious

36. **Aaliyah:** (Arabic): an ascender; (Muslim): exalted; (American): immigrant to a new home

37. **Gabriella:** (Israel & Hebrew): God gives strength; (Italian): woman of God

38. **Allison**: (English): noble, truthful, strong character

39. **Nevaeh:** (American): gift from God, heaven spelled backwards

40. **Alexis**: (English): helper, defender; (Biblical): protector of mankind

41. **Audrey**: (English): noble strength

42. **Savannah:** (Spanish): open plain, field

43. **Sarah:** (Hebrew, Spanish & Biblical): princess

44. **Alyssa:** (Greek): logical

45. **Claire:** (English): clear; (French): bright

46. **Taylor:** (English & French): a tailor

47. **Riley**: (English): from the rye clearing; (Irish): a small stream

48. Camilla: (Italian): a noble virgin, a ceremonial attendant

49. Arianna: (Greek & Italian): holy

50. Ashley: (English & Biblical): lives in the ash tree

51. Brianna: (Irish): strong; (Celtic & English): she ascends

52. Sophie: (Greek & Biblical): wisdom

53. Peyton: (English): village

54. Bella: (Hebrew): devoted to God; (Spanish & Latin America): beautiful

55. Khloe: (Greek): verdant, blooming

56. Genesis: (Hebrew): origin, birth; (Israel): beginning

57. Alexa: (Greek, English & Latin America): defender of mankind

58. Serenity: (Latin & English): peaceful

59. Kylie: (Australian): a boomerang

60. Aubree: (English): one who rules with elf-wisdom

61. Scarlett: (English): red

62. Stella: (French, Italian & Greek): star

63. Maya: (Indian): an illusion or dream; (Hebrew): woman of the water

64. Katherine: (Irish): clear; (English): pure; (Greek): pure, virginal

65. Julia: (French): youthful; (Latin America): soft-haired, youthful

66. Lucy: (Latin America): bringer of light

67. Madelyn: (Greek): high tower

68. Autumn: (English & Latin America): the fall season

69. Makayla: (English & Irish): like God

70. Kayla: (Irish & Greek): pure and beloved

71. Mackenzie: (Irish & Scottish): fair, favored one

72. Lauren: (French): crowned with laurel

73. Gianna: (Italian): diminutive form of Giovanna, which means God is gracious

74. Ariana: (Greek & Italian): holy

75. Faith: (English): faithful; (Latin America): to trust

76. Alexandra: (Greek, English & Latin America): defender of mankind

77. Melanie: (Greek): dark-skinned beauty

78. Sydney: (French): from Saint Denis

79 Bailey: (English): bailiff, steward, public official

80. Caroline: (Mexican): beautiful woman; (French & English): song of happiness

81. Naomi: (Hebrew & Israel): pleasant

82. Morgan: (Celtic): lives by the sea; (Welsh): bright sea

83. Kennedy: (Gaelic): a helmeted chief

84. Ellie: (English): a diminutive form of Ellen, which means light

85. Jasmine: (Persian): a climbing plant; (English): a fragrant flower

86. Eva: (Hebrew, Israel, Indian & Spanish): one who gives life

87. Skylar: (English): a scholar

88. Kimberly: (English): ruler

89. Violet: (French): resembling the flower

90. Molly: (Israel & English): bitter

91. Aria: (Italian): melody

92. Jocelyn: (Latin): cheerful, happy

93. Trinity: (Latin): the holy three

94. London: (English): capital of England; fortress of the moon

95. Lydia: (Greek): beautiful maiden

96. Madeline: (Greek): high tower

97. Reagan: (Celtic): regal; (Irish): son of the small ruler

98. Piper: (English): plays the flute

99. Andrea: (Greek & Latin): courageous, strong

100. Annabelle: (Italian): graceful and beautiful

Chapter 3. The Evolution of Names Since 1900

While reading this book, you may wonder how (and why) names have evolved over time - and why some of your choices sound really strange to your parents and grandparents. In Chapter 2, we listed the most popular baby names in the United States last year. In this chapter, we will take a look back at the same data at ten-year increments, beginning in 1900.

This exercise is fun for several reasons. First, it will allow you to see the types of names that were popular when your parents and grandparents were making the same decision that you are making today (when no one, and I mean, *no one*, named their baby Axel). Second, it reveals the names that are truly timeless - and those that only stayed popular for a few years. Third, it may spark your interest in names that you might otherwise not have considered, either for your child's first or middle name. You've just begun your search; before you consider a trendy name, it's worth looking back at some genuine classics, which were inspired by the leaders and celebrities of their time.

All data is from the official records of the U.S. Social Security Administration. For each year, names are presented in the order of popularity, from 1 to 20.

1900 - Boys Names

1. **John:** (Israel): God is gracious; Jehovah has been gracious
2. **William:** (English, German & French): protector
3. **James:** (English): supplant, replace; (Israel): supplanter
4. **George:** (English): farmer
5. **Charles:** (English): strong, manly
6. **Robert:** (English, French, German & Scottish): famed, bright, shining
7. **Joseph:** (Biblical): God will increase; (Hebrew): may Jehovah add/give
8. **Frank**: (English): free man
9. **Edward:** (English): wealthy guardian; (German): strong as a boar
10. **Henry:** (English, German & French): rules his household
11. **Thomas:** (Hebrew, Greek & Dutch): twin
12. **Walter**: (German): the commander of the army
13. **Harry:** (German): home or house ruler
14. **Willie**: (English, German & French): a diminutive form of William, which means protector
15. **Arthur:** (English): bear, stone
16. **Albert:** (English & German): noble, bright
17. **Fred:** (German): peaceful ruler
18. **Clarence**: (English & Latin America): clear, luminous
19. **Paul:** (English & French): small, apostle in the Bible
20. **Harold:** (Scandinavian): ruler of the army

1900 - Girls Names

1. **Mary:** (Biblical, English & Slovakian): bitter
2. **Helen:** (Greek): light
3. **Anna/Ana:** (Hebrew): favor or grace; (Native American): mother; (Israel): gracious
4. **Margaret:** (Greek & Latin America): a pearl
5. **Ruth:** (Hebrew & Israel): companion, friend
6. **Elizabeth:** (English): my God is bountiful; (Hebrew & Biblical): consecrated to God
7. **Florence:** (English): flowering; (Latin America): prosperous
8. **Ethyl:** (English): noble
9. **Marie:** (Latin): bitter
10. **Lillian**: (Latin): resembling the lily
11. **Annie:** diminutive form of Anne, which means favor or grace
12. **Edna:** (Celtic): fire; (Hebrew): rejuvenation; (Israel): spirit renewed
13. **Emma:** (English, Danish & German): whole, complete, universal

14. **Alice**: (Spanish): of the nobility
15. **Bessie**: (English): my God is bountiful
16. **Bertha**: (Germany): bright
17. **Grace**: (Latin America): grace of God; (American): land of grace
18. **Rose**: (English, French & Scottish): flower, a rose; (German): horse, fame
19. **Clara**: (French & Catalonia): clear, bright
20. **Mildred**: (English): gentle counselor

1910 - Boys Names

1. **John:** (Israel): God is gracious; Jehovah has been gracious
2. **James:** (English): supplant, replace; (Israel): supplanter
3. **William:** (English, German & French): protector
4. **Robert:** (English, French, German & Scottish): famed, bright, shining
5. **George:** (English): farmer
6. **Joseph:** (Biblical): God will increase; (Hebrew): may Jehovah add/give
7. **Charles:** (English): strong, manly
8. **Frank**: (English): free man
9. **Edward:** (English): wealthy guardian; (German): strong as a boar
10. **Henry:** (English, German & French): rules his household
11. **Willie:** (English, German & French): a diminutive form of William, which means protector
12. **Thomas:** (Hebrew, Greek & Dutch): twin
13. **Walter**: (German): the commander of the army
14. **Albert:** (English & German): noble, bright
15. **Paul:** (English & French): small, apostle in the Bible
16. **Harry:** (German): home or house ruler
17. **Arthur:** (English): bear, stone
18. **Harold**: (Scandinavian): ruler of the army
19. **Raymond**: (German): wise protector
20. **Clarence**: (English & Latin America): clear, luminous

1910 - Girls Names

1. **Mary:** (Biblical, English & Slovakian): bitter
2. **Helen:** (Greek): light
3. **Margaret:** (Greek & Latin America): a pearl
4. **Dorothy** (Greek): gift of God
5. **Ruth:** (Hebrew & Israel): companion, friend
6. **Anna/Ana:** (Hebrew): favor or grace; (Native American): mother; (Israel): gracious
7. **Elizabeth:** (English): my God is bountiful; (Hebrew & Biblical): consecrated to God
8. **Mildred**: (English): gentle counselor
9. **Marie:** (Latin): bitter
10. **Alice:** (Spanish): of the nobility
11. **Frances**: (Latin America: free
12. **Florence:** (English): flowering; (Latin America): prosperous
13. **Ethyl**: (English): noble
14. **Lillian**: (Latin): resembling the lily
15. **Gladys:** (Welsh): lame
16. **Rose:** (English, French & Scottish): flower, a rose; (German): horse, fame
17. **Evelyn:** (Celtic): light; (English & Hebrew): life, hazelnut
18. **Edna:** (Celtic): fire; (Hebrew): rejuvenation; (Israel): spirit renewed
19. **Annie:** (Hebrew): a diminutive form of Anne, which means favor or grace
20. **Louise**: (German): famous warrior

1920 - Boys Names

1. **John:** (Israel): God is gracious; Jehovah has been gracious
2. **William:** (English, German & French): protector
3. **Robert:** (English, French, German & Scottish): famed, bright, shining
4. **James:** (English): supplant, replace; (Israel): supplanter
5. **Charles:** (English): strong, manly
6. **George:** (English): farmer
7. **Joseph:** (Biblical): God will increase; (Hebrew): may Jehovah add/give
8. **Edward:** (English): wealthy guardian; (German): strong as a boar
9. **Frank**: (English): free man
10. **Richard**: (English, French & German): a strong and powerful ruler
11. **Thomas:** (Hebrew, Greek & Dutch): twin
12. **Harold**: (Scandinavian): ruler of the army
13. **Walter**: (German): the commander of the army
14. **Paul:** (English & French): small, apostle in the Bible
15. **Raymond**: (German): wise protector
16. **Donald:** (Celtic & Gaelic): dark stranger; (Irish, English & Scottish): great leader
17. **Henry:** (English, German & French): rules his household
18. **Arthur:** (English): bear, stone
19. **Albert:** (English & German): noble, bright
20. **Jack:** (English): God is gracious; (Hebrew): supplanter

1920 - Girls Names

1. **Mary:** (Biblical, English & Slovakian): bitter
2. **Dorothy** (Greek): gift of God
3. **Helen:** (Greek): light
4. **Margaret:** (Greek & Latin America): a pearl
5. **Ruth:** (Hebrew & Israel): companion, friend
6. **Mildred**: (English): gentle counselor
7. **Virginia:** (English, Spanish, Italian & Latin America): pure
8. **Elizabeth:** (English): my God is bountiful; (Hebrew & Biblical): consecrated to God
9. **Frances**: (Latin America) free
10. **Anna/Ana:** (Hebrew): favor or grace; (Native American): mother; (Israel): gracious
11. **Betty:** (English): a diminutive form of Elizabeth, which means my God is bountiful, consecrated to God
12. **Evelyn:** (Celtic): light; (English & Hebrew): life, hazelnut
13. **Marie:** (Latin): bitter
14. **Doris:** (Greek): sea
15. **Alice:** (Spanish): of the nobility
16. **Florence:** (English): flowering; (Latin America): prosperous
17. **Irene:** (Greek & Spanish): peaceful
18. **Lillian**: (Latin): resembling the lily
19. **Louise**: (German): famous warrior
20. **Rose:** (English, French & Scottish): flower, a rose; (German): horse, fame

1930 - Boys Names

1. **Robert:** (English, French, German & Scottish): famed, bright, shining
2. **James:** (English): supplant, replace; (Israel): supplanter
3. **John:** (Israel): God is gracious; Jehovah has been gracious
4. **William:** (English, German & French): protector
5. **Richard**: (English, French & German): a strong and powerful ruler
6. **Charles:** (English): strong, manly
7. **Donald:** (Celtic & Gaelic): dark stranger; (Irish, English & Scottish): great leader
8. **George:** (English): farmer

9. **Joseph:** (Biblical): God will increase; (Hebrew): may Jehovah add/give
10. **Edward:** (English): wealthy guardian; (German): strong as a boar
11. **Thomas:** (Hebrew, Greek & Dutch): twin
12. **Paul:** (English & French): small, apostle in the Bible
13. **Frank**: (English): free man
14. **Jack:** (English): God is gracious; (Hebrew): supplanter
15. **David:** (Hebrew, Scottish & Welsh): beloved
16. **Raymond**: (German): wise protector
17. **Kenneth:** (Celtic, Scottish & Irish): handsome; (English): royal obligation
18. **Harold:** (Scandinavian): ruler of the army
19. **Walter:** (German): the commander of the army
20. **Billy**: (English, German & French): a diminutive form of William, which means protector

1930 - Girls Names

1. **Mary:** (Biblical, English & Slovakian): bitter
2. **Betty:** (English): a diminutive form of Elizabeth, which means my God is bountiful, consecrated to God
3. **Dorothy** (Greek): gift of God
4. **Helen:** (Greek): light
5. **Margaret:** (Greek & Latin America): a pearl
6. **Barbara:** (Latin America): stranger
7. **Patricia:** (Spanish & Latin America): noble
8. **Joan**: (Hebrew): gift from God; (English): God is gracious
9. **Doris:** (Greek): sea
10. **Ruth:** (Hebrew & Israel): companion, friend
11. **Shirley**: (English): bright meadow
12. **Virginia:** (English, Spanish, Italian & Latin America): pure
13. **Dolores:** (Spanish): woman of sorrow
14. **Jean:** (Hebrew): God is gracious
15. **Elizabeth:** (English): my God is bountiful; (Hebrew & Biblical): consecrated to God
16. **Frances**: (Latin America) free
17. **Lois:** (Israel): good; (German): famous warrior
18. **Joyce:** (English & Latin America): cheerful, merry
19. **Evelyn:** (Celtic): light; (English & Hebrew): life, hazelnut
20. **Alice:** (Spanish): of the nobility

1940 - Boys Names

1. **James:** (English): supplant, replace; (Israel): supplanter
2. **Robert:** (English, French, German & Scottish): famed, bright, shining
3. **John:** (Israel): God is gracious; Jehovah has been gracious
4. **William:** (English, German & French): protector
5. **Richard**: (English, French & German): a strong and powerful ruler
6. **Charles:** (English): strong, manly
7. **David:** (Hebrew, Scottish & Welsh): beloved
8. **Thomas:** (Hebrew, Greek & Dutch): twin
9. **Donald:** (Celtic & Gaelic): dark stranger; (Irish, English & Scottish): great leader
10. **Ronald:** (English, Gaelic & Scottish): rules with counsel
11. **George:** (English): farmer
12. **Joseph:** (Biblical): God will increase; (Hebrew): may Jehovah add/give
13. **Larry:** (Dutch & Latin America): laurels
14. **Jerry**: (English): a diminutive form of Jerald, which means one who rules with the spear
15. **Kenneth**: (Celtic, Scottish & Irish): handsome; (English): royal obligation
16. **Edward:** (English): wealthy guardian; (German): strong as a boar
17. **Paul:** (English & French): small, apostle in the Bible
18. **Michael:** (Biblical & Hebrew): like God

19. **Gary**: (English): mighty spearman
20. **Frank**: (English): free man

1940 - Girls Names

1. **Mary:** (Biblical, English & Slovakian): bitter
2. **Barbara:** (Latin America): stranger
3. **Patricia:** (Spanish & Latin America): noble
4. **Judith:** (Hebrew): praised; (Israel): from Judah
5. **Betty:** (English): a diminutive form of Elizabeth, which means my God is bountiful, consecrated to God
6. **Carol:** (French): melody, song
7. **Nancy:** (Hebrew & English): grace
8. **Linda:** (Spanish): pretty; (English): lime tree; (German): snake, lime tree
9. **Shirley:** (English): bright meadow
10. **Sandra:** (Greek): helper of humanity; (English): unheeded prophetess
11. **Margaret:** (Greek & Latin America): a pearl
12. **Dorothy** (Greek): gift of God
13. **Joyce:** (English & Latin America): cheerful, merry
14. **Joan**: (Hebrew): gift from God; (English): God is gracious
15. **Carolyn:** (English): joy, song of happiness
16. **Judy:** (Hebrew): praised; (Israel): from Judah
17. **Sharon:** (Hebrew & Israel): a flat clearing
18. **Helen:** (Greek): light
19. **Janet:** (Hebrew & English): gift from God
20. **Elizabeth:** (English): my God is bountiful; (Hebrew & Biblical): consecrated to God

1950 - Boys Names

1. **James:** (English): supplant, replace; (Israel): supplanter
2. **Robert:** (English, French, German & Scottish): famed, bright, shining
3. **John:** (Israel): God is gracious; Jehovah has been gracious
4. **Michael:** (Biblical & Hebrew): like God
5. **William:** (English, German & French): protector
6. **David:** (Hebrew, Scottish & Welsh): beloved
7. **Richard**: (English, French & German): a strong and powerful ruler
8. **Thomas:** (Hebrew, Greek & Dutch): twin
9. **Charles:** (English): strong, manly
10. **Gary**: (English): mighty spearman
11. **Larry:** (Dutch & Latin America): laurels
12. **Ronald:** (English, Gaelic & Scottish): rules with counsel
13. **Joseph:** (Biblical): God will increase; (Hebrew): may Jehovah add/give
14. **Donald:** (Celtic & Gaelic): dark stranger; (Irish, English & Scottish): great leader
15. **Kenneth:** (Celtic, Scottish & Irish): handsome; (English): royal obligation
16. **Steven:** (English & Greek): crowned one
17. **Dennis**: (Greek): wild, frenzied
18. **Paul:** (English & French): small, apostle in the Bible
19. **Stephen**: (English & Greek): crowned one
20. **George:** (English): farmer

1950 - Girls Names

1. **Linda:** (Spanish): pretty; (English): lime tree; (German): snake, lime tree
2. **Mary:** (Biblical, English & Slovakian): bitter
3. **Patricia:** (Spanish & Latin America): noble
4. **Barbara:** (Latin America): stranger
5. **Susan:** (Hebrew): graceful lily; (Israel): lily

6. **Nancy**: (Hebrew & English): grace
7. **Deborah**: (Hebrew & Israel): honey bee
8. **Sandra**: (Greek): helper of humanity; (English): unheeded prophetess
9. **Carol**: (French): melody, song
10. **Kathleen**: (English, Irish & French): diminutive of Katherine, which means pure
11. **Sharon**: (Hebrew & Israel): a flat clearing
12. **Karen**: (Greek): pure
13. **Donna**: (Italian): lady
14. **Brenda**: (Gaelic): little raven; (Scandinavian): sword
15. **Margaret**: (Greek & Latin America): a pearl
16. **Diane**: (Latin America): hunter
17. **Pamela**: (Greek, English & Indian): honey
18. **Janet**: (Hebrew & English): gift from God
19. **Shirley**: (English): bright meadow
20. **Carolyn**: (English): joy, song of happiness

1960 - Boys Names

1. **David**: (Hebrew, Scottish & Welsh): beloved
2. **Michael**: (Biblical & Hebrew): like God
3. **James**: (English): supplant, replace; (Israel): supplanter
4. **John**: (Israel): God is gracious; Jehovah has been gracious
5. **Robert**: (English, French, German & Scottish): famed, bright, shining
6. **Mark**: (Latin): dedicated to Mars, the god of war
7. **William**: (English, German & French): protector
8. **Richard**: (English, French & German): a strong and powerful ruler
9. **Thomas**: (Hebrew, Greek & Dutch): twin
10. **Steven**: (English & Greek): crowned one
11. **Timothy**: (Greek & English): to honor God
12. **Joseph**: (Biblical): God will increase; (Hebrew): may Jehovah add/give
13. **Charles**: (English): strong, manly
14. **Jeffrey**: (English): a man of peace
15. **Kevin**: (Irish & Gaelic): handsome, beautiful; (Celtic): gentle
16. **Kenneth**: (Celtic, Scottish & Irish): handsome; (English): royal obligation
17. **Daniel**: (Hebrew & Biblical): God is my judge; (Irish & Welsh): attractive
18. **Paul**: (English & French): small, apostle in the Bible
19. **Donald**: (Celtic & Gaelic): dark stranger; (Irish, English & Scottish): great leader
20. **Brian**: (Gaelic): noble birth; (Celtic): great strength

1960 - Girls Names

1. **Mary**: (Biblical, English & Slovakian): bitter
2. **Susan**: (Hebrew): graceful lily; (Israel): lily
3. **Linda**: (Spanish): pretty; (English): lime tree; (German): snake, lime tree
4. **Karen**: (Greek): pure
5. **Donna**: (Italian): lady
6. **Lisa**: (German): devoted to God; (Israel): consecrated to God
7. **Patricia**: (Spanish & Latin America): noble
8. **Debra**: (Hebrew & Israel): honey bee
9. **Cynthia**: (Greek): moon
10. **Deborah**: (Hebrew & Israel): honey bee
11. **Sandra**: (Greek): helper of humanity; (English): unheeded prophetess
12. **Barbara**: (Latin America): stranger
13. **Brenda**: (Gaelic): little raven; (Scandinavian): sword
14. **Pamela**: (Greek, English & Indian): honey
15. **Nancy**: (Hebrew & English): grace

16. **Sharon:** (Hebrew & Israel): a flat clearing
17. **Cheryl:** (English): beloved
18. **Elizabeth:** (English): my God is bountiful; (Hebrew & Biblical): consecrated to God
19. **Teresa/Theresa:** (Finnish): summer, harvester; (Greek): reaper
20.**Lori:** (English): crowned with laurels

1970 - Boys Names

1. **Michael:** (Biblical & Hebrew): like God
2. **James:** (English): supplant, replace; (Israel): supplanter
3. **David:** (Hebrew, Scottish & Welsh): beloved
4. **John:** (Israel): God is gracious; Jehovah has been gracious
5. **Robert:** (English, French, German & Scottish): famed, bright, shining
6. **Christopher:** (Biblical): Christ-bearer; (English): he who holds Christ in his heart
7. **William:** (English, German & French): protector
8. **Brian**: (Gaelic): noble birth; (Celtic): great strength
9. **Mark**: (Latin): dedicated to Mars, the god of war
10. **Richard**: (English, French & German): a strong and powerful ruler
11. **Jeffrey**: (English): a man of peace
12. **Scott**: (Scottish): wanderer
13. **Jason:** (Greek): to heal
14. **Kevin:** (Irish & Gaelic): handsome, beautiful; (Celtic): gentle
15. **Steven:** (English & Greek): crowned one
16. **Joseph:** (Biblical): God will increase; (Hebrew): may Jehovah add/give
17. **Thomas:** (Hebrew, Greek & Dutch): twin
18. **Eric:** (Scandinavian): honorable ruler
19. **Daniel:** (Hebrew & Biblical): God is my judge; (Irish & Welsh): attractive
20. **Timothy:** (Greek & English): to honor God

1970 - Girls Names

1. **Jennifer**: (English & Welsh): fair one; (English & Celtic): white wave
2. **Lisa:** (German): devoted to God; (Israel): consecrated to God
3. **Kimberly:** (English): ruler
4. **Michelle:** (French & Hebrew): like God, close to God
5. **Amy**: (English, French & Latin America): beloved
6. **Angela:** (Spanish, French, Italian & Latin America): angel
7. **Melissa:** (Greek): honey bee
8. **Tammy:** a diminutive form of Tamara, which means spice, palm tree
9. **Mary:** (Biblical, English & Slovakian): bitter
10. **Tracy:** (English): brave
11. **Julie:** (French): youthful; (Latin America): soft-haired, youthful
12. **Karen:** (Greek): pure
13. **Laura:** (English, Spanish & Latin America): crowned with laurel, from the laurel tree
14. **Christine:** (English): follower of Christ
15. **Susan:** (Hebrew): graceful lily; (Israel): lily
16. **Dawn:** (English): aurora; (Greek): sunrise
17. **Stephanie**: (Greek): crowned in victory
18. **Elizabeth:** (English): my God is bountiful; (Hebrew & Biblical): consecrated to God
19. **Heather:** (English): a flowering plant
20. **Kelly:** (Gaelic & Irish): warrior; (Scottish): wood

1980 - Boys Names

1. **Michael:** (Biblical & Hebrew): like God
2. **Christopher:** (Biblical): Christ-bearer; (English): he who holds Christ in his heart

3. **Jason:** (Greek): to heal
4. **David:** (Hebrew, Scottish & Welsh): beloved
5. **James:** (English): supplant, replace; (Israel): supplanter
6. **Matthew**: (Hebrew & Biblical): gift of the Lord
7. **Joshua:** (Hebrew & Biblical): Jehovah saves
8. **John:** (Israel): God is gracious; Jehovah has been gracious
9. **Robert:** (English, French, German & Scottish): famed, bright, shining
10. **Joseph:** (Biblical): God will increase; (Hebrew): may Jehovah add/give
11. **Daniel:** (Hebrew & Biblical): God is my judge; (Irish & Welsh): attractive
12. **Brian**: (Gaelic): noble birth; (Celtic): great strength
13. **Justin:** (English & French): just, true; (Irish): judicious
14. **William:** (English, German & French): protector
15. **Ryan:** (Gaelic): little king; (Irish): kindly, young royalty
16. **Eric:** (Scandinavian): honorable ruler
17. **Nicholas:** (Greek): victorious people
18. **Jeremy:** (Israel): God will uplift
19. **Andrew:** (English, Scottish & Biblical): manly; brave
20. **Timothy:** (Greek & English): to honor God

1980 - Girls Names

1. **Jennifer**: (English & Welsh): fair one; (English & Celtic): white wave
2. **Amanda:** (Latin): much loved
3. **Jessica:** (Israel): God is watching; (Hebrew): rich, God beholds
4. **Melissa:** (Greek): honey bee
5. **Sara(h):** (Hebrew, Spanish & Biblical): princess
6. **Heather**: (English): a flowering plant
7. **Nicole:** (French): victory of the people
8. **Amy:** (English, French & Latin America): beloved
9. **Elizabeth:** (English): my God is bountiful; (Hebrew & Biblical): consecrated to God
10. **Michelle:** (French & Hebrew): like God, close to God
11. **Kimberly:** (English): ruler
12. **Angela:** (Spanish, French, Italian & Latin America): angel
13. **Stephanie**: (Greek): crowned in victory
14. **Tiffany:** (Greek): lasting love
15. **Christina**: (English): follower of Christ
16. **Lisa:** (German): devoted to God; (Israel): consecrated to God
17. **Rebecca:** (Biblical): servant of God
18. **Crystal/Krystal:** (English): jewel; (Latin America): a clear brilliant glass
19. **Kelly:** (Gaelic & Irish): warrior; (Scottish): wood
20. **Erin:** (Irish): peace

1990 - Boys Names

1. **Michael:** (Biblical & Hebrew): like God
2. **Christopher:** (Biblical): Christ-bearer; (English): he who holds Christ in his heart
3. **Matthew**: (Hebrew & Biblical): gift of the Lord
4. **Joshua:** (Hebrew & Biblical): Jehovah saves
5. **Daniel:** (Hebrew & Biblical): God is my judge; (Irish & Welsh): attractive
6. **David:** (Hebrew, Scottish & Welsh): beloved
7. **Andrew:** (English, Scottish & Biblical): manly; brave
8. **James:** (English): supplant, replace; (Israel): supplanter
9. **Justin:** (English & French): just, true; (Irish): judicious
10. **Joseph:** (Biblical): God will increase; (Hebrew): may Jehovah add/give
11. **Ryan:** (Gaelic): little king; (Irish): kindly, young royalty
12. **John:** (Israel): God is gracious; Jehovah has been gracious

13. **Robert:** (English, French, German & Scottish): famed, bright, shining
14. **Nicholas:** (Greek): victorious people
15. **Anthony:** (English & Biblical): worthy of praise
16. **William:** (English, German & French): protector
17. **Jonathan**: (Hebrew): Jehovah has given: (Israel): gift of God
18. **Kyle:** (Gaelic): young; (Irish): young at heart
19. **Brandon:** (Irish): little raven
20. **Jacob**: (Biblical): supplanter; (Hebrew): he grasps the heel

1990 - Girls Names

1. **Jessica:** (Israel): God is watching; (Hebrew): rich, God beholds
2. **Ashley:** (English & Biblical): lives in the ash tree
3. **Brittany:** (English & Celtic): from Britain
4. **Amanda:** (Latin): much loved
5. **Samantha:** (Hebrew & Biblical): listener of God
6. **Sara(h):** (Hebrew, Spanish & Biblical): princess
7. **Stephanie:** (Greek): crowned in victory
8. **Jennifer**: (English & Welsh): fair one; (English & Celtic): white wave
9. **Elizabeth:** (English): my God is bountiful; (Hebrew & Biblical): consecrated to God
10. **Lauren:** (French): crowned with laurel
11. **Megan:** (Irish): soft and gentle; (Greek): strong and mighty
12. **Emily:** (Latin America): admiring
13. **Nicole:** (French): victory of the people
14. **Kayla:** (Irish & Greek): pure and beloved
15. **Amber:** (Arabic): precious jewel, yellow-brown color
16. **Rachel:** (Hebrew): ewe; (Israel): innocent lamb
17. **Courtney:** (English): courteous
18. **Danielle:** (Hebrew): God is my judge
19. **Heather**: (English): a flowering plant
20. **Melissa:** (Greek): honey bee

2000 - Boys Names

1. **Jacob:** (Biblical): supplanter; (Hebrew): he grasps the heel
2. **Michael:** (Biblical & Hebrew): like God
3. **Matthew**: (Hebrew & Biblical): gift of the Lord
4. **Joshua:** (Hebrew & Biblical): Jehovah saves
5. **Christopher:** (Biblical): Christ-bearer; (English): he who holds Christ in his heart
6. **Nicholas:** (Greek): victorious people
7. **Andrew:** (English, Scottish & Biblical): manly; brave
8. **Joseph:** (Biblical): God will increase; (Hebrew): may Jehovah add/give
9. **Daniel:** (Hebrew & Biblical): God is my judge; (Irish & Welsh): attractive
10. **Tyler:** (English): maker of tiles
11. **William:** (English, German & French): protector
12. **Brandon:** (Irish): little raven
13. **Ryan:** (Gaelic): little king; (Irish): kindly, young royalty
14. **John:** (Israel): God is gracious; Jehovah has been gracious
15. **Zachary:** (Hebrew): Jehovah has remembered; (Israel): remembered by the Lord
16. **David:** (Hebrew, Scottish & Welsh): beloved
17. **Anthony:** (English & Biblical): worthy of praise
18. **James:** (English): supplant, replace; (Israel): supplanter
19. **Justin:** (English & French): just, true; (Irish): judicious
20. **Alexander:** (Greek): protector of mankind

2000 - Girls Names

1. **Emily:** (Latin America): admiring
2. **Hannah:** (English & Hebrew): favor, grace; (Biblical): grace of God
3. **Madison:** (English): son of Matthew
4. **Ashley:** (English & Biblical): lives in the ash tree
5. **Sara(h):** (Hebrew, Spanish & Biblical): princess
6. **Alexis**: (English): helper, defender; (Biblical): protector of mankind
7. **Samantha:** (Hebrew & Biblical): listener of God
8. **Jessica:** (Israel): God is watching; (Hebrew): rich, God beholds
9. **Elizabeth:** (English): my God is bountiful; (Hebrew & Biblical): consecrated to God
10. **Taylor:** (English & French): a tailor
11. **Lauren:** (French): crowned with laurel
12. **Alyssa:** (Greek): logical
13. **Kayla:** (Irish & Greek): pure and beloved
14. **Abigail**: (Hebrew): father rejoiced; (Biblical): source of joy
15. **Brianna:** (Irish): strong; (Celtic & English): she ascends
16. **Olivia:** (Spanish & Italian): olive; (Biblical): peace of the olive tree
17. **Emma:** (English, Danish & German): whole, complete, universal
18. **Megan:** (Irish): soft and gentle; (Greek): strong and mighty
19. **Grace:** (Latin America): grace of God; (American): land of grace
20. **Victoria:** (Latin America): winner

2010 - Boys Names

1. **Jacob**: (Biblical): supplanter; (Hebrew): he grasps the heel
2. **Ethan:** (Hebrew & Biblical): firm, strong
3. **Michael:** (Biblical & Hebrew): like God
4. **Jayden:** (American): God has heard
5. **William:** (English, German & French): protector
6. **Alexander:** (Greek): protector of mankind
7. **Noah:** (Biblical): rest, peace; (Hebrew): comfort, long-lived
8. **Daniel:** (Hebrew & Biblical): God is my judge; (Irish & Welsh): attractive
9. **Aiden:** (Irish, Celtic & Gaelic): fire, fiery
10. **Anthony:** (English & Biblical): worthy of praise
11. **Joshua:** (Hebrew & Biblical): Jehovah saves
12. **Mason:** (French & English): stone worker
13. **Christopher:** (Biblical): Christ-bearer; (English): he who holds Christ in his heart
14. **Andrew:** (English, Scottish & Biblical): manly; brave
15. **David:** (Hebrew, Scottish & Welsh): beloved
16. **Matthew**: (Hebrew & Biblical): gift of the Lord
17. **Logan**: (Irish): small cove; (Scottish): Finnian's servant; (Gaelic): from the hollow
18. **Elijah:** (Biblical): the Lord is my God; (Hebrew): Jehovah is God
19. **James:** (English): supplant, replace; (Israel): supplanter
20. **Joseph:** (Biblical): God will increase; (Hebrew): may Jehovah add/give

2010 - Girls Names

1. **Isabella:** (Hebrew): devoted to God; (Spanish): God is bountiful; (Biblical): consecrated to God
2. **Sophia:** (Greek & Biblical): wisdom
3. **Emma:** (English, Danish & German): whole, complete, universal
4. **Olivia:** (Spanish & Italian): olive; (Biblical): peace of the olive tree
5. **Ava:** (Latin America): like a bird
6. **Emily:** (Latin America): admiring
7. **Abigail**: (Hebrew): father rejoiced; (Biblical): source of joy
8. **Madison:** (English): son of Matthew

9. **Chloe:** (Greek): verdant, blooming
10 **Mia:** (Italian): my; (Biblical): mine
11. **Addison:** (English): son of Adam
12. **Elizabeth:** (English): my God is bountiful; (Hebrew & Biblical): consecrated to God
13. **Ella:** (English); beautiful fairy; (Spanish): she
14. **Natalie:** (French): to be born at Christmas; (Slovakian): to be born
15. **Samantha:** (Hebrew & Biblical): listener of God
16. **Alexis**: (English): helper, defender; (Biblical): protector of mankind
17. **Lily/Lilly:** (Hebrew, English & Latin America): lily, blossoming flower
18. **Grace:** (Latin America): grace of God; (American): land of grace
19. **Hailey:** (English): hero, field of hay
20. **Alyssa:** (Greek): logical

Chapter 4. Christian & Biblical Names

Across the U.S., Christian and Biblical names continue to be perennial favorites for both boys and girls. Depending upon your preference, you can follow this trend in a traditional or nonconventional way. Some names, such as Anna and Abigail, are extremely popular, while others, such as Bathsheba and Hagar, are relatively rare. Nevertheless, their place in history and religion gives them a strong global appeal. In this chapter, we present dozens of Christian and Biblical names in alphabetical order. Find the ones that suit your preference - and add them to your list.

Christian & Biblical Names for Boys

Aaron: (Jewish): enlightened; (Hebrew): lofty, exalted
Abel: (Hebrew & Biblical): breathe, son

Abner: (Israel & Hebrew): father is light, father of light
Abraham: (Hebrew & Biblical): exalted father

Abram: (Hebrew): high father; (Israel): father of nations
Adam: (Hebrew): red; (Israel): man of the earth; (English): of the red earth

Alexander: (Greek): protector of mankind
Amos: (Hebrew): strong, carried, brave: (Israel): troubled

Andrew: (English, Scottish & Biblical): manly; brave
Anthony: (English & Biblical): worthy of praise

Apollos: (Israel): one who destroys
Asa: (Hebrew): physician; (Japanese): born at dawn

Asher: (Hebrew & Israel): happy, blessed
Azariah: (Hebrew & Israel): God helps

Barak: (Hebrew & Israel): flash of lightening
Barnabus: (Hebrew & Israel): comfort

Bartholomew: (English, Hebrew & Biblical): son of a farmer
Benjamin: (English, Hebrew & Biblical): son of my right hand

Cain: (Israel): craftsman; (Hebrew): spear; (Welsh): clear water; (Irish): archaic
Caleb: (Israel): faithful; (Hebrew): dog or bold

Christian: (English & Irish): follower of Christ
Christopher: (Biblical): Christ-bearer; (English): he who holds Christ in his heart

Claudius: (English): lame
Cornelius: (Irish): strong willed, wise; (Latin America): horn-colored

Daniel: (Hebrew & Biblical): God is my judge; (Irish & Welsh): attractive
David: (Hebrew, Scottish & Welsh): beloved

Demetrius: (Greek): goddess of fertility, one who loves the earth
Ebenezer: (Hebrew & Israel): rock of help

Eli: (Hebrew): ascended, uplifted, high; (Greek): defender of man
Elijah: (Biblical): the Lord is my God; (Hebrew): Jehovah is God

Emmanuel: (Hebrew): God with us
Ephraim: (Hebrew & Israel): fruitful

Esau: (Hebrew): hairy, famous bearer; (Israel): he that acts or finishes
Ethan: (Hebrew & Biblical): firm, strong

Evan: (English): God is good; (Welsh): young; (Celtic): young fighter
Ezekiel: (Hebrew & Israel): strength of God

Ezra: (Hebrew & Israel): helper
Gabriel: (Israel): hero of God; (Hebrew): man of God; (Spanish): God is my strength

Gideon: (Hebrew & Israel): great warrior
Ira: (Hebrew & Israel): watchful

Isaac: (Biblical): he will laugh
Isaiah: (Hebrew): the Lord is generous; (Israel): salvation by God

Ishmael: (Hebrew, Israel & Spanish): God listens, God will hear
Jacob: (Biblical): supplanter; (Hebrew): he grasps the heel

Jaden: (American): God has heard
James: (English); supplant, replace; (Israel): supplanter

Jeremiah: (Hebrew): may Jehovah exalt; (Israel): sent by God
Jeremy: (Israel): God will uplift

Jesse: (Hebrew): wealthy; (Israel): God exists; (English): Jehovah exists
Jethro: (Hebrew & Israel): excellence

Joab: (Israel): paternity, voluntary
Joel: (Hebrew): Jehovah is God; (Israel): God is willing

John: (Israel): God is gracious; Jehovah has been gracious
Jonah: (Hebrew & Israel): a dove

Jonathan: (Hebrew): Jehovah has given: (Israel): gift of God
Jordan: (Hebrew): to flow down; (Israel): descendant

Josiah: (Hebrew): Jehovah has healed; (Israel): God has healed
Joshua: (Hebrew & Biblical): Jehovah saves

Judas: (Hebrew & Israel): praised
Jude: (Israel): one who is praised

Justin: (English & French): just, true; (Irish): judicious
Justus: (Israel): fairness, justice

Lazarus: (Hebrew & Israel): God will help
Levi: (Hebrew & Israel): attached, united as one

Lucas: (Gaelic, English & Latin America): light
Luke: (Greek & Latin America): light

Marcus: (Gaelic): hammer; (Latin America): warlike
Mark: (Latin America): warlike

Matthew: (Hebrew & Biblical): gift of the Lord
Michael: (Biblical & Hebrew): like God

Micah: (Israel): like God
Moses: (Hebrew & Biblical): saved from the water

Nathan: (Hebrew): he gives; (Israel): gift of God
Nathaniel: (Hebrew & Israel): gift of God

Nicholas: (Greek): victorious people
Noah: (Biblical): rest, peace; (Hebrew): comfort, long-lived

Omar: (Arabian): ultimate devotee; (Hebrew): eloquent speaker
Paul: (English & French): small, apostle in the bible

Peter: (Greek & English): a small stone or rock, apostle in the bible
Philip: (French, Greek & English): lover of horses

Phineas: (Hebrew): oracle; (Israel): loudmouth
Reuben: (Hebrew & Israel): behold - a son

Rufus: (Latin America): redhead
Samson: (Hebrew & Israel): bright as the sun

Samuel: (Israel): God hears; (Hebrew): name of God
Saul: (Israel): borrowed; (Hebrew & Spanish): asked for

Sean: (Irish): God is gracious
Seth: (Hebrew): anointed; (Israel): appointed

Silas: (Latin America): man of the forest
Simon: (Israel): it is heard

Solomon: (Hebrew & Israel): peaceful
Stephen: (English & Greek): crowned one

Thaddeus: (Hebrew): valiant, wise: (Greek): praise, one who has courage
Thomas: (Hebrew, Greek & Dutch): twin

Timothy: (Greek & English): to honor God
Tobias: (Hebrew & Israel): God is good

Victor: (Spanish & Latin America): winner
Vincent: (English & Latin America): conquering, victorious

Zachary/Zachariah: (Hebrew): Jehovah has remembered; (Israel): remembered by the Lord
Zebulun: (Hebrew & Israel): habitation

Christian & Biblical Names for Girls

Abigail: (Hebrew): father rejoiced; (Biblical): source of joy
Ada: (English): wealthy; (Hebrew): ornament; (German): noble; (African): first daughter

Angela: (Spanish, French, Italian & Latin America): angel
Anna/Ana: (Hebrew): favor or grace; (Native American): mother; (Israel): gracious

Bathsheba: (Hebrew): oath, voluptuous, famous bearer; (Biblical): seventh daughter
Bernice: (French & Greek): one who brings victory

Bethany: (Hebrew & Israel): a life-town near Jerusalem
Beulah: (Hebrew & Israel): married

Candace: (English): pure, glittering white
Carmel: (Hebrew): garden; (Israel): woodland; (Celtic): from the vineyard

Charity: (English): kindness, generous, goodwill
Chloe: (Greek): verdant, blooming

Claudia: (Spanish & Latin America): lame
Cordelia: (English, Welsh & Celtic): of the sea

Deborah: (Hebrew & Israel): honey bee
Diana: (Greek): divine, goddess of the moon and the hunt

Dinah: (Hebrew & Israel): judgment
Drucilla/Drusilla: (Bible): fruitful, dewy-eyed; (Latin America): mighty

Eden: (Hebrew): delight; (Israel): paradise
Edna: (Celtic): fire; (Hebrew): rejuvenation; (Israel): spirit renewed

Elisha: (Hebrew): God is salvation; (Israel): God is gracious
Elizabeth: (English): my God is bountiful; (Hebrew & Biblical): consecrated to God

Esther: (Hebrew & African): star
Eunice: (Greek): happy, victorious

Eva: (Hebrew, Israel, Indian & Spanish): one who gives life
Eve: (Hebrew): to breathe

Faith: (English): faithful; (Latin America): to trust
Grace/Gracie: (Latin America): grace of God; (America): land of grace

Hagar: (Hebrew): forsaken, flight, famous bearer; (Israel): flight
Hannah: (English & Hebrew): favor, grace; (Biblical): grace of God

Honey: (English): sweet
Hope: (English): trust, faith

Jewel: (English & French): precious gem
Joanna: (Hebrew & French): gift from God

Joy: (French, English & Latin America): rejoicing
Judith: (Hebrew): praised; (Israel): from Judah

Julia: (French): youthful; (Latin America): soft-haired, youthful
Leah: (Hebrew): weary

Lia: (Greek): bearer of good news
Lily: (Hebrew, English & Latin America): lily, blossoming flower

Lois: (Israel): good
Lydia: (Greek): maiden

Magdalena: (Hebrew): from the tower; (Spanish): bitter
Mara: (English, Italian, Hebrew & Israel): bitter

Martha: (Israel): lady
Mary: (Biblical, English & Slovakian): bitter

Merry: (English): joyful, mirthful
Miriam: (Hebrew): rebellious; (Israel): strong-willed

Myra: (Greek): fragrant
Naomi: (Hebrew & Israel): pleasant

Neriah: (Israel): light lamp of the Lord
Olive: (Irish): olive; (Latin America): olive branch, peace

Orpah: (Israel): fawn
Paula: (Latin America): small

Phoebe: (Greek): bright, shining one
Priscilla: (Latin America): ancient

Rebecca: (Biblical): servant of God
Rachel: (Hebrew): ewe; (Israel): innocent lamb

Rhoda: (Greek): roses
Rose: (English, French & Scottish): flower, a rose; (German): horse, fame

Ruby: (English & French): a precious jewel, a ruby
Ruth: (Hebrew & Israel): companion, friend

Sapphira: (Hebrew): sapphire; (Israel): beautiful
Sara(h): (Hebrew, Spanish & Biblical): princess

Sela(h): (Israel): pause and reflect
Sharon: (Hebrew & Israel): a flat clearing

Shiloh: (Hebrew): the one to whom it belongs; (Israel): peaceful
Susannah: (Hebrew): graceful lily; (Israel): lily

Tabitha: (Hebrew): beauty, grace; (Israel): a gazelle
Tamara: (Hebrew): palm tree; (Israel): spice

Zina: (English): welcoming
Zillah: (Hebrew): shade

Zipporah: (Hebrew & Israel): bird
Zemira: (Hebrew & Israel): praised

Chapter 5. Names from Literature & Mythology

Many times, when you encounter a baby name that is mature, sophisticated, with a global appeal, it has its roots in literature and mythology. As expected, the popularity of these names has varied over time (and across geographical borders). Nevertheless, names from literature and mythology continue to hold a strong appeal for American parents who are passionate about history and the arts. In this chapter, we present a comprehensive list of names from literature and mythology in alphabetical order. See if your baby's name is on the list!

Boys Names from Literature & Mythology

Adonis: (Greek): beautiful
Ajax: (Greek): warrior

Ammon: (Egyptian): god of a unified Egypt
Amory: (German): ruler

Andre: (French): manly, brave
Angus: (Irish): vigorous one

Apollo: (Latin): strength, sun god
Ares: (Greek): god of war

Aristotle: (Greek): thinker with a great purpose
Arthur: (English): bear, stone

Atlas: (Greek): lifted, carried
Atticus: (Latin): a man from Athens

Balthazar: (English): the comedy of errors a merchant
Barrington: (English): town of Barr

Beau: (French): handsome, beautiful
Beowulf: (English): intelligent wolf

Burke: (German): birch tree
Carleton: (English): town of Charles

Casper: (Persian): treasurer; (German): imperial
Castor: (Greek): bereaved brother of Helen

Cato: (Latin): sagacious, wise one, good judgment
Chance: (English & French): good luck, keeper of records

Charles: (English): strong, manly
Clement: (French): compassionate

Cody: (Irish): helpful; (English): a cushion, helpful
Connor: (Irish): strong willed, much wanted

Cullen: (Irish & Gaelic): handsome; (Celtic): cub; (English): city in Germany
Damon: (English): calm, tame

Darcy: (Irish & Celtic): dark one
Dion: (French): mountain of Zeus

Dylan: (English & Welsh): born from the ocean, son of the wave; (Gaelic): faithful
Eamon: (Irish): blessed guardian

Ellison: (English): son of Elias
Faust: (Latin): fortunate

Finn: (English): blond
Fraser: (Scottish): strawberry flowers

Galen: (Gaelic): tranquil; (English): festive party: (Greek): healer, calm
Griffin: (Latin): prince, (Welsh): strong in faith

Hans: (German & Hebrew): gift from God; (Scandinavian): God is gracious
Heathcliff: (English): cliff near the heath

Hector: (Greek): anchor; (Spanish): tenacious
Henderson: (Scottish): son of Henry

Hermes: (Greek): stone pile
Hewitt: (English): little smart one

Holden: (English): from a hollow in the valley
Homer: (Greek & English): pledge, promise

Israel: (Israel): prince of God; (Hebrew): may God prevail
Janus: (Latin American): god of beginnings

Jarvis: (German): skilled with a spear
Jason: (Greek): to heal

Jasper: (Hebrew, French & English): precious stone
Johann: (German): God's gracious gift

Jonathan: (Hebrew): Jehovah has given: (Israel): gift of God
Jude: (Hebrew & Israel): praised

Jules: (French): youthful, downy-haired
Julian: (Spanish, French & Greek): youthful

Justin: (English & French): just, true; (Irish): judicious
Kana: (Japanese): powerful

Laird: (Scottish): lord; (Irish): head of household
Leander: (Greek): man of lions

Lewis: (German): famous warrior
Leo: (Italian & English): a lion

Loki: (Scandinavian): trickster god
Macon: (English): to make

Magnus: (Latin): great
Malloy: (Irish): noble chief

McKenna: (English): handsome, fiery
Merlin: (Welsh): of the sea fortress

Milo: (English): soldier
Oberon: (German): bear heart

Odin: (Scandinavian): ruler
Oliver: (French, English, Danish & Latin America): the olive tree; (German): elf army

Orion: (Greek): a hunter in Greek mythology
Orlando: (Spanish): land of gold: (German): famous throughout the land

Otto: (German): wealthy or prosperous
Pan: (Greek): god of flocks

Paris: (Persian): angelic face; (Greek): downfall; (French): the capital city of France
Philip: (French, Greek & English): lover of horses

Phineas: (Hebrew): oracle; (Israel): loudmouth
Pierre: (French): a rock

Plato: (Greek): strong shoulders
Pollux: (Latin American): brother of Helen

Puck: (English): elf
Quentin: (French, English & Latin America): fifth

Quillan: (Gaelic): resembling a cub
Raiden: (Japanese): god of thunder and lightning

Rhett: (English): stream
Ridley: (English): from the red meadow

Robin: (English): a diminutive form of Robert, which means famed, bright, shining
Romeo: (Italian, Spanish, Latin America & African American): from Rome

Rufus: (Latin America): redhead
Samson: (Hebrew & Israel): bright as the sun

Santiago: (Spanish): named for Saint James
Sawyer: (English): one who works with wood

Sebastian: (Greek): the revered one
Sheridan: (Irish, English & Celtic): untamed; (Gaelic): bright

Silas: (Latin America): man of the forest
Stern: (English): austere

Stuart: (Scottish): steward; (English): bailiff; (Irish): keeper of the estate
Taft: (French): from the homestead

Thor: (Norse): god of thunder
Tristan: (English, Celtic & French): outcry, tumult; (Welsh): noisy; (Irish): bold

Troy: (French): curly haired; (Irish): foot soldier
Tyr: (Norway): god of war

Ulysses: (Latin): hateful
Valentino: (Italian): brave or strong; (Latin America): health or love

Virgil: (English): flourishing; (Latin America): strong
Vulcan: (Latin): the god of fire

Wolf: (English): the animal, wolf
Yancy: (Native American): Englishman

Zeus: (Greek): powerful one

Girls Names from Literature & Mythology

Agatha: (Latin): virtuous, good
Aimee: (English, French & Latin America): beloved

Aja: (Indian): goat
Alejandra: (Spanish): defender of mankind

Anat: (Hebrew & Israel): a singer
Annika: (Dutch): gracious

Antoinette: (French): flower
Aphrodite: (Greek): beauty, love goddess

Apollonia: (Greek): strength
Artemis: (Greek): goddess of the moon

Astraea: (Greek): justice
Athena: (Greek): wisdom, goddess of war

Aurora: (Latin): dawn
Ava: (Latin America): like a bird

Avalon: (Latin): island
Beatrice: (Italian): blesses; (French): bringer of joy

Belisama: (Celtic): goddess of rivers and lakes
Branwen: (Welsh): raven

Bronte: (Greek): thunder
Calliope: (Greek): beautiful voice

Camilla: (Italian): a noble virgin, a ceremonial attendant
Candace: (English): pure, glittering white

Cassandra: (Greek): prophet of doom
Cecilia: (Latin): blind

Chloe: (Greek): verdant, blooming
Cleo/Clio: (English): father's glory

Clair: (English): clear; (French): bright
Cleopatra: (Greek): glory to the father; (African American): queen

Cloris: (Greek): goddess of flowers
Colette: (English): victorious people

Constance: (American): strong-willed
Cordelia: (English, Welsh & Celtic): of the sea

Cynthia: (Greek): moon
Dalia: (Hebrew): tree branch

Daphne: (Greek): of the laurel tree
Dekla: (Latvian): a trinity goddess

Demeter: (Greek): lover of the earth
Echo: (Greek): sound returned

Electra: (Greek): bright, the shining one
Elinor: (English): torch

Eudora: (Greek): honored gift
Eunice: (Latin): victory

Faith: (English): faithful; (Latin America): to trust
Felicia: (French & Latin America): happiness

Felicity: (French, English & Latin America): happiness
Flora: (English): flower: (Latin): flowering

Freya: (Norse): lady
Geraldine: (French, English & German): rules by the spear

Gillian: (English): child of the gods; (Irish): young at heart
Guinevere: (Celtic): white lady; (English): white wave

Harriet: (English & German): rules the home
Helen: (Greek): light

Helene: (French): in the light of the sun
Hera: (Greek): goddess of marriage

Hester: (Greek): star
Hestia: (Greek): goddess of the hearth

Ida: (English): hardworking
Ina: (Polynesian): moon goddess

Isadore/Isadora: (Greek): gift from the goddess Isis
Ishtar: (Arabic): mythical goddess of love and fertility

Isis: (Egyptian): most powerful goddess
Janine: (Hebrew): gift from God

Josephina: (Hebrew): God will add
Juliana: (Spanish): soft-haired

Juno: (Roman): mythical queen of the heavens
Justina: (Greek): just

Justine: (English): just, upright; (Latin America): fairness
Kamala: (Hawaiian & Indian): lotus

Kelly: (Gaelic & Irish): warrior; (Scottish): wood
Laurie: (English): crowned with laurels

Leda: (Greek): mother creator
Lilith: (Babylonian): woman of the night

Livia: (English): life
Lorelei: (German): from the rocky cliff

Lucy: (Latin America): bringer of light
Maeve: (Irish): intoxicating, joyous

Maia: (French): May, (Greek): mother
Marian: (French): bitter

Marianne: (French): bitter
Martha: (Israel): lady

Melia: (German): industrious
Melissa: (Greek): honey bee

Minerva: (Latin): wise
Ming: (Chinese): brilliant light

Mirabel: (Spanish): of uncommon beauty
Morgan: (Celtic): lives by the sea; (Welsh): bright sea

Muriel: (Arabian): myth; (Celtic): shining sea
Natasha: (Greek): rebirth

Nyssa: (Greek): the beginning
Octavia: (Latin America): eighth; (Italian): born eighth

Odessa: (Latin America): the odyssey
Olga: (Slovakian): holy

Ophelia: (Greek): useful, wise
Pandora: (Greek): gifted and talented woman

Patience: (English): patient, enduring
Patricia: (Spanish & Latin America): noble

Penelope: (Greek): weaver
Phoebe: (Greek): bright, shining one

Pomona: (Latin): goddess of fruit trees
Portia: (Latin): offering

Quilla: (Incan): goddess of the moon
Raven: (English): to be black, blackbird

Regina: (Italian, Spanish & Latin America): queen
Rhea: (Greek): rivers

Rosemary: (English): bitter rose
Sabrina: (English): legendary princess

Selene: (Greek): of the moon
Sheila: (English & Irish): blind; (Italian): music

Tess: (English): harvester
Thea: (Greek): gift of God

Ursula: (Danish & Scandinavian): female bear
Venus: (Greek): love goddess, little bird

Winifred: (Irish): friend of peace; (Welsh): reconciled, blessed
Yara: (Brazilian): goddess of the river; (Iranian): courage

Zenia: (Greek): hospitable
Zora: (Slavic): sunrise

Zoya: (Greek): life

Chapter 6. Names from Popular Culture & the Entertainment Industry

Every year, parents seek new inspiration for their babies' names from the world of music, movies, sports, and television. As a result, the rise of a popular athlete, singer, or reality star can have a strong - and immediate - impact on a parent's choice of names. In some cases, such as Adele and Audrey, the phenomenon brings new interest to classic names that had fallen out of favor. In other cases, such as Buffy and Miley, the phenomenon brings new names to the forefront that would otherwise not be considered.

My only caveat about names from popular culture is their shelf-life. Sixty years ago, millions of parents named their baby girls after Marilyn Monroe; however, its popularity waned within a few years. Nevertheless, some trends **do** manage to stick. After *Love Story* was released in 1970, millions of parents named their baby girls after the doomed heroine Jennifer ..... and the name continued to remain a top choice for more than 25 years.

When reviewing these names, try to be objective - and determine if you would still like the name if it was *not* associated with a famous person, character, movie, or song. Also consider the popularity of the name - and whether you want your child to be one of the seven girls named Mila in her kindergarten class. In the end, there is no right or wrong answer - simply what feels right to **you**.

Boys Names from Popular Culture & the Entertainment Industry

Ace: (Latin): unity
Adrian: (German, Spanish & Italian): dark

Aiken: (English): sturdy, made of oak
Anderson: (Scottish): son of Andrew

Angus: (Irish): vigorous one
Apollo: (Latin): strength, sun god

Ashton: (Hebrew): shining light; (English): ash tree settlement
Ari: (Hebrew): lion of God

Armand: (French): of the army
Armstrong: (English): strong arm

Arsenio: (Greek): masculine, virile
Austin/Austen: (English): from the name Augustin, which means revered

Avi: (Hebrew): my God, father; (Latin America): Lord of mine
Axl: (German & Hebrew): father of peace; (German): source of all life

Barak/Barack: (Hebrew & Israel): flash of lightening
Barrett: (English & German): strength of a bear

Beck: (English): the brook
Beckett: (English) : brook

Beckham: (Englidh): from the Beck homestead
Bjorn: (Scandinavian): a form of Bernard, which means strong as a bear

Bodhi: (Indian): awakens
Boone: (French): good

Boston: (English): the city Boston
Bowie: (Celtic): yellow-haired

Brady: (Gaelic & Irish): spirit; (Irish): broad-shouldered
Brandon: (Irish): little raven

Braxton: (English): from Brock's town
Brody: (Irish): brother, from the muddy place; (Scottish): second son

Bruno: (German): brown-haired
Bryce: (Scottish): speckled

Cameron: (Irish & Gaelic): crooked nose
Carlisle: (English): from the walled city

Carlton: (English): town of Charles
Casper: (Persian): treasurer; (German): imperial

Cassius: (Latin): empty, hollow, vain
Cato: (Latin): sagacious, wise one, good judgment

Cedric: (English): battle chieftain
Chandler: (French): candle maker

Chase: (English): hunter
Chauncey: (Latin): chancellor

Clay: (English): clay maker, immortal
Colbert: (French): famous and bright

Cole: (Irish): warrior
Conan: (English): resembling a wolf; (Gaelic): high and mighty

Cooper: (English): barrel maker
Cosmo: (Greek): the order of the universe

Creed: (English): belief, guiding principle
Crosby: (English): town crossing

Cullen: (Irish & Gaelic): handsome; (Celtic): cub; (English): city in Germany
Cyrus: (English): far-sighted

Damon: (English): calm, tame
Dane: (Hebrew & Scandinavian): God will judge; (English): brook

Darius: (Greek): kingly, wealthy; (American): pharaoh
Dax: (English & French): water

Dawayne: (Irish): dark
Deepak: (Hindu): little lamp

Denzel: (English): fort; African: wild
Dermot: (Irish): free from envy

Dexter: (Latin): right-handed, skillful; (Latin America): flexible
Dixon: (English): power, brave ruler

Dierks: (Danish): ruler of the people
Drake: (English): male duck, dragon,

Draper: (English): fabric maker
Dre: (American): a diminutive form of Andre, which means manly, brave

Drew: (English): courageous, valiant
Duncan: (Scottish): brown warrior

Dylan: (English & Welsh): born from the ocean, son of the wave
Edward: (English): blesses guardian

Eli: (Hebrew): ascended, uplifted, high; (Greek): defender of man
Elton: (English): old town

Elvis: (Scandinavian): wise
Emmett: (English): whole, universal

Evander: (Greek): benevolent ruler
Ewan: (Celtic, Scotch & Irish): young

Ezra: (Hebrew & Israel): helper
Finn: (English): blond

Fox: (English): fox
Frasier: (French): strawberry, curly-haired

Franco: (Italian): of France
Garth: (Scandinavian): keeper of the garden

Giovanni/Gian: (Italian); God is gracious
Godric: (English): power of God

Graham: (Scottish): from the gray home
Gray: (English): gray-haired

Grayson: (English): son of the bailiff
Gus: (German): revered

Guy: (French): guide; (Hebrew): valley; (Celtic): sensible; (Latin America): living spirit
Heath: (English): from the heath wasteland|

Helio: (Greek): god of the sun
Hogan: (Irish & Gaelic): young, young at heart

Horatio: (French): hour, time
Hudson: (English): son of the hooded man

Hurley: (Irish): sea tide
Iggy: (Latin): fiery

Ioan: (Greek, Bulgarian & Romanian): a form of John, which means God is gracious
Jaden/Jayden: (American): God has heard

Jagger: (English): a carter, to carry
Jasper: (Persian): treasurer

Javier/Xavier: (Spanish): owner of a new house
Jay: (German): swift; (French): blue jay; (English): to rejoice; (Latin America): a crow

Jermaine: (French): a man from Germany; (Latin): brotherly
Jett: (English): resembling the black gemstone

Jonas: (Hebrew): gift from God; (Spanish): dove; (Israel): accomplishing
Juan Pablo: (Spanish): God is gracious/borrowed

Justin: (English & French): just, true; (Irish): judicious
Kareem: (Arabic): noble, distinguished

Keanu: (Hawaiian): of the mountain breeze
Keaton: (English): from the town of hawks

Kidd: (English): resembling a young goat
Kiefer: (German): one who makes barrels

Kieran: (Gaelic): the little dark one
Kingston: (English): from the king's village

Knox: (English): from the hills
Kobe/Kobi/Koby: (African): supplanter; (American): from California

Kramer: (German): shopkeeper
Laird: (Scottish): lord; (Irish): head of household

Lamar: (German): famous land; (French): of the sea
Leib: (Yiddish): roaring lion

Leif: (Scandinavian): beloved descendent
Levi/Levin: (Hebrew & Israel): attached, united as one

Levon: (Armenian): lion
Luc: (Latin): surrounded by light

Luka: (Latin America): light; (Russian): of Luciana
Maddox: (English): son of the Lord; (Celtic): beneficent

Magnus: (Latin): great
Marlon: (French): falcon, of the sea fortress

Marston: (English): from the town near the marsh
Mason: (French & English): stone worker

Maximus: (Greek): greatest
Miller: (English): one who works at the mill

Milo: (English): soldier
Montel: (Italian): mountain

Moroccan: (African): one from Morocco
Nash: (American): adventurer

Naveen: (Hindu): new; (Irish): beautiful, pleasant
Neo: (Greek & American): new

Niles: (English): champion
Orlando: (Spanish): land of gold: (German): famous throughout the land

Oz: (Hebrew): having great strength
Ozzy: (English): divine ruler

Quincy: (English): fifth; (French): estate belonging to Quintus
Quinn: (Celtic): wise; (Irish): fifth, counsel, intelligent

Pax: (English): peaceful
Penn: (Latin): pen, quill

Percy: (English): piercing the valley
Perry: (English): a familiar form of Peter, which means a small stone or rock

Peyton: (English): from the village of warriors
Peeta: (Indian): yellow silk cloth

Pharell/Pharrell: (American): of proven courage
Phineas: (Hebrew): oracle; (Israel): loudmouth

Presley: (English): priest's land
Radcliff: (English): red cliff

Rain/Raine: (American): blessings from above; (French & Latin): ruler; (English): lord, wise
Regis: (Latin): regal; (Latin America): rules

Reilly: (Gaelic): outgoing
Rio: (Portuguese): river

Ripley: (English): from the noisy meadow
River: (English): from the river

Rupert: (German): bright fame
Robin: (English): a diminutive form of Robert, which means famed, bright, shining

Rocco: (Italian & German): rest
Rocket: (English): fast

Roman: (Spanish & Latin America): from Rome
Ryder: (English): knight

Sanjay: (American): a combination of Sanford and Jay
Satchel: (French): Saturn

Sawyer: (English): one who works with wood
Sayid: (African): lord and master

Shane: (Hebrew): gift from God; (Irish): God is gracious
Shepherd: (English): one who herds sheep

Seven: (American): the number seven
Silas: (Latin America): man of the forest

Slater: (English): one who works with slate
Speck: (German): bacon

Spencer: (English): provider
Stanford: (English): from the stony ford

Sully: (English): from the southern meadow
Taye: (Ethiopian): *one who has been seen*

Terence: (Latin America): tender, gracious
Terrell: (German): thunder ruler

Tex: (English): of Texas
Tiger: (English): powerful cat

Trey: (English & Latin): third-born child
Trigg: (Norse): truthful

Tripp: (English): traveler
Troy: (French): curly haired; (Irish): foot soldier

True: (English): loyal
Tucker: (English): tucker of cloth

Tyrell: (American & English): thunder ruler
Tyson: (French): explosive; (English): son of Tye

Upton: (English): upper town
Urban: (Latin): city dweller, courteous

Usher: (Latin): from the mouth of the river; (English): doorkeeper
Vaughn: (Celtic): small

Wentworth: (English): village, from the white one's estate
Wesley: (English): from the west meadow

West: (English): from the west
Weston: (English): west town

Ziggy: (Latvian & Russian): a form of Siegfried, which means victorious peace

Girls Names from Popular Culture & the Entertainment Industry

Aaliyah/Aliyah: (Arabic): an ascender; (Muslim): exalted; (American): immigrant to a new home
Addison: (English): son of Adam

Adele: (German & French): noble, kind
Alanis: (English): attractive

Alexis: (English): helper, defender; (Biblical): protector of mankind
Alyssa: (Greek): logical

Amber: (Arabic): precious jewel, yellow-brown color
America: (English): ruler of the home

Angelina: (Italian): little angel
Anjelica: (Greek): a diminutive form of Angela, which means angel

Aria: (Italian): melody
Arial: (Hebrew): lioness of God

Arianna: (Greek & Italian): holy
Ashanti: (African): great African woman

Ashley: (English & Biblical): lives in the ash tree
Audrey: (English): noble strength

Audrina: (English): nobility, strength
Avril: (English): born in April

Bailey: (English): bailiff, steward, public official
Bella: (Hebrew): devoted to God; (Spanish & Latin America): beautiful

Bettina: (English): consecrated to God
Beyonce: (American): one who surpasses others

Bijou: (French): as precious as a jewel
Blair: (Irish & Celtic): from the plain, (Gaelic): child of the fields; (Scottish): peat moss

Blythe: (English): happy
Brandy: (English): firebrand

Bree: (Celtic): broth; (Irish): hill, strong one
Bristol: (English): bridge

Brittany: (English & Celtic): from Britain
Bronwyn: (Welsh): dark and pure; (English): white-skinned

Brooke: (English): lives by the stream
Brooklyn: (English): water, stream

Buffy: (American): buffalo, from the plains
Carmen: (English): garden; (Spanish & Latin America): song

Carrie: (American): melody, song
Cameron/Camryn: (Irish & Gaelic): crooked nose

Camilla/Camille: (Italian): a noble virgin, a ceremonial attendant
Campbell: (Scottish): crooked mouth

Callie/Cally: (Greek): beautiful; (English); lark
Carlie/Carly: (American): strong one; (Latin America): little, womanly

Celine: (Latin): of the heavens
Charisma: (Greek): grace

Charlize: (French): manly
Cher: (English): beloved

Chloe: (Greek): verdant, blooming
Clove: (German): spice

Clover: (English): meadow flower
Contessa: (Italian): a countess

Cordelia: (English, Welsh & Celtic): of the sea
Courtney: (English): courteous

Crimson: (English): deep red color
Dana: (English, Danish, Irish & Hebrew): a person from Denmark

Danica: (Slavic): the morning star
Destiny: (English): fate

Dharma: (Indian): ultimate law of all things
Dionne: (Greek): divine queen

Dominique: (French): belonging to God
Drew: (Greek): courageous, strong

Edie: (English): blessed
Effie: (Greek): melodious talk

Elle: (English): torch
Elliott: (Israel): close to God; (English): the Lord is my God

Evangeline: (Greek): like an angel
Faith: (English): faithful; (Latin America): to trust

Fantasia: (Latin): from a fantasy land
Felicity: (French, English & Latin America): happiness

Fiona: (Gaelic): fair, a white-shouldered woman
Florence: (English): flowering; (Latin America): prosperous

Gabrielle: (French): strength of God
Giada: (Italian): jade

Giselle: (French): pledge
Giuliana: (Italian):youthful

Golda/Goldie: (English): resembling the precious metal
Gwyneth: (Welsh): blessed with happiness

Hallie/Halle: (English): hay meadow
Hannah: (English & Hebrew): favor, grace; (Biblical): grace of God

Harlow: (American): impetuous
Harper: (English): musician, harp player

Haven: (English): safe place
Hayden: (English & Welsh): in the meadow or valley

Haylee/Hailey: (English): from the hay meadow, hero
Hazel: (English & Irish): the hazel tree

Hermione: (Greek): earthly
Hillary: (English & Greek): joyous, cheerful

Hoda: (Indian): child of God
Honor: (Spanish & Irish): honor; (Latin America): integrity

Ilsa: (German): abbreviation of Elizabeth, which means God is bountiful
Ireland: (Irish): country of the Irish

Ivanka: (Slavic): God is gracious
Ivy: (English): vine

Jada: (Israel): wise
Jamie: (English): supplanter, representative

Jamielynn: (American): a combination of Jamie and Lynn
January: (American): born in January

Jewel: (English & French): precious gem
Jorja: (English): farmer

Juno: (Roman): mythical queen of the heavens
Katniss: (American): female warrior

Keira: (Celtic): black-haired
Keisha: (African): favorite

Kendall: (English & Celtic): from the bright valley
Kendra: (English): having royal power

Kerri: (Irish): dusky, dark
Kimora: (American): royal

Kristi: (Greek): anointed, follower of Christ
Kyle: (Irish): attractive

Kylie: (Australian): a boomerang
Lacy/Lacey: (Irish): surname; (English): derived from lace

Lake: (American): body of water, from the lake
Layla: (Indian): born at night; (Arabian): dark beauty

Leighton: (English): herb garden, town by the meadow
Liberty: (English): free, independent

Lorelei: (German): from the rocky cliff
Madonna: (Italian): my lady

Malia: (American): calm, peaceful
Mariah: (English): biter

Martina: (Latin America): warlike
Meredith: (Welsh): great ruler, protector of the sea

Michelle: (French & Hebrew): like God, close to God
Miley: (American): virtuous

Miranda: (Latin): worthy of admiration
Mischa: (Russian): like God

Monique: (French): one who provides wise counsel
Monroe: (Gaelic): from the red swamp; (Scottish): from the river; (Irish): near the river roe

Montana: (Latin America): mountainous
Murphy: (Irish): sea warrior

Mya: (American): emerald
Nadia: (Slovakian): hopeful

Neve: (Irish): radiant
Nicole: (French): victory of the people

Nicolette: (French): a form of Nicole, which means victory of the people
Nikita: (Russian): victorious people

Nona: (English): ninth
Octavia: (Latin America): eighth; (Italian): born eighth

Oprah: (Hebrew): resembling a fawn
Quinn: (Celtic): wise; (Irish): fifth, counsel, intelligent

Paris: (Persian): angelic face; (Greek): downfall; (French): the capital city of France
Penelope: (Greek): weaver

Peyton: (English): village
Philippa/Pippa: (English): friend of horses

Phoebe: (Greek): bright, shining one
Piper: (English): plays the flute

Portia: (Latin): offering
Posy: (English): God will increase

Primrose: (English): the first rose, primrose flower
Precious: (American): treasured

Prudence: (English): prudent or cautious
Rachel: (Hebrew): ewe; (Israel): innocent lamb

Rain/Raina: (American): blessings from above; (French & Latin): ruler; (English): lord, wise
Reba: (Hebrew): fourth

Rebel: (American): outlaw
Reese/Reece: (English &Welsh): ardent, fiery, enthusiastic

Remy: (French): oarsman or rower, from Rheims
Rhianna: (English): goddess; (Welsh): nymph

Rhoda: (Greek): roses
Rielle: (Hebrew): a feminine form of Gabriel, which means God is my strength

Riley: (Irish): a small stream
Rory: (Irish): famous brilliance, famous ruler; (Gaelic): red-haired

Rosario: (Filipino & Spanish): rosary
Roseanna: (Greek): graceful rose

Roseanne: (Greek): graceful rose
Rue: (English): bitter, medicinal plant

Rumer: (English): gypsy
Santana: (Spanish): saintly

Sasha: (English): defender of mankind
Scarlett: (English): red

Sela(h): (Israel): pause and reflect
Selena: (Greek): of the moon

Serena: (English): calm, serene
Shakira: (Arabic): grateful

Shanae: (Hebrew): God is gracious
Shania: (Native American): on my way

Shannon/Shannen: (Gaelic): having ancient wisdom
Sherri: (Israel): beloved; (French): dear one

Sheryl: (English): beloved
Shiloh: (Israel): peaceful

Sinead: (Irish): gift from God
Sienna: (Italian): reddish brown in color

Signourney: (English): victorious conquerer
Simone: (French): one who listens well

Solange: (French): religious and dignified
Soledad: (Spanish): solitary

Summer: (English): the summer season
Sunshine: (English): brilliant rays from the sun

Suri: (Todas): pointy nose
Sydney: (French): from Saint Denis

Tameka: (Aramaic): twin
Tanya: (Slovakian): a fairy queen

Taylor: (English & French): a tailor
Temperance: (English): temperate, moderate

Thora: (Scandinavian): thunder
Tiana: (Greek): princess

Tipper: (Irish): water pourer
Topagna: (Native American): from above

Tory/Tori: (American): victorious
Trisha: (English & Latin): noble

Tyra: (Scandinavian): God of battle; (Scottish): land
Uma: (Hindi): mother

Unique: (Latin): only one; (American): unlike others
Venus: (Greek): love goddess, little bird

Vera: (Russian): verity, truth
Vivianne: (English): the lady of the lake

Whitney: (English & African American): white island
Willow: (English): willow tree

Wynonna/Winona: (American): oldest daughter
Xena: (Greek): hospitable

Yasmine/Yasmeen: (Persian): resembling the jasmine flower
Zahara: (Arabic): shining, luminous

Zoe (or Zoey): (Greek): life, alive

Chapter 7. Named After U.S. Presidents, First Ladies & Their Daughters

The names of U.S. Presidents and First Ladies are favorites for many prospective parents. This is particularly true in election years, when the country "meets" the candidates' spouses and families for the first time. In this chapter, we will explore the names of U.S. Presidents, First Ladies and daughters that have stood the test of time; they also provide a fascinating glimpse into the distinguished men and women who have lived in the White House during the past two centuries.

U.S. Presidents

Abraham: (Hebrew & Biblical): exalted father
Andrew: (English, Scottish & Biblical): manly; brave

Arthur: (English): bear, stone
Barack: (Hebrew & Israel): flash of lightening

Benjamin: (English, Hebrew & Biblical): son of my right hand
Calvin: (English & Latin America): bald

Carter: (English): cart driver
Chester: (English): a rock fortress

Clinton: (English): town on a hill
Dwight: (English): a diminutive form of DeWitt, which means blond hair

Ford: (English): from the river crossing
Franklin: (English): free man

Garfield: (English): battlefield
George: (English): farmer

Gerald: (German): one who rules with the spear
Grant: (Latin): great

Grover: (English): grove
Harding: (English): brave, manly

Harrison: (English): son of Harry
Harry: (German): home or house ruler

Hayes: (English): from the hedged place
Herbert: (German): glorious soldier

Howard: (English): guardian of the home
Jackson: (English): son of Jack; (Scottish): God has been gracious

James: (English): supplant, replace; (Israel): supplanter
Jefferson: (English): son of Jeffrey, which means divine peace

John: (Israel): God is gracious; Jehovah has been gracious
Johnson: (Scottish & English): son of John

Kennedy: (Scottish): ugly head; (Irish & Gaelic): helmeted
Lincoln: (English): Roman colony at the pool; (Latin America): village

Lyndon: (English): flexible
Madison: (English): son of Matthew

Martin: (Latin): dedicated to Mars, the god of war
McKinley: (English): offspring of the fair hero

Monroe: (Gaelic): from the red swamp; (Scottish): from the river; (Irish): near the river roe
Nixon: (English): son of Nick

Quincy: (English): fifth; (French): estate belonging to Quintus
Pierce: (English): rock

Reagan: (Celtic): regal; (Irish): son of the small ruler
Richard: (English, French & German): a strong and powerful ruler

Ronald: (English, Gaelic & Scottish): rules with counsel
Roosevelt: (Danish): from the field of roses

Rutherford: (English): from the cattle's ford
Taft: (French): from the homestead

Taylor: (English & French): a tailor
Theodore: (Greek): divine gift

Thomas: (Hebrew, Greek & Dutch): twin
Truman: (English): loyal, trusted man; (German): faithful man

Tyler: (English): maker of tiles
Ulysses: (Latin) : hateful

Warren: (English): to preserve; (German): protector, loyal
Washington: (English): town near water

William: (English, German & French): protector
Wilson: (English & German): son of William

Woodrow: (English): forester, row of houses
Zachary: (Hebrew & Israel): remembered by God

First Ladies & Presidential Daughters

Abigail: (Hebrew): father rejoiced; (Biblical): source of joy
Amy: (English, French & Latin America): beloved

Anjelica: (Greek): a diminutive form of Angela, which means angel
Anna/Anne: (Hebrew): favor or grace; (Native American): mother; (Israel): gracious

Barbara: (Latin America): stranger
Caroline: (Spanish): beautiful woman; (French & English): song of happiness

Chelsea: (English): seaport
Claudia: (Spanish & Latin America): lame

Dolly: (American): cute child
Edith: (English): joyous, a treasure

Eleanor: (English): torch
Eliza: (French): consecrated to God

Elizabeth: (English): my God is bountiful; (Hebrew & Biblical): consecrated to God
Ellen: (Greek): light

Emily: (Latin America): admiring
Florence: (English): flowering; (Latin America): prosperous

Frances: (Latin America): free
Grace: (Latin America): grace of God; (American): land of grace

Harriet: (English & German): rules the home
Helen: (Greek): light

Hillary: (English & Greek): joyous, cheerful
Ida: (English): hardworking

Jacqueline: (French): to protect
Jane: (Hebrew): gift from God; (English): gracious, merciful

Jenna: (English): small bird
Julia: (French): youthful; (Latin America): soft-haired, youthful

Laura: (English, Spanish & Latin America): crowned with laurel, from the laurel tree
Leticia: (Spanish): joy, gladness

Lou/Louisa: (German): famous warrior
Lucrecia: (Spanish): brings light

Lucy: (Latin America): bringer of light
Malia: (American): calm, peaceful

Mamie: (American): a diminutive form of Margaret, which means pearl
Margaret: (Greek & Latin America): a pearl

Martha: (Israel): lady
Mary: (Biblical, English & Slovakian): bitter

Maureen: (Irish): star of the sea, from the sea of bitterness
Michelle: (French & Hebrew): like God, close to God

Nancy: (Hebrew & English): grace
Priscilla: (Latin): from an ancient family

Rose: (English, French & Scottish): flower, a rose; (German): horse, fame
Rosalind: (Spanish): beautiful one

Sasha: (English): defender of mankind
Sara(h): (Hebrew, Spanish & Biblical): princess

Chapter 8. Names from Disney

In reality, this material could easily be included in Chapter 6, which presents baby names from popular culture and the entertainment industry. But, on a practical basis, Disney has a greater reach - and longer staying power - than most musical, athletic, and movie franchises, which is why we have given it a chapter all its own.

Within a few months of a Disney release, the names of its characters begin to ascend the list of popular baby names. As a result, they bring the same benefits and pitfalls of other trendy names: everyone knows why you chose it..... and they probably chose it, too!

In the past few years, here are the most popular names from Disney movies (in alphabetical order). See if one of them is right for *your* little princess.

Boys Names from Disney

Abu: (African): father
Aladdin: (Arabian): faithful

Andrew/Andy: (English, Scottish & Biblical): manly; brave
Apollo: (Latin): strength, sun god

Archimedes: (Greek): to think about first
Arthur: (English): bear, stone

Ben: (English): son of my right hand
Bruce: (French & English): woods, thick brush

Chip: (English): chipping sparrow
Christopher: (Biblical): Christ-bearer; (English): he who holds Christ in his heart

Clayton: (English): mortal
Dale: (German): valley; (English): lives in the valley

Dashiell: (French): page boy
David: (Hebrew, Scottish & Welsh): beloved

Donald: (Celtic & Gaelic): dark stranger; (Irish, English & Scottish): great leader
Doug: (Scottish): dark river

Eli: (Hebrew): ascended, uplifted, high; (Greek): defender of man
Fagin: (Gaelic): ardent; (Irish): eager

Fenton: (English): from the farm on the fens
Finn: (English): blond

Flynn: (Irish): heir to the red-headed
Gaetan: (French & Italian): from Italy

Gaston: (French): a man from Gastony
Gideon: (Hebrew & Israel): great warrior

Gus: (German): revered
Hercules: (Greek): son of Zeus

Hermes: (Greek): stone pile
Horace: (French): hour, time

Iago: (Welsh): Spanish supplanter
Ian: (Scottish): gift from God

Jack: (English): God is gracious; (Hebrew): supplanter
Jafar: (Hindu): little stream

Jake: (Hebrew): he grasps the heel
Jasper: (Persian): treasurer

Jock: (Scottish): God is gracious
Ken: (Welsh): clear water; (English): royal obligation; (Irish): handsome; (Japanese): strong

Kevin: (Irish & Gaelic): handsome, beautiful; (Celtic): gentle
Lafayette: (Israel): to God to the mighty

Lawrence: (Latin America): crowned with laurel
Louis: (French): famous warrior

Lucifer: (Israel): bringing light
Lyle: (French & English): from the island

Maurice: (Latin): dark-skinned
Maximus: (Greek): greatest

Mickey: (Irish, English & Hebrew): diminutive of Michael, which means like God
Milo: (English): soldier

Nemo: (Greek): glen, glade
Oliver: (French, English, Danish & Latin America): the olive tree; (German): elf army

Orville: (French): golden city; (English): spear-strength
Oswald: (English): the power of God

Otto: (German): wealthy or prosperous
Pascal: (French): born at Easter

Pegasus: (Greek): winged horse
Percy: (English): piercing the valley

Peter: (Greek & English): a small stone or rock, apostle in the Bible
Philip: (French, Greek & English): lover of horses

Preston: (English): from the priest's farm
Randall: (German): the wolf shield

Remy: (French): oarsman or rower, from Rheims
Rex: (Latin): king

Robin: (English): a small bird
Roscoe: (Norwegian): deer forest

Rufus: (Latin America): redhead
Russell: (French): a little red-haired boy

Sebastian: (Greek): the revered one
Sid/Sidney: (English): wide island

Simba: (African): lion
Terrence: (Latin America): tender, gracious

Timon: (Hebrew): honor
Timothy: (Greek & English): to honor God

Tito: (Italian): honor
Winston: (English): joy stone

Woodey: (English): wooded meadow
Zeus: (Greek): powerful

Girls Names from Disney

Abigail: (Hebrew): father rejoiced; (Biblical): source of joy
Adelaide: (French & German): noble, kind

Adella: (German & French): noble, kind
Alana: (Irish): beautiful, peaceful

Alice: (Spanish): of the nobility
Amelia: (English & Latin America): industrious, striving

Anastasia: (Greek): resurrection
Andrina: (English): courageous, valiant

Anita: (Italian, Hebrew & Latin America): gracious
Ariel: (Hebrew): lioness of God

Arista: (Latin): harvest
Audrey: (English): noble strength

Aurora: (Latin): dawn
Bambi: (Italian): child

Barbie: (Latin America): a diminutive form of Barbara, which means stranger
Belle: (French): beautiful

Bianca: (Italian): white, fair
Bonnie: (English): good; (French): sweet; (Scottish): pretty, charming

Calliope: (Greek): beautiful voice
Carlotta: (Italian): a derivative of Charlotte, which means feminine

Celia: (Italian): heavenly
Charlotte: (French): feminine

Cinderella: (French & English): of the ashes
Clarabelle: (French & Catalonia): clear, bright/(French): beauty

Cleo: (English); father's glory
Colette: (English): victorious people

Daisy: (English); day's eve; (American): daisy flower
Dinah: (Hebrew & Israel): judgment

Donna: (Italian): lady
Dori/Dory: (Greek): gift

Elizabeth: (English): my God is bountiful; (Hebrew & Biblical): consecrated to God
Ellie: (English): a diminutive form of Ellen, which means light

Esmeralda: (Spanish): resembling a prized emerald
Eudora: (Greek): honored gift

Evangeline: (Greek): like an angel
Faline: (Irish): in charge

Fauna: (French): fawn, a young deer
Felicia/Felice/Phylicia: (French & Latin America): happiness

Flora: (English): flower: (Latin): flowering
Frances: (Latin America): free

Genia/Genie: (Greek): well-born
Giselle: (French): pledge

Georgette: (French): farmer
Gypsy: (English): wanderer

Helga: (German): wealthy, blessed
Hera: (Greek): Goddess of marriage

Jane: (Hebrew): gift from God; (English): gracious, merciful
Jasmine: (English): a fragrant flower

Jessica/Jessie: (Israel): God is watching; (Hebrew): rich, God beholds
Kala: (Hawaiian): princess

Kay: (Greek): rejoice; (Scottish & Welsh): fiery
Kirby: (Scandinavian): church village

Laverne: (French): woodland, like the spring
Lilo: (American): generous one

Ling: (Chinese): dainty
Marian: (French): bitter

Marie: (Latin): bitter
Megara: (Greek): wife of Hercules

Melody: (Greek): beautiful song
Minnie: (Irish): bitter; (Hebrew): wished for a child

Morgana: (Welsh & Celtic): dweller of the sea
Mulan: (Chinese): magnolia blossom

Myrtle: (Greek): the tree, victory; (English): the flowering shrub
Nala: (African): successful; (Tanzanian): queen

Olivia: (Spanish & Italian): olive; (Biblical): peace of the olive tree
Penny: (English): duck

Perdita: (English): lost
Rosie: (English, French & Scottish): flower, a rose; (German): horse, fame

Roz: (Polish): rose
Sally/Sallie: (English): princess

Sara(h): (Hebrew, Spanish & Biblical): princess
Seraphina: (Israel): burning fire; (Hebrew): fiery-ringed

Snow: (American): frozen rain
Thalia: (Greek): plentiful, blooming

Tia: (Greek); princess; (Spanish): princess, aunt; (African American): aunt
Tiana: (Greek): princess

Ursula: (Danish & Scandinavian): female bear
Vanessa: (Greek): resembling a butterfly

Violet: (French): resembling the flower
Wendy: (English): white-skinned, literary

Wilhemina: (German): resolute protector
Willow: (English): willow tree

Winifred: (Irish): friend of peace; (Welsh): reconciled, blessed

Chapter 9. Names that are Ideals or Concepts

A fascinating trend is the use of personal ideals - such as Charity and Fidelity - as baby names. These noble concepts are valued in all cultures, which gives the names a global appeal. Additionally, most of them are relatively rare, which increases their cachet. In this chapter, we present a list of ideal or concept names for boys and girls in alphabetical order. Perhaps one of them will be right for your little angel.

Concept Names for Boys

Creed: (English): belief, guiding principle
Earnest: (English): industrious

Ernest: (German): serious, determined, truth
Freeborn: (English): child of freedom

Freeman: (English): free
Goode: (English): upstanding

Hero: (Greek): great defender
Journey: (American): one who likes to travel

Justice/Justus: (English): fair and moral
Legend: (American): memorable

Loyal: (English): faithful, loyal
Rebel: (American): outlaw

Unique: (Latin): only one; (American): unlike others
Unity: (English): unity, togetherness

Young: (Korean): forever, unchanging

Concept Names for Girls

Angel: (Spanish & Greek): angelic
Bliss: (English): joy, happiness

Cadence: (Latin): rhythmic and melodious
Charity: (English): kindness, generous, goodwill

Charisma: (Greek): grace
Chastity: (Latin): pure

Cherish: (English): to be held dear, values
Destiny: (English): fate

Dharma: (Indian): ultimate law of all things
Epiphany: (Greek): manifestation

Ever: (English): strong as a boar
Faith: (English): faithful; (Latin America): to trust

Felicity: (French, English & Latin America): happiness
Fidelity: (Latin): faithful, true

Flair: (English): natural talent
Flame: (American): passionate, fiery

Grace: (Latin America): grace of God; (American): land of grace
Harmony: (Latin America): a beautiful blending

Haven: (English): safe place
Heaven: (American): from the heavens

Honor: (Spanish & Irish): honor; (Latin America): integrity
Hope: (English): trust, faith

Journey: (American): one who likes to travel
Joy: (French, English & Latin America): rejoicing

Liberty: (English): free, independent
Love: (English): full of affection

Maven: (English): having great knowledge
Mercy: (English): compassion; (French): merciful

Merry: (English): joyful, mirthful
Patience: (English): patient, enduring

Peace: (English): peaceful
Prudence: (English): prudent or cautious

Rebel: (American): outlaw
Salome: (Hebrew): peace and tranquility

Serenity: (Latin & English): peaceful
Unique: (Latin): only one; (American): unlike others

Unity: (American): unity, togetherness
Victory: (Latin): victory

Chapter 10. Names from Nature

People differ greatly in their temperament and ideals. Many times, our only commonality is the planet we inhabit - and the beautiful flowers, oceans, colors, and gemstones that we all enjoy. As a result, names from nature are perennial favorites for boys and girls in all cultures. In this chapter, we present an intriguing collection of names that honor the incomparable beauty of nature.

Boys Names from Nature

Basil: (Greek & Latin): royal, kingly
Bay: (Vietnamese): born on a Saturday; (American): a natural body of water

Birch: (English): white, shining
Brock: (English): badger

Clay: (English): clay maker, immortal
Cliff: (English): from the ford near the cliff

Colt: (American): baby horse; (English): from the dark town
Drake: (English): male duck, dragon

Eagle: (Native American): resembling the bird
Finch: (Irish): resembling the small bird

Flint: (English): stream, hard quartz rock
Forrest: (English & French): from the woods

Fox: (English): fox
Glade: (English): from the clearing in the woods

Glenn: (Scottish): glen, valley
Hawk: (English): hawk

Hawkins: (English): resembling a small hawk
Heath: (English): from the heath wasteland

Hunter: (English): one who hunts
Hyde: (English): animal hide

Jett: (English): resembling the black gemstone
Leif: (Scandinavian): beloved descendent

Raine: (American): blessings from above; (Latin): ruler; (English): lord, wise
Ridge: (English): from the ridge

River: (English): from the river
Robin: (English): a small bird

Sage: (English & French): wise one; (English): from the spice
Sailor: (American): sailor

Silver: (English): precious metal, the color silver
Storm: (English): tempest; (American): impetuous nature

Thorne: (English): from the thorn bush
Wolf: (English): the animal, wolf

Girls Names - Flowers, Fruit & Spices

Amaranth: (Greek): an unfading flower
Apple: (American): sweet fruit

Blossom: (English): fresh, flowerlike
Brandy: (English): a woman wielding a sword, an alcoholic drink

Calla: (Greek): resembling a lily, beautiful
Candy: (American): bright, sweet; (Hebrew): famous bearer

Cayenne: (French): hot and spicy
Cherise: (French): cherry, dear one

Cherry: (French): dear one; (American): cherry
Cinnamon: (American): reddish-brown spice

Clover: (English): meadow flower
Coral: (English): a reef formation

Daisy: (English); day's eve; (American): daisy flower
Fern: (English): the fern plant

Flora: (English): flower: (Latin): flowering
Gardenia: (English): a sweet-smelling flower

Ginger: (English): the spice
Heather: (English): a flowering plant

Holly: (French, English & Germany): shrub
Honey: (English): sweet

Iris: (Greek): colorful, rainbow; (Hebrew & English): the flower
Ivy: (English): vine

Jasmine: (Persian): a climbing plant; (English): a fragrant flower
Laurel: (English & French): crowned with laurel, from the laurel tree

Lavender: (English): a purple flowering plant
Leighton: (English): herb garden, town by the meadow

Lilac: (Latin America): bluish purple; (American): a flowering bluish purple shrub
Lily: (Hebrew, English & Latin America): lily, blossoming flower

Lotus: (Greek): the flower
Meadow: (American): beautiful field

Olive: (Irish): olive; (Latin America): olive branch, peace
Peaches: (English): fruit

Petunia: (English): resembling the flower
Poppy: (English & Latin America): the poppy flower

Rose: (English, French & Scottish): flower, a rose; (German): horse, fame
Rosemary: (English): bitter rose

Saffron: (English): resembling the yellow flower
Sage: (English & French): wise one; (English): from the spice

Violet: (Italian): violet flower
Willow: (English): willow tree

Zinnia: (English): the flower: (Latin America): beautiful

Girls Names - Colors

Amber: (Arabic): precious jewel, yellow-brown color
Blue: (English): the color blue

Crimson: (English): deep red color
Coral: (English): a reef formation

Cyan: (American): light blue or green
Ebony: (American): dark strength

Fuschia: (Latin): resembling the color
Goldie: (English): resembling the precious metal

Indigo: (Latin America): dark blue
Ivory: (English & Latin America): white, pure

Lavender: (English): a purple flowering plant
Mauve: (American): purplish color

Scarlett: (English): red
Sienna: (Italian): reddish brown in color

Silver: (English): the color silver
Violet: (Italian): violet flower

Girls Names - Gemstones

Amber: (Arabic): precious jewel, yellow-brown color
Amethyst: (Greek): a semi-precious stone **Beryl:** (Greek & English): green jewel

Azura/Azure: (Persian): a blue, semi-precious stone
Cameo: (Italian): sculptured jewel; (English & Latin America): a shadow or carved gem portrait

Crystal/Krystal: (English): jewel; (Latin America): a clear brilliant glass
Diamond: (English): bridge protector: (Greek): unbreakable

Emerald: (English, Spanish & French): a bright green gem
Garnet: (English): gem, armed with a spear; (French): keeper of grain

Gemma: (French & Italian): jewel
Jade: (Spanish): jewel, green gemstone

Jewel: (English & French): precious gem
Onyx: (Greek): the onyx stone

Opal: (English & Indian): precious gem
Pearl: (English): gemstone

Ruby: (English & French): a precious jewel, a ruby
Sapphire: (Greek): the sapphire gem; (Hebrew): sapphire gem, beautiful

Topaz/Topaza: (Mexican): golden gem

Girls Names - Weather, Seasons, Nature & Animals

April: (English): opening buds of spring; (Latin America): opening, fourth month
Aurora: (Latin): dawn

Autumn: (English & Latin America): the fall season
Bay: (Vietnam): born on a Saturday

Brooke: (English): lives by the stream
Bunny: (Greek): a diminutive form of Beatrice, which means blessed, happy

Dawn: (English): aurora; (Greek): sunrise
Dove: (American): bird of peace

Easter: (American): from the holiday or Christian festival
Fauna: (French): fawn, a young deer

Fawn: (French & English): young deer
January: (American): the first month of the year

June: (Dominican Republic): born in June
Lake: (American): body of water, from the lake

Lark: (English): a lark; (American): songbird
Luna: (Latin & Latin America): the moon

Marina: (Greek & Slovakian): from the sea
May: (English): name of month; (Hebrew & Latin America): from Mary

Rain/Raine: (American): blessings from above; (French & Latin): ruler; (English): lord, wise
Rainbow: (English): rainbow

Raven: (English): to be black, blackbird
River: (Latin & French): stream, water

Robin: (English): a small bird
Sailor: (American): sailor

Skye: (English): sky
Snow: (American): frozen rain

Spring: (English): the spring season
Starr: (English & American): star

Stormy: (English): tempest; (American): impetuous nature
Summer: (American): the summer season

Sunshine: (English): brilliant rays from the sun
Una: (Welsh & Celtic): white wave; (Native America): remember; (English): one

Ursula: (Danish & Scandinavian): female bear
Winter: (American): the season

Wren: (Welsh): ruler; (English): small bird

Chapter 11. Last Names as First Names

In the past decade, one of the most popular trends is the use of last names as first names for both boys and girls. This approach offers parents a creative way to honor a cherished surname or to give their child a gender neutral (unisex) moniker that will be easy to remember. Alternatively, these choices also make excellent middle names.

In this chapter, we have included the most popular last names that are gender neutral (in alphabetical order). Use the list to narrow your search - or as inspiration for your own unique choices.

Abbott: (Hebrew): father
Addison: (English): son of Adam

Alton: (English): from the old town
Ames: (French): friend

Anderson: (Scottish): son of Andrew
Ashton: (Hebrew): shining light; (English): ash tree settlement

August: (German): revered
Avery: (English): counselor, sage, wise

Bailey: (English): bailiff, steward, public official
Brown: (English): brown color, dark-skinned

Bellamy: (French): handsome
Bowen: (Gaelic): small son; (Irish): archer

Black: (English): dark-skinned
Blake: (English): pale, fair

Brooks: (English): running water, son of Brooke
Brogan: (Gaelic & Irish): from the ditch

Brady: (Irish): a large-breasted woman
Blair: (Irish & Celtic): from the plain, (Gaelic): child of the fields; (Scottish): peat moss

Campbell: (Gaelic): crooked mouth; (French): from the beautiful field
Cullen: (Irish & Gaelic): handsome; (Celtic): cub; (English): city in Germany

Chase: (English): hunter
Curran: (Celtic): hero

Casey: (Celtic & Gaelic): brave; (Irish): observant, alert, brave; (Spanish): honorable
Cameron: (Irish & Gaelic): crooked nose

Carson: (English): son who lives in the swamp
Cain: (Israel): craftsman; (Hebrew): spear; (Welsh): clear water; (Irish): archaic

Carter: (English): cart driver
Chen: (Chinese): great, dawn

Cramer: (English): full
Crosby: (English): town crossing

Drew: (English): courageous, valiant
Davis: (English & Scottish): David's son

Drake: (English): male duck, dragon
Dixon: (English): power, brave ruler

Emerson: (English): brave, powerful
Elliott: (Israel): close to God; (English): the Lord is my God

Easton: (English): from east town
Ennis: (Irish): island; (Gaelic): the only choice

Ford: (English): river crossing
Franklin: (English): free man

Foster: (English & French): one who keeps the forest
Gallagher: (Irish & Gaelic): eagle helper

Fletcher: (English): one who makes arrows
Fleming: (English): from Denmark

Fitzgerald: (English): the son of Gerald
Fitzpatrick: (English): son of Patrick

Flynn: (Irish): ruddy complexion
Ford: (English): from the river crossing

Grant: (Latin): great
Gannon: (Irish & Gaelic): fair-skinned

Grayson: (English): son of the bailiff
Graham: (Scottish): from the gray home

Haines: (English): from the vine-covered cottage
Hayden: (English & Welsh): in the meadow or valley

Hilton: (English): town on a hill
Henderson: (Scottish): son of Henry

Hunter: (English): one who hunts
Holt: (English): wood, by the forest

Hogan: (Irish & Gaelic): young, young at heart
Howard: (English): guardian of the home

Jordan: (Hebrew): to flow down; (Israel): descendant
Jensen: (Scandinavian): God is gracious

Jackson: (English): son of Jack; (Scottish): God has been gracious
Johnson: (Scottish & English): son of John

Jagger: (English): a carter, to carry
Jefferson: (English): son of Jeffrey, which means divine peace

Kane: (Welsh): beautiful; (Gaelic): little warrior
Keaton: (English): from the town of hawks

Kendall: (English & Celtic): from the bright valley
Kennedy: (Scottish): ugly head; (Irish & Gaelic): helmeted

Kirkland: (English): from the church's land
Kramer: (German): shopkeeper

Landon: (English): grassy plain; from the long hill
Lawrence: (Latin America): crowned with laurel

Lincoln: (English): Roman colony at the pool; (Latin America): village
Logan: (Irish): small cove; (Scottish): Finnian's servant; (Gaelic): from the hollow

London: (English): fortress of the moon
Lewis: (German): famous warrior

Mackenzie: (Irish & Scottish): fair, favored one
Meyer: (Jewish & Hebrew): shining

Morgan: (Celtic): lives by the sea; (Welsh): bright sea
Marlowe: (English): from the hill by the lake

Macdonald: (Scottish): son of Donald
Malloy: (Irish): noble chief

Madison: (English): son of Matthew
Monroe: (Gaelic): from the red swamp; (Scottish & Irish): near the river roe

Marshall: (French): caretaker of horses; (English): a steward
Martin: (Latin): dedicated to Mars, the god of war

Miller: (English): one who works at the mill
Maxwell: (English): capable, great spring

Nash: (American): adventurer
North: (English): from the north

Moore: (French): dark-skinned; (Irish & French): surname
Murphy: (Gaelic): warrior of the sea

Nolan: (Irish & Gaelic): famous; (Celtic): noble
Nelson: (English, Celtic, Irish & Gaelic): son of Neil

Nash: (American): adventurer
Newman: (English): a newcomer

Oliver: (French, English, Danish & Latin America): the olive tree; (German): elf army
Osborne: (Norse): a bear of God

Payton: (English): village
Paxton: (English): from the peaceful farm; (Latin America): town of peace

Parker: (English): keeper of the park or forest
Porter: (French): gate keeper; (Latin America): door guard

Reagan: (Celtic): regal; (Irish): son of the small ruler
Riley: (Irish): a small stream

Ryan: (Gaelic): little king; (Irish): kindly, young royalty
Rowan: (Irish): red-haired; (English & Gaelic): from the rowan tree

Reese: (Welsh): enthusiastic
Rylan: (English); dweller in the rye field

Quinn: (Celtic): wise; (Irish): fifth, counsel, intelligent
Quentin: (French, English & Latin America): fifth

Shea: (Irish): majestic, fairy place
Smith: (English): artisan, tradesman

Scully: (Irish): herald; (Gaelic): town crier
Silver: (English): the color silver

Sawyer: (English): one who works with wood
Sheldon: (English): from the steep valley

Tanner: (English & German): leather worker
Terrell: (German): thunder ruler

Tate: (English): cheerful
Tyler: (English): maker of tiles

Taylor: (English & French): a tailor
Thomas: (Hebrew, Greek & Dutch): twin

West: (English): from the west
Winter: (American): the season

Wyatt: (English): guide, wide, wood, famous bearer; (French): son of the forest guide
Wilson: (English & German): son of William

Chapter 12. Named After Famous Places

This chapter explores a fascinating trend that has emerged in the past two decades: the use of city, state, and country names for both boys and girls. Some of these choices are fairly common, such as Augusta and Charlotte, while others are esoteric, such as Aspen and Darby. Nevertheless, the trend is real, the names are eclectic, and the variety can't be beat. So, sit back and explore the most popular baby names (in alphabetical order) that are based on famous places.

Famous Places - Boys

Austin: (English): from the name Augustin, which means revered
Ames: (French): friend

Alton: (English): from the old town
Aiken: (English): sturdy, made of oak

Boston: (English): the city Boston
Beaumont: (French): beautiful mountain

Berkeley: (English & Irish): from the birch meadow
Benson: (English): son of Benedict

Bentley: (English): from the bent grass meadow
Barrington: (English): town of Barr

Chester: (English): a rock fortress
Clayton: (English): mortal

Camden: (Irish, Scottish, English & Gaelic): from the winding valley
Carlin: (Irish, Gaelic & Scottish): little champion

Clyde: (Irish): warm
Carlisle: (English): from the walled city

Cody: (Irish): helpful; (English): a cushion, helpful
Chandler: (French): candle maker

Colton: (English): coal town, from the dark town
Columbus: (Greek): curious

Derby: (English): deer park; (Irish): from the village of dames
Devon: (English & Irish): a poet, a county in England

Diego: (Spanish): Saint James
Dallas: (Irish & Gaelic): wise; (Scottish & Celtic): from the waterfall

Easton: (English): from east town
Everett: (English): hardy, brave, strong

Fairbanks: (English): from the bank along the path
Fargo: (American): jaunty

Frederick: (German): peaceful ruler
Flint: (English): stream, hard quartz rock

Fremont: (French): protector of freedom
Fuller/Fullerton: (English): from Fuller's town

Jordan: (Hebrew): to flow down; (Israel): descendant
Jackson: (English): son of Jack; (Scottish): God has been gracious

Hartley: (English): from the stage meadow
Hadley: (English & Irish): from the heath covered meadow

Holland: (American): from the Netherlands
Houston: (Gaelic): from Hugh's town: (English): from the town on the hill

Kent: (English & Welsh): white; (Celtic): chief
Kingston: (English): from the king's village

Lincoln: (English): Roman colony at the pool; (Latin America): village
Lawrence: (Latin America): crowned with laurel

Logan: (Irish): small cove; (Scottish): Finnian's servant; (Gaelic): from the hollow
Landon: (English): grassy plain, from the long hill

London: (English): fortress of the moon
Livingston: (English): Leif's town

Mitchell: (Hebrew): gift from God
Maxwell: (English): capable, great spring

Mason: (French & English): stone worker
Merrill: (English): falcon, shining sea

Orlando: (Spanish): land of gold
Oliver: (French, English, Danish & Latin America): the olive tree; (German): elf army

Ramsey: (Scottish): island of ravens
Redford: (English): over the red river, from the reedy ford

Raleigh: (English): deer meadow
Radcliff/Radcliffe: (English): red cliff

Salem: (Hebrew): peace
Salisbury: (English): fort at the willow pool

Trenton: (English): town of Trent
Tanner: (English & German): leather worker

Texas: (Native American): one of many friends, from the state of Texas
Tennessee: (Native American): from the state of Tennessee

York: (Celtic, English & Latin America): from the yew tree
Vernon: (Latin): youthful, young at heart; (French & English): alder tree grove

Warren: (English): to preserve; (German): protector, loyal
Wesley: (English & Berman): from the west meadow

Famous Places - Girls

Aurora: (Latin): dawn
Augusta: (Latin): venerable, majestic

Afton: (English): from the Afton River
Ada: (English): wealthy; (Hebrew): ornament; (German): noble; (African): first daughter

Asia: (Greek & English): resurrection, rising sun
Arizona: (Native American): from the little spring, from the state of Arizona

Aspen: (English): from the aspen tree
Alexandria: (Greek, English & Latin America): defender of mankind

Brooklyn: (English): water, stream
Bristol: (English): bridge

Catalina: (Spanish): pure
Carolina: (Mexican): beautiful woman; (French & English): song of happiness

Chelsea: (English): seaport
Charlotte: (French): feminine

Cheyenne: (French): dog; (Native American): an Algonquin tribe
China: (Chinese): fine porcelain

Dakota: (Native American): friend, ally
Darby: (Irish & Gaelic): free man; (English): deer park

Eden: (Hebrew): delight; (Israel): paradise
Echo: (Greek): sound returned

Florence: (English): flowering; (Latin America): prosperous
Fallon: (Irish): of a ruling family

Georgia: (Greek & German): farmer
Geneva: (French): juniper berry: (German): of the race of woman

Helena: (Greek): light
Hailey/Hailee/Haley: (English): hero, field of hay

Ireland: (Irish): of a ruling family
India: (English): from India

Jordan: (Hebrew): to flow down; (Israel): descendant
Logan: (Irish): small cove; (Scottish): Finnian's servant; (Gaelic): from the hollow

Kent: (English & Welsh): white; (Celtic): chief
Kenya: (Israel): animal horn

Lincoln: (English): Roman colony at the pool; (Latin America): village
Lane: (English): narrow road, from the long meadow

Madison: (English): son of Matthew
Montana: (Latin America): mountainous

Nazareth: (Hebrew): religion
Nevada: (English): covered in snow

Odessa: (Latin America): the odyssey
Octavia: (Latin America): eighth; (Italian): born eighth

Paris: (Persian): angelic face; (Greek): downfall; (French): the capital city of France
Phoenix: (Greek): rising bird

Regina: (Italian, Spanish & Latin America): queen
Racine: (French): root

Sierra: (Spanish): mountain; (Irish): dark
Savannah: (Spanish): open plain, field

Virginia: (English, Spanish, Italian & Latin America): pure
Vienna: (Latin America): from wine country

Sydney: (English): wide island
Sahara: (Arabian): wilderness

Victoria: (Latin America): winner
Valencia: (Spanish): brave

Chapter 13. One Syllable Names

When I meet prospective parents, I tend to hear the same question over and over again: "Why aren't there any great one-syllable names?" This chapter answers that question in a fairly conclusive way: there are dozens of excellent baby names that are short, sweet, and just one syllable. A better question - how can you choose just one?

One Syllable Names for Boys

Abe: (Jewish): father of nations
Ace: (Latin): unity

Bart: (Hebrew): ploughman; (English): from the barley farm
Beau: (French): handsome, beautiful

Ben: (English): son of my right hand
Black: (English): dark-skinned

Blade: (English): wielding a sword or knife
Blake: (English): pale, fair

Blaze: (Latin): one who stammers; (English): flame
Boone: (French): good

Boyd: (Celtic): blond-haired
Brant: (English): steep, tall

Brent: (English): from the hill
Brett: (French, English & Celtic): a native of Brittany

Brice: (Welsh): alert, ambitious
Brock: (English): badger

Brooks: (English): running water, son of Brooke
Brown: (English): brown color, dark-skinned

Bruce: (French & English): woods, thick brush
Bryce: (Scottish): speckled

Buck: (German & English): male deer
Bud: (English): brotherly

Burke: (German): birch tree
Byrd: (English): bird-like

Cade: (American): pure
Cain: (Israel): craftsman; (Hebrew): spear; (Welsh): clear water; (Irish): archaic

Carl: (English): man; (German): strong one
Cash: (Latin): money

Chad: (English): battle
Chance: (English & French): good luck, keeper of records

Charles: (English): strong, manly
Chase: (English): hunter

Clark: (English): cleric, scholar, clerk
Claude: (English): lame

Claus: (Greek): people's victory
Clay: (English): clay maker, immortal

Cliff: (English): from the ford near the cliff
Clive: (English): one who lives near the cliff

Cole: (Irish): warrior; (English): having dark features
Colt: (American): baby horse; (English): from the dark town

Craig: (Scottish): dwells at the crag; (Welsh): rock
Creed: (English): belief, guiding principle

Dale: (German): valley; (English): lives in the valley
Dane: (Hebrew & Scandinavian): God will judge; (English): brook

Dax: (English & French): water
Dean: (English): head, leader

Dell: (English): from the small valley
Dierks: (Danish): ruler of the people

Dirk: (German): a diminutive form of Derek, which means gifted ruler
Dobbs: (English): fiery

Dolph: (German): diminutive form of Adolph, which means noble wolf
Doyle: (Irish): dark river

Drake: (English): male duck, dragon
Drew/Dru: (English): courageous, valiant

Duane: (Gaelic): a dark and swarthy man
Dwight: (English): a diminutive form of DeWitt, which means blond hair

Earl: (Irish): pledge; (English): nobleman
Fenn: (English): from the marsh

Finn: (English): blond
Fitch: (English): resembling an ermine

Flynn: (Irish): ruddy complexion
Ford: (English): from the river crossing

Fox: (English): fox
Frank: (English): free man

Fred: (German): peaceful ruler
Fynn: (Russian): the Offin River

Gabe: (English): strength of God
Gage/Gaige: (French): a pledge or pawn

Garth: (Scandinavian): keeper of the garden
Gene: (English): a well-born man

George: (English): farmer
Giles: (Greek): resembling a young goat

Gill: (Gaelic): servant
Glenn: (Scottish): glen, valley

Grant: (Latin): great
Gray: (English): gray-haired

Gus: (German): revered
Guy: (French): guide; (Hebrew): valley; (Celtic): sensible; (Latin America): living spirit

Haines: (English): from the vine-covered cottage
Hal: (English): ruler of the army

Hank: (Dutch & German): rules his household
Hans: (German & Hebrew): gift from God; (Scandinavian): God is gracious

Heath: (English): from the heath wasteland
Holt: (English): wood, by the forest

Hoyt: (Irish): mind, spirit
Hugh: (English): intelligent

Hurst: (Irish): dense grove, thicket
Hyde: (English): animal hide

Ike: (Hebrew): full of laughter
Ives: (Scandinavian): the archer's bow

Jack: (English): God is gracious; (Hebrew): supplanter
Jake: (Hebrew): he grasps the heel

James: (English); supplant, replace; (Israel): supplanter
Jan: (Dutch): a form of John, which means God is gracious

Jax: (American): son of Jack
Jay: (German): swift; (French): blue jay; (English): to rejoice; (Latin America): a crow

Jean: (French): a form of John, which means God is gracious
Jess: (Israel): wealthy

Jett: (English): resembling the black gemstone
Jobe: (Hebrew): afflicted

Joel: (Hebrew): Jehovah is God; (Israel): God is willing
John: (Israel): God is gracious; Jehovah has been gracious

Juan: (Hebrew): gift from God; (Spanish): God is gracious
Jules: (French): youthful, downy-haired

Kai: (American): ocean; (Welsh): keeper of the keys; (Scottish): fire
Kale: (English): manly and strong

Kane: (Welsh): beautiful; (Gaelic): little warrior
Karl: (English & Icelandic): man; (French): strong, masculine; (Danish): one who is free

Keefe: (Irish): handsome, loved
Keene: (German): bold, sharp; (English): smart

Keith: (Scottish): wood; (Irish): warrior descending; (Welsh): dwells in the woods
Kent: (English & Welsh): white; (Celtic): chief

King: (English): royal ruler
Kirk: (Norse): a man of the church

Knight: (English): noble soldier
Knox: (English): from the hills

Kris: (Swedish): Christ-bearer
Kurt: (German): brave counselor

Kipp: (English): from the small pointed hill
Kyle: (Gaelic): young; (Irish): young at heart

Lane: (English): narrow road
Laird: (Scottish): lord; (Irish): head of household

Lance: (German): spear; (French): land
Lear: (English): Shakespearean king

Lee/Leigh: (English): meadow
Leif: (Scandinavian): beloved descendent

Lloyd: (Celtic, Welsh & English): gray
Locke: (English): forest

Luke: (Greek & Latin America): light
Lyle: (French & English): from the island

Lynch: (Irish): mariner
Lynn: (English): waterfall

Mark: (Latin): dedicated to Mars, the god of war
Max: (English): greatest

Mead: (English): meadow
Merle: (French): blackbird; (English): falcon

Miles: (German): merciful; (Latin): a soldier
Moore: (French): dark-skinned; (Irish & French): surname

Nash: (American): adventurer
Neal/Neil: (Irish, English & Celtic): a champion

Ned: (English & French): diminutive of Edward, which means wealthy guardian
Niles: (English): champion

Noel: (French): Christmas
North: (English): from the north

Oz: (Hebrew): having great strength
Puck: (English): elf

Pace: (English): a peaceful man
Paine/Payne: (Latin): a peasant

Paul: (English & French): small, apostle in the Bible
Pax: (English): peaceful

Pell: (English): a clerk
Penn: (Latin): pen, quill

Pierce: (English): rock
Platt: (French): flatland

Ponce: (Spanish): fifth
Prince: (Latin): chief, prince

Quinn: (Gaelic): one who provides counsel
Royce: (Irish & French): king, regal; (Scottish, Gaelic & Scottish): red, red-haired

Rafe: (Irish): a tough man
Rain/Raine: (American): blessings from above; (French & Latin): ruler; (English): lord, wise

Ralph: (English): wolf counsel
Rand: (German): the wolf shield

Raul: (French): a form of Ralph, which means wolf counsel
Ray: (French): regal: (Scottish): grace; (English): wise protector

Reed/Reid: (English & French): red-haired
Rex: (Latin): king

Rhett: (English): stream
Rhys/Reese/Reece: (English &Welsh): ardent, fiery, enthusiastic

Rhodes: (Greek): where roses grow
Ridge: (English): from the ridge

Roan: (English): from the Rowan tree
Roark: (Gaelic): champion

Rolf: (German): wolf counsel
Ross: (Scottish): from the peninsula

Saige/Sage: (English & French): wise one; (English): from the spice
Saul: (Israel): borrowed: (Hebrew & Spanish): asked for

Scott: (Scottish): wanderer
Sean/Shawn: (Irish): God is gracious

Seth: (Hebrew): anointed; (Israel): appointed
Shane: (Hebrew): gift from God; (Irish): God is gracious

Shea: (Irish): majestic, fairy place
Slade: (English): child of the valley

Sloan: (English): raid; (Irish, Celtic, Scottish & Gaelic): fighter, warrior
Smith: (English): artisan, tradesman

Stern: (English): austere
Stony: (English): stone

Storm: (English): tempest; (American): impetuous nature
Sven: (Scandinavian): youth

Taft: (French): from the homestead
Thor: (Norse): god of thunder

Thorne: (English): from the thorn bush
Todd: (Scottish): fox

Trent: (Welsh): dwells near the rapid stream
Trey: (English & Latin): third-born child

Trigg: (Norse): truthful
Tripp: (English): traveler

Troy: (French): curly haired; (Irish): foot soldier
True: (English): loyal

Twain: (English): divided in two
Ty: (English): from the fenced-in pasture

Vance: (English): windmill dweller
Vaughn: (Celtic): small

Wade: (English): ford, cross the river
Wayne: (English): craftsman, wagon maker

Webb: (English): weaver
West: (English): from the west

Whit: (English): white-skinned
Wolf: (English): the animal, wolf

Yale: (Welsh): from the fertile upland
Yan/Yann: (Russian): a form of John, which means God is gracious

York: (Celtic, English & Latin America): from the yew tree
Yves: (French): a young archer

Zale: (Greek): having the strength of the sea
Zane: (Hebrew): gift from God; (Arabian): beloved

Zeke: (English): strengthened by God
Zeus: (Greek): powerful one

One Syllable Names for Girls

Anne: (Hebrew & Israel): favor or grace
Bea: (America): blessed

Belle: (French): beautiful
Bess: (English): my God is bountiful

Beth: (Scottish): lively
Blair: (Irish & Celtic): from the plain, (Gaelic): child of the fields; (Scottish): peat moss

Blaine: (Gaelic, Irish & Celtic): thin
Blake: (English): pale blond or dark; (Scottish): dark-haired

Bliss: (English): joy, happiness
Blue: (English): the color blue

Blythe: (English): happy
Brea: (French): champion

Bree: (Celtic): broth; (Irish): hill, strong one
Bryce: (Welsh): alert, ambitious

Brie: (French): from the northern region of France
Britt: (Swedish): high goddess

Brooke: (English): lives by the stream
Brynn: (Welsh): hill

Cate: (English): blessed, pure, holy
Cher: (English): beloved

Clove: (German): spice
Cree: (Native American): name of tribe

Dale: (English): valley
Dawn: (English): aurora; (Greek): sunrise

Dove: (American): bird of peace
Drew: (Greek): courageous, strong

Dulce: (Latin): very sweet
Fran: (Latin America): free

Eve: (Hebrew): to breathe
Faith: (English): faithful; (Latin America): to trust

Fawn: (French & English): young deer
Faye: (French): fairy; (Irish): raven; (English): faith, confidence

Fern: (English): the fern plant
Fleur: (French): flower

Flynn: (Irish): heir to the red-headed
Gayle: (English): merry, lively

Gay: (English): merry, happy
Grace: (Latin America): grace of God; (American): land of grace

Greer: (Scottish): alert, watchful
Gwen: (Celtic): mythical son of Gwastad

Hope: (English): trust, faith
Jade: (Spanish): jewel, green gemstone

Jayne: (Indian): victorious; (Hebrew): gift from God; (English): Jehovah has been gracious
Jean: (Hebrew): God is gracious

Jill: (English): girl, sweetheart
Joan: (Hebrew): gift from God; (English): God is gracious

Joy: (French, English & Latin America): rejoicing
June: (Dominican Republic): born in June

Kate: (Irish, English & French): diminutive of Katherine, which means pure, virginal
Kay: (Greek): rejoice; (Scottish & Welsh): fiery

Kent: (English & Welsh): white; (Celtic): chief
Kim: (Welsh): leader

Kyle: (Irish): attractive
Lane: (English): narrow road, from the long meadow

Lake: (American): body of water, from the lake
Lark: (English): a lark; (American): songbird

Leigh: (English): from the meadow
Liv: (Norwegian): protector

Love: (English): full of affection
Lynn(e): (English): woman of the lake, waterfall

Madge: (English): pearl
Maeve: (Irish): intoxicating, joyous

Maude: (French): strong in war; (Irish): strong battle maiden
Mauve: (American): purplish color

May: (English): name of month; (Hebrew & Latin America): from Mary
Nell: (English): torch

Neve: (Irish): radiant; (Hebrew): life
Noor: (Aramaic): light

Paige: (French): assistant, attendant
Pearl: (English): gemstone

Queen: (English): queen
Quinn: (Celtic): queenly

Rae: (Scottish): grace; (German): wise protection
Rain/Raine: (American): blessings from above; (French & Latin): ruler; (English): lord, wise

Reese: (Welsh): enthusiastic
Rose: (English, French & Scottish): flower, a rose; (German): horse, fame

Rue: (Greek): herb of grace
Ruth: (Hebrew & Israel): companion, friend

Saige/Sage: (English): sage
Scout: (French): scout

Shane: (Hebrew): gift from God; (Irish): God is gracious
Shawn: (Irish): a form of Sean, which means God is gracious

Skye: (English): sky
Sloan: (English): raid; (Irish, Celtic, Scottish & Gaelic): fighter, warrior

Starr: (English & American): star
Tess: (English): harvester

Tish: (Latin): joy
Tyne: (English): of the river Tyne

Vail: (English): valley
Wren: (Welsh): ruler; (English): small bird

Chapter 14. Four-Syllable Names

On a practical basis, this chapter is the flip side of Chapter 13, which presents dozens of one syllable names for boys and girls. Here, we will focus on the longest, most elegant and sophisticated names that are at least four syllables. Why, you may ask, would someone choose this type of name for their child, which is hard to pronounce and spell? Many times, a long name is the best fit for a short and simple last name, such as Smith, Tom, Wu, or Lee. Other times, the parents are seeking a formal name that the child can "grow into," such as Elizabeth. In the meantime, they will call the child one of many possible nicknames, such as Liz, Betty, or Beth.

One fascinating aspect about this list: many of these longer names are older, from other cultures, and not particularly common (with a few notable exceptions). Nevertheless, for parents seeking elegant, sophisticated, and mature names that are also somewhat unusual, this chapter has several hidden gems.

Four-Syllable Names for Boys

Alejandro: (Spanish): defender of mankind
Alexander: (Greek): protector of mankind

Aloysius: (German): famous warrior
Amadeus: (Latin): loves God

Amerigo: (Teutonic): industrious
Arsenio: (Greek): masculine, virile

Archimedes: (Greek): to think about first
Aristotle: (Greek): thinker with a great purpose

Aurelius: (Latin): golden
Azariah: (Hebrew & Israel): God helps

Bartholomew: (English, Hebrew & Biblical): son of a farmer
Bonaventure: (Latin): one who undertakes a blessed venture

Cornelius: (Irish): strong willed, wise; (Latin America): horn-colored
Ezekiel: (Hebrew & Israel): strength of God

Deangelo: (Italian): a combination of De and Angelo; little angel
Demetrius: (Greek): goddess of fertility, one who loves the earth

Ebenezer: (Hebrew & Israel): rock of help
Emmanuel: (Hebrew): God with us

Fabrizio: (Italian): craftsman
Galileo: (Hebrew): one who comes from Galilee

Genovese: (Italian): from Genoa, Italy
Geronimo: (Greek & Italian): a famous chef

Giovanni/Gian: (Italian); God is gracious
Horatio: (French): hour, time

Indiana: (English): from the land of the Indians, the state of Indiana
Macallister: (Gaelic): the son of Alistair

Jedidiah: (Hebrew): one who is loved by God
Jeremiah: (Hebrew): may Jehovah exalt; (Israel): sent by God

Maximilian: (Latin): greatest
Montgomery: (French): rich man's mountain

Napoleon: (French): fierce one
Nehemiah: (Hebrew): compassion of Jehovah

Octavius: (Latin): eighth
Odysseus: (Greek): wrathful

Olivier: (French, English, Danish & Latin America): the olive tree; (German): elf army
Onofrio: (Italian): a defender of peace

Santiago: (Spanish): named for Saint James
Valentino: (Italian): brave or strong; (Latin America): health or love

Zachariah: (Hebrew): Jehovah has remembered; (Israel): remembered by the Lord
Michelangelo*: (Italian): a combination of Michael and Angelo

Four-Syllable Names for Girls

Adelina: (French & Spanish): of the nobility
Alejandra: (Spanish): defender of mankind

Adriana: (Spanish, Greek & Italian): woman with dark and rich features
Alexandra/Alexandria*: (Greek, English & Latin America): defender of mankind

America: (English): ruler of the home
Anastasia: (Greek): resurrection

Angelina: (Italian): little angel
Anjelica: (Greek): a diminutive form of Angela, which means angel

Antonia: (Greek): flourishing or flowering
Apollonia*: (Greek): strength

Aphrodite: (Greek): beauty, love goddess
Arabella: (Latin): answered prayer, beautiful altar

Arianna: (Greek & Italian): holy
Arizona: (Native American): from the little spring, from the state of Arizona

Belisama: (Celtic): goddess of rivers and lakes
Davina: (Scottish): feminine form of David, which means beloved one

Carolina: (Mexico): beautiful woman; (French & English): song of happiness
Catalina: (Spanish): pure

Caledonia: (Latin): woman of Scotland
Calliope: (Greek): beautiful voice

Cleopatra: (Greek): glory to the father; (African American): queen
Concordia: (Latin): peace

Corinthia: (Greek): woman of Clorinth
Eliana: (Hebrew): the Lord answers our prayers

Elizabeth: (English): my God is bountiful; (Hebrew & Biblical): consecrated to God
Eloisa: (Latin): famous warrior

Emmanuelle: (Hebrew): God is with us
Epiphany: (Greek): manifestation

Ernestina: (German): determined, serious
Esmeralda: (Spanish): resembling a prized emerald

Eugenia: (Greek): well-born
Evangeline: (Greek): like an angel

Fabiana: (Latin): bean grower
Felicity: (French, English & Latin America): happiness

Fidelity: (Latin): faithful, true
Frederica: (German): peaceful ruler

Gabriella: (Israel & Hebrew): God gives strength; (Italian): woman of God
Gardenia: (English): a sweet-smelling flower

Giovanna: (Italian): God is gracious
Guadalupe: (Spanish): from the valley of wolves

Henrietta: (German): ruler of the house
Ileana: (Roman): torch; (Greek): from the city of lion

Isabella: (Hebrew): devoted to God; (Spanish): God is bountiful; (Biblical): consecrated to God
Isadora: (Greek): gift from the goddess Isis

Javiera: (Spanish): owner of a new house
Josephina: (Hebrew): God will add

Julietta: (French): youthful, young at heart
Lavinia: (Latin): purified

Magdalena: (Hebrew): from the tower; (Spanish): bitter
Mahogany: (Spanish): rich, strong

Mariana: (Spanish): star of the sea; (French): bitter
Marietta: (French): star of the sea

Nefertiti: (Egyptian): queenly
Parthenia: (Greek): virginal

Octavia: (Latin America): eighth; (Italian): born eighth
Okalani: (Hawaiian): from the heavens

Olivia: (Spanish & Italian): olive; (Biblical): peace of the olive tree
Olympia: (Greek): from Mount Olympus

Orabella: (Latin): a form of Arabella, which means answered prayer
Oriana: (Latin): born at sunrise

Penelope: (Greek): weaver
Pheodora: (Greek): supreme gift

Philomena: (Greek): friend of strength
Pollyanna: (American): overly optimistic

Seraphina: (Latin): a winged angel
Serenity: (Latin & English): peaceful

Tatiana: (Slavic): fairy queen
Tayanita: (Cherokee): beaver

Theodora: (English): gift of God
Thomasina: (Hebrew): a twin

Tijuana: (Spanish): border town in Mexico
Timothea: (English): honoring God

Valencia: (Spanish & Italian): brave; (Latin America): health or love
Venecia: (Italian): from Venice

Veronica: (Latin): displaying a true image
Victoria: (Latin America): winner

Virgilia: (Latin): staff bearer
Wilhelmina: (German): resolute protector

*****Note**: The names Alexandria, Appolonia and Michelangelo are five-syllables, rather than four.

Chapter 15. Gender Neutral (Unisex) Names

Throughout this book, you have probably stopped at least once or twice and thought: "Wow, I didn't know *that* was a girl's name." To me, that is the most distinctive trend that is worth noting - the fact that few names are reserved for only one sex.

Fifty years ago, that wasn't the case. If you asked someone to suggest a gender neutral name, they would probably say Pat, Lee, Dale, or Frances - and then draw a blank. Now, there are dozens of popular names that are equally used by both sexes. We've included this chapter for two reasons:

1. to offer suggestions for parents who want a gender neutral name

2. to note the names that truly **are** unisex, for prospective parents who might not be aware of this trend. Sadly, I have met several parents who chose a name on this list, thinking that it was exclusively female. A few years later, they were stunned to learn that there were three little boys in their daughter's kindergarten class with the same name.

And, that, ultimately, is the only pitfall of unisex names - they don't "announce" your child's gender the way most conventional names do. Nevertheless, these names are definitely hot and trendy - and well worth a second look.

The Top Unisex Names (with gender divisions) from the 2012 Social Security Administration statistics:

1. **Rowan:** (Irish): red-haired; (English & Gaelic): from the rowan tree (37% female)
2. **Quinn:** (Celtic): queenly; (Gaelic): one who provides counsel (68% female)
3. **Kai:** (American): ocean; (Welsh): keeper of the keys; (Scottish): fire (13% female)
4. **Sawyer:** (English): one who works with wood (17% female)
5. **Charlie:** (English) a diminutive form of Charles, which means strong (41% female)
6. **Avery**: (English): wise ruler (81% female)
7. **Finley:** (Irish): blond-haired soldier (66% female)
8. **Elliott:** (Israel): close to God; (English): the Lord is my God (17% female)
9. **Emery:** (German): industrious (80% female)
10. **Emerson:** (English): brave, powerful (61% female)
11. **Rory:** (Irish): famous brilliance, famous ruler; (Gaelic): red-haired (31% female)
12. **Riley:** (English): from the rye clearing; (Irish): a small stream (59% female)
13. **Marlowe:** (English): from the hill by the lake (88% female)
14. **River:** (Latin & French): stream, water (36% female)
15. **Arden**: (English): passionate, enthusiastic, valley of the eagle (74% female)
16. **Peyton:** (English): from the village of warriors (68% female)
17. **Remy**: (French): oarsman or rower, from Rheims (46% female)
18. **Sage:** (English & French): wise one; (English): from the spice (66% female)
19. **Ellis:** (English & Hebrew): my God is Jehovah (35% female)
20. **Addison**: (English): son of Adam (70% female)

A Comprehensive List of Gender Neutral Names (in alphabetical order)

Addison: (English): son of Adam
Alpha: (Greek): first-born child

Aspen: (English): from the aspen tree
Bailey: (English): bailiff, steward, public official

Blair: (Irish & Celtic): from the plain, (Gaelic): child of the fields; (Scottish): peat moss
Blaine: (Gaelic, Irish & Celtic): thin

Blake: (English): pale blond or dark; (Scottish): dark-haired
Blue: (English): the color blue

Brady: (Irish): a large-breasted woman
Brett: (French, English & Celtic): a native of Brittany

Brice/Bryce: (Welsh): alert, ambitious
Camden/Camdyn: (Irish, Scottish, English & Gaelic): from the winding valley

Cameron: (Irish & Gaelic): crooked nose
Campbell: (Gaelic): crooked mouth; (French): from the beautiful field

Cary/Carey: (Greek): pure
Chris: (English & Irish): follower of Christ

Clancy/Clancey: (Celtic): son of the red-haired warrior
Cleo/Clio: (Greek): to praise, acclaim

Coby/Koby/Kobe: (Hebrew): supplanter
Cody: (English): cushion

Corey/Cory: (Irish): from the hollow, of the churning waters
Dale: (German): valley; (English): lives in the valley

Drew: (Greek): courageous, valiant
Derry: (English, Irish, German & Gaelic): red-haired, from the oak grove

Dakota: (Native American): friend to all
Easton: (English): from east town

Ellison: (English): son of Elias
Ellory/Ellery: (Cornish): resembling a swan

Gale/Gail/Gayle: (English): merry, lively
Flynn: (Irish): heir to the red-head; ruddy complexion

Garnet: (English): gem, armed with a spear; (French): keeper of grain
Gentry: (English): gentleman

Hadley: (English & Irish): from the heath covered meadow
Hagen: (Gaelic): youthful

Halsey: (English): Hal's island
Harlow: (English): from the army on the hill

Harper: (English): one who plays or makes harps
Haven: (English): safe place

Hayden: (English): from the hedged valley
Hunter: (English): hunter

Jai: (Tai): heart
Jamie: (Spanish): supplanter

Jensen: (Scandinavian): God is gracious
Jordan: (Hebrew): to flow down; (Israel): descendant

Kacey/Casey: (Irish): brave
Keaton: (English): from the town of hawks

Kelsey: (English): from the island of ships
Kendall: (English & Celtic): from the bright valley

Kent: (English & Welsh): white; (Celtic): chief
Kennedy: (Gaelic): a helmeted chief

Kerry: (Irish): dark-haired
Kim: (Vietnamese): as precious as gold; (Welsh): leader

Kimball: (Greek): hollow vessel
Kinsey: (English): victorious prince

Kirby: (Scandinavian): church village
Kyle: (Irish): attractive

Laine/Lane: (English): narrow road
Lee/Leigh: (English): meadow

Landon: (English): from the long hill
Linden: (English): from linden hill

London/Londyn: (English): capital of England; fortress of the moon
Lynn(e): (English): waterfall

Mackenzie: (Scottish): son of Kenzie
McKinley: (English): offspring of the fair hero

Mika/Micah: (Finnish): like God; (Japanese): new moon
Monroe: (Gaelic): from the red swamp; (Scottish): from the river; (Irish): near the river roe

Morgan: (Celtic): lives by the sea; (Welsh): bright sea
Murphy: (Irish): sea warrior

O'Shea: (Irish): child of Shea
Orion: (Greek): a hunter in Greek mythology

Page/Paige: (French): youthful assistant
Parker: (English): keeper of the park

Paris: (Persian): angelic face; (Greek): downfall; (French): the capital city of France
Pembroke: (Welsh): headland

Presley: (English): priest's land
Quincy: (English): fifth-born child; (French): estate belonging to Quintus

Rain: (American): blessings from above; (Latin): ruler; (English): lord, wise
Reese/Reece: (English & Welsh): ardent, fiery, enthusiastic

Randy: (German): the wolf shield
Rene/Renee: (French): reborn

Rio: (Spanish & Portuguese): river
Rylan/Ryland: (English): the place where rye is grown

Sailor: (American): sailor
Santana: (Spanish): saintly

Shane: (Hebrew): gift from God; (Irish): God is gracious
Shawn: (Irish): a form of Sean, which means God is gracious

Sheridan: (Irish, English & Celtic): untamed; (Gaelic): bright, a seeker
Shiloh: (Hebrew): he who was sent, God's gift, the one to whom it belongs; (Israel): peaceful

Silver: (English): precious metal, the color silver
Sloan: (English): raid; (Irish, Celtic, Scottish & Gaelic): fighter, warrior

Spencer/Spenser: (English): dispenser of provisions
Storm/Stormy: (English): tempest; (American): impetuous nature

Sydney: (English): wide island
Tai: (Chinese): large; (Vietnamese): prosperous

Teagan: (Gaelic): handsome, attractive
Toby: (Hebrew): God is good

Unique: (Latin): only one; (American): unlike others
Whitley: (English): from the white meadow

Chapter 16. Cultural Preferences: Popular Names for African-American Babies

In a country as large and diverse as the United States, parents often choose baby names that honor their cultural heritage and unique family traditions. By doing so, they bring a depth and richness to our society that is fresh and exciting. Other times, parents choose mainstream names that are equally popular among other racial and ethnic groups. We will explore these trends in this chapter by presenting the most popular names for babies in African-American households.

In reading this chapter, please note the source of the data, which prevents us from projecting it to a national level. By design, the Social Security Administration does not break down this information by race; they simply publish the number of times that a name is used across all racial and ethnic groups. Only five states report the information by race: Virginia, Colorado, Arkansas, Texas, and New York. For that reason, we are presenting the top names strictly from those states, in alphabetical order (rather than by popularity). Depending upon where you live - and the level of diversity in your community, these names may (or may not) be particularly common. They do, however, show the amazing range of names that are popular in African-American families in five distinctly different parts of the country.

Popular Names for African-American Boys

Aaron: (Jewish): enlightened; (Hebrew): lofty, exalted
Adrian: (German, Spanish & Italian): dark; (Greek): rich

Akil: (Arabian): intelligent
Alonzo: (Spanish & American): ready for battle

Andre: (French): manly, brave
Anel: (Greek): messenger of God, angel

Anthony: (English & Biblical): worthy of praise
Antoine: (French): a flourishing man

Armstrong: (English): strong arm
Barrington: (English): fenced town

Benjamin: (English, Hebrew & Biblical): son of my right hand
Booker: (English): bible, book maker

Caleb: (Israel): faithful; (Hebrew): dog or bold
Calvin: (English & Latin America): bald

Cameron: (Irish & Gaelic): crooked nose
Cassius: (Latin): empty, hollow, vain

Chikae: (African American): God's power
Christian: (English & Irish): follower of Christ

Christopher: (Biblical): Christ-bearer; (English): he who holds Christ in his heart
Cleavon: (English): cliff

Clinton: (English): town on a hill
Cody: (Irish): helpful; (English): a cushion, helpful

Cornelius: (Irish): strong willed, wise; (Latin America): horn-colored
Cory/Corey: (English & Irish): hill, hollow

D'angelo/Deangelo: (Italian): a combination of De and Angelo, which means little angel
D'shawn/Dashawn: (English): God is willing

D'wayne/Dawayne: (Irish): dark, small
Damon: (English): calm, tame

Daniel: (Hebrew & Biblical): God is my judge; (Irish & Welsh): attractive
Darius: (Greek): kingly, wealthy; (American): pharaoh

Darvell: (French): from the eagle town
David: (Hebrew, Scottish & Welsh): beloved

Delroy: (French): belonging to the king
Demarco: (African American): of Mark: (South African): warlike

Demond: (African American): of man
Devin/Devaughn/Devon: (Irish): poet

Dewayne: (American): a combination of De and Wayne, which means wagon maker
Dion: (Greek & French): mountain of Zeus; (African American): God

Dixon: (English): power, brave ruler
Dre: (American): a diminutive form of Andre, which means manly, brave

Edward: (English): wealthy guardian; (German): strong as a boar
Elijah: (Biblical): the Lord is my God; (Hebrew): Jehovah is God

Elon: (Biblical & African American): spirit, God loves me
Emmett/Emmitt: (English): whole, universal

Ennis: (Irish): island; (Gaelic): the only choice; (Greek): mine
Ethan: (Hebrew & Biblical): firm, strong

Gabriel: (Israel): hero of God; (Hebrew): man of God; (Spanish): God is my strength
Garfield: (English): battlefield

Glover: (English): one who makes gloves
Harim/Hareem: (Arabic): superior

Isaiah: (Hebrew): the Lord is generous; (Israel): salvation by God
James: (English): supplant, replace; (Israel): supplanter

Jamal/Jamaal/Jamall/Jamaul: (Arabic): handsome
Jamar: (American): handsome

Jayden: (American): God has heard
Jaylen: (English); to rejoice

Jefferson: (English): son of Jeffrey, which means divine peace
Jeremiah: (Hebrew): may Jehovah exalt; (Israel): sent by God

Jermaine: (French): a man from Germany; (Latin): brotherly
Jordan: (Hebrew): to flow down; (Israel): descendant

Joseph: (Biblical): God will increase; (Hebrew): may Jehovah add/give
Joshua: (Hebrew & Biblical): Jehovah saves

Josiah: (Hebrew): Jehovah has healed; (Israel): God has healed
Justin: (English & French): just, true; (Irish): judicious

Kadeem: (Arabic): servant
Kendrick: (English): royal ruler; (Gaelic): champion

Kenton: (English): from the king's town
Kevin: (Irish & Gaelic): handsome, beautiful; (Celtic): gentle

Kwame: (Akan): born on a Saturday
Lamar: (German): famous land; (French): of the sea

Lamont: (Scandinavian): lawyer
Lance: (German): spear; (French): land

Lashaun: (American): enthusiastic
Levon: (Armenian): lion

Lincoln: (English): Roman colony at the pool; (Latin America): village
Lovell: (French & English): young wolf

Luther: (German): soldier of the people
Malik: (African & Arabic): king, master

Marquis: (French): nobleman
Marvin: (Welsh): friend of the sea

Matthew: (Hebrew & Biblical): gift of the Lord
Michael: (Biblical & Hebrew): like God

Montel: (Italian): mountain
Moses: (Hebrew & Biblical): saved from the water

Nathan: (Hebrew & Israel): gift of God
Nelson: (English, Celtic, Irish & Gaelic): son of Neil

Nero: (Latin & Spanish): stern
Noah: (Biblical): rest, peace; (Hebrew): comfort, long-lived

Omarr: (Arabian): ultimate devotee; (Hebrew): eloquent speaker
Orlando: (Spanish): land of gold: (German): famous throughout the land

Orpheus: (Greek): an excellent musician
Otis: (German & Greek): wealthy

Quashawn: (American): tenacious
Quentin: (Latin): fifth

Quincy: (English): fifth-born child; (French): estate belonging to Quintus
Quinton/Quinten/Quintin: (Latin): from the queen's town

Pearson: (English): son of Peter
Perry: (English): a familiar form of Peter, which means a small stone or rock

Raymone: (Spanish): a wise or mighty protector
Rocket/Rockett/Rockitt: (English): fast

Romeo: (Italian, Spanish, Latin America & African American): from Rome
Roscoe: (Norwegian): deer forest

Rufus: (Latin America): redhead
Samuel: (Israel): God hears; (Hebrew): name of God

Santana: (Spanish): saintly
Sebastian: (Greek): the revered one

Shawn/Shaun: (Irish): a form of Sean, which means God is gracious
Steadman: (English): one who lives at the farm

Stephen/Steven/Stevie: (English & Greek): crowned one
Sylvester/Sly: (Latin): man from the forest

Taye: (Ethiopian): one who has been seen
Terrell: (German): thunder ruler

Trenton: (English): town of Trent
Treyvon: (American): a form of Trevon, which is a combination of Trey and Von

Tye/Ty: (English): from the fenced-in pasture
Tyler: (English): maker of tiles

Tyrell: (American & English): thunder ruler
Tyrone/Tyronne: (French): from Owen's land

Tyson: (French): explosive; (English): son of Tye
Vance: (English): windmill dweller

Wardell: (English): from the guardian's hill
Waverly: (English): quaking aspen

Wayan: (Indonesian): first son
Wendall/Wendell: (German): a wanderer

Wesley: (English & German): from the west meadow
Winton: (English): from the enclosed pastureland

William: (English, German & French): protector
Xavier: (Basque): owner of a new house; (Arabic): one who is bright

Zachariah/Zacarias/Zachary: (Hebrew): Jehovah has remembered; (Israel): remembered by the Lord

Popular Names for African-American Girls

Aaliyah/Aliyah: (Arabic): an ascender; (Muslim): exalted; (American): immigrant to a new home
Aisha/Aiesha: (African): womanly, lively; (Muslim): life, lively

Alexandra: (Greek, English & Latin America): defender of mankind
Alexis: (English): helper, defender; (Biblical): protector of mankind

Alyssa: (Greek): logical
Amaya: (Japanese & Arabic): night rain

Amber: (Arabic): precious jewel, yellow-brown color
Angel: (Spanish & Greek): angelic

Aniyah: (Polish & Hebrew): God has shown favor
Aretha: (Greek): virtuous

Beyonce: (English & American): one who surpasses others
Brianna: (Irish): strong; (Celtic & English): she ascends

Cambria: (Latin): woman of Wales
Cassandra: (Greek): prophet of doom

Chantal: (French): song
Charmaine: (English): song; (French): beautiful orchard

Cherise: (French): cherry, dear one
Chloe: (Greek): verdant, blooming

Dana: (English, Danish, Irish & Hebrew): a person from Denmark
Davina: (Scottish): feminine form of David, which means beloved one

Dendara: (Egyptian): from the town on the river
Deondra: (American): a combination of Dee and Andrea

Destiny: (English): fate
Diamond: (English): bridge protector; (Greek): unbreakable

Dionne: (Greek): divine queen
Essence: (English): scent

Fawn: (French & English): young deer
Gabrielle: (French): strength of God

Gemma: (French & Italian): jewel
Gwendolyn: (Welsh): fair

Hannah: (English & Hebrew): favor, grace; (Biblical): grace of God
Haylee: (English): from the hay meadow, hero

Imani: (Kenya): faith
Isis: (Egyptian): most powerful goddess

Jada: (Israel): wise
Jacinta: (Spanish): resembling the hyacinth

Jailyn: (American): a combination of Jae and Lynn
Jalisa: (American): a combination of Jae and Lisa

Jasmine: (Persian): a climbing plant; (English): a fragrant flower
Jayla: (Arabia): charity; (African American): one who is special

Jordan: (Hebrew): to flow down; (Israel): descendant
Kayla: (Irish & Greek): pure and beloved

Kennedy: (Gaelic): a helmeted chief
Keisha/Keesha: (African): favorite

Kenya: (Israel): animal horn
Kiara: (Irish): small and dark

Krystal: (American): clear, brilliant glass
Lacrecia: (Latin): bringer of light

Lakeisha: (American): joyful, happy
Lashawna: (American): filled with happiness

Latisha: (Latin): a form of Lucretia, which means bringer of light
Laverne: (French): woodland, like the spring

Layla: (Arabic): beauty of the night
Levona: (Hebrew): spice, incense

Madison: (English): son of Matthew
Makayla: (English & Irish): like God

Marietta: (French): star of the sea
Malia: (American): calm, peaceful

Malika: (African): queen, princess
Nevaeh: (American): gift from God, heaven spelled backwards

Octavia: (Latin America): eighth; (Italian): born eighth
Odessa: (Latin America): the odyssey

Paulina: (Latin America): small
Precious: (American): treasured

Serena: (Latin): peaceful disposition; (African American): calm, tranquil
Sapphire: (Hebrew): sapphire; (Israel): beautiful

Shahina: (Arabic): falcon
Shakila: (Arabic): beautiful one

Shakira: (Arabic): grateful
Shana: (Hebrew): God is gracious

Shandy: (English): rambunctious
Shanelle: (American): a form of Chanel, which means from the canal

Shani: (African): marvelous
Shania: (Native American): on my way

Shanika: (American): a combination of Sha and Nika
Shasta: (Native American): from the triple-peaked mountain

Sheba: (Hebrew): an ancient country in Arabia
Sheena: (Gaelic): God's gracious gift

Sierra: (Spanish): mountain; (Irish): dark
Sydney: (French): from Saint Denis

Talisa/Talissa: (American): consecrated to God
Talisha: (American): damsel, innocent

Tamara: (Hebrew): palm tree; (Israel): spice
Taylor: (English & French): a tailor

Tia: (Greek); princess; (Spanish): princess, aunt; (African American): aunt
Tiana: (Greek): princess

Tiffany: (Greek): lasting love
Trinity: (Latin): the holy three

Xaviera: (Arabic): bright
Yolanda: (Greek): resembling the violet flower

Zakiyyah: (Muslim): sharp, intellectual, pious, pure
Zola: (Mexican): Earth; (French): famous bearer

Chapter 17. Cultural Preferences: Popular Names for Hispanic Girls in the U.S.

On a practical basis, this chapter continues the theme that we started in Chapter 16 - it presents the most popular names for babies in Hispanic households in the U.S. (in states that break down this information by race). The selections include a fascinating mix of old and new favorites that blend the richness of the Spanish culture with a decidedly American flair.

In reading this chapter, please note the source of the data, which prevents us from projecting it to a national level. By design, the Social Security Administration does not break down this information by race; they simply publish the number of times that a name is used across all racial and ethnic groups. Only five states report the information by race: Virginia, Colorado, Arkansas, Texas, and New York. For that reason, we are presenting the top names strictly from those states, in alphabetical order (rather than by popularity). Depending upon where you live - and the level of diversity in your community, these names may (or may not) be particularly common. They do, however, show the amazing range of names that are popular in Hispanic families in five distinctly different parts of the country.

Popular Names for Hispanic Boys

Aaron: (Jewish & Hebrew): enlightened
Adrian: (German, Spanish & Italian): dark

Agustin: (Spanish): majestic dignity
Alan: (English & Irish): handsome; (Celtic): harmony, stone or noble

Alejandro: (Spanish): defender of mankind
Alex: (Greek): protector of mankind

Alexander: (Greek): protector of mankind
Alonzo: (Spanish & American): ready for battle

Andres: (Spanish): manly, courageous
Angel: (Spanish & Greek): angelic

Antonio: (Italian & Spanish): a flourishing man, worthy of praise
Axel: (German & Hebrew): father of peace; (German): source of all life

Bautista: (Italian): John the Baptist
Benjamin: (English, Hebrew & Biblical): son of my right hand

Bruno: (German): brown-haired
Caleb: (Israel): faithful; (Hebrew): dog or bold

Carlos: (Spanish): a free man
Che: (Spanish): a derivative of Jose, which means God will add

Christopher: (Biblical): Christ-bearer; (English): he who holds Christ in his heart
Cordero: (Spanish): little lamb

Cristobal: (Spanish): bearer
Cruz: (Spanish): of the cross

Damian: (Greek): one who tames others
Daniel: (Hebrew & Biblical): God is my judge; (Irish & Welsh): attractive

Dante: (Latin): enduring, everlasting
Dario: (Spanish): affluent

David: (Hebrew, Scottish & Welsh): beloved
Diego: (Spanish): Saint James

Dylan: (English & Welsh): born from the ocean, son of the wave; (Gaelic): faithful
Eduardo: (Spanish): wealthy protector or guardian

Elias: (Latin & Hebrew): the Lord is my God
Emiliano: (Italian & Latin): rival, industrious

Emilio: (Spanish): flattering
Emmanuel: (Hebrew): God with us

Enrique: (Spanish): ruler of the estate
Esteban: (Spanish): crowned in victory

Facundo: (Spanish): significant, eloquent
Felipe: (Spanish): one who loves horses

Fernando: (Spanish): daring, adventurous
Francisco: (Spanish): a man from France, free

Franco: (Spanish): frank, free
Gabriel: (Israel): hero of God; (Hebrew): man of God; (Spanish): God is my strength

Gael: (English): merry, lively
Geronimo: (Greek & Italian): a famous chef

Gonzalo:(Spanish): wolf
Hugo: (English): intelligent

Ian: (Scottish): gift from God
Ignacio: (Italian): fiery

Iker: (Spanish): visitation
Isaac: (Biblical): he will laugh

Ivan: (Slavic): God is gracious
Jacobo: (Spanish): supplanter

Javier/Xavier: (Spanish): owner of a new house
Jesus: (Hebrew): God is my salvation

Joaquin: (Hebrew): God will establish
Jorge: (Spanish): farmer

Josue: (Spanish & Hebrew): God is salvation
Juan: (Hebrew): gift from God; (Spanish): God is gracious

Juan David: (Spanish): God is gracious/beloved
Juan Diego: (Spanish): God is gracious/Saint James

Juan Esteban: (Spanish): God is gracious/crowned in victory
Juan Jose: (Spanish): God is gracious/God shall add

Juan Ignacio: (Spanish): God is gracious/fiery
Juan Manuel: (Spanish): God is gracious/like God

Juan Pablo: (Spanish): God is gracious/borrowed
Julian: (Spanish, French & Greek): youthful

Kevin: (Irish & Gaelic): handsome, beautiful; (Celtic): gentle
Lautaro: (Spanish): crowned with laurel

Leonardo: (German): brave as a lion
Lorenzo: (Italian & Spanish): crowned with laurel

Lucas: (Gaelic, English & Latin America): light
Luciano: (Spanish): light

Luis: (Spanish): famous warrior
Manuel: (Spanish): God is with us

Marcos: (Spanish): of mars; (Portuguese): the god of war
Martin: (Latin): dedicated to Mars, the god of war

Mateo: (Italian): gift of God Nicolas:
Matias: (Spanish & Hebrew): gift of God

Matthew: (Hebrew & Biblical): gift of the Lord
Mauricio: (Spanish): moorish; (Portuguese): dark-skinned

Maximiliano: (Italian): greatest
Maximo (Italian): greatest

Miguel: (Spanish): like God
Miguel Angel: (Spanish): like God/angelic

Nicolas: (Greek): victorious people
Pablo: (Spanish): borrowed

Patricio: (Spanish): patrician, noble
Pedro: (Spanish): solid and strong as a rock

Rafael/Raphael: (Spanish): one who is healed by God
Ricardo: (Spanish): strong and powerful ruler

Rodrigo: (Spanish): famous ruler
Sebastian: (Greek): the revered one

Samuel: (Israel): God hears; (Hebrew): name of God
Santiago: (Spanish): named for Saint James

Santino: (Italian): little angel
Salvador: (Spanish & Italian): savior

Simon: (Israel): it is heard
Thiago: (Spanish, Portuguese & Brazilian): Saint James

Tomas: (German): a form of Thomas, which means twin
Vicente: (Spanish): conquering, victorious

Valentino: (Italian): brave or strong; (Latin America): health or love

Popular Names for Hispanic Girls

Abigail: (Hebrew): father rejoiced; (Biblical): source of joy
Abril: (Spanish): April

Adrianna: (Spanish, Greek & Italian): woman with dark and rich features
Agustina: (Latin America): majestic, grand

Alejandra: (Spanish): defender of mankind
Alexa: (Greek, English & Latin America): defender of mankind

Allison: (English): noble, truthful, strong character
Alma: (Latin & Italian): nurturing, kind

Amalia: (Latin America): industrious; hard working
Amanda: (Latin): much loved

Ana: (Hebrew): favor or grace; (Native American): mother; (Israel): gracious
Andrea: (Greek & Latin): courageous, strong

Antonia: (Greek): flourishing or flowering
Antonella: (Latin America): praiseworthy

Ariana: (Greek & Italian): holy
Bianca: (Italian): white, fair

Camila: (Italian): a noble virgin, a ceremonial attendant
Carla: (Portuguese & Latin America): strong one

Carmella: (Hebrew & Israel): golden; (Spanish): garden
Carolina: (Mexican): beautiful woman; (French & English): song of happiness

Catalina: (Spanish): pure
Clara: (French & Catalonia): clear, bright

Constanza: (American): strong-willed
Corazon: (Spanish): of the heart

Cota: (Spanish): lively
Daniela: (Hebrew & Spanish): God is my judge

Danna: (Indian): gift
Elena: (Spanish): the shining light

Elisa: (Hebrew): my God is bountiful
Emilia: (Spanish): flattering

Emily: (Latin America): admiring
Emma: (English, Danish & German): whole, complete, universal

Fabiana: (Latin): bean grower
Fernanda: (Spanish): adventurous

Filipa: (Spanish): friend of horses
Fiorella: (Italian): little flower

Florencia: (Spanish): flowering, blooming
Gabriella: (Israel & Hebrew): God gives strength; (Italian): woman of God

Guadalupe: (Spanish): from the valley of wolves
Isabella: (Hebrew): devoted to God; (Spanish): God is bountiful; (Biblical): consecrated to God

Isidora: (Spanish): gifted with many ideas
Jazmin: (Japanese): the flower

Josefina: (Hebrew): God will add
Jovana: (Spanish): daughter of the sky

Julia: (French): youthful; (Latin America): soft-haired, youthful
Juliana: (Spanish): soft-haired

Julieta: (French): youthful, young at heart
Kiara: (Irish): small and dark

Laura: (English, Spanish & Latin America): crowned with laurel, from the laurel tree
Lola: (Spanish): woman of sorrow

Lucia: (Latin America): bringer of light
Luciana: (Latin America): bringer of light

Luna: (Latin & Latin America): the moon
Magdalena: (Hebrew): from the tower; (Spanish): bitter

Maite: (Spanish): loved
Manuela: (Spanish): God is with us

Maria: (Latin): bitter
Mariana: (French): bitter

Martina: (Latin America): warlike
Mercedes: (Latin): reward, payment; (Spanish): merciful

Mia: (Italian): my; (Biblical): mine
Michelle: (French & Hebrew): like God, close to God

Miranda: (Latin): worthy of admiration
Monserrat: (Latin): jagged mountain

Natalia: (French): to be born at Christmas; (Slovakian): to be born
Nicole: (French): victory of the people

Noa: (Israel): movement
Olivia: (Spanish & Italian): olive; (Biblical): peace of the olive tree

Paloma: (Spanish): dove-like
Paola: (Italian): little

Paula: (Latin America): small
Paulina: (Latin America): small

Rafaella: (Hebrew): healed by God
Regina: (Italian, Spanish & Latin America): queen

Renata: (French): a form of Renee, which means reborn
Romina: (Arabian): from the Christian land

Salome: (Hebrew): peace and tranquility
Samantha: (Hebrew & Biblical): listener of God

Santina: (Spanish): little saint
Sara(h): (Hebrew, Spanish & Biblical): princess

Sofia: (Greek & Biblical): wisdom
Ximena: (Greek): heroine

Valentina: (Spanish & Italian): brave; (Latin America): health or love
Valeria: (French): brave, fierce one; (English): strong, valiant

Valery: (French): brave, fierce one; (English): strong, valiant
Vanessa: (Greek): resembling a butterfly

Victoria: (Latin America): winner
Violeta: (Bulgarian): violet

Zita: (Spanish): little rose
Zoe: (Greek): life, alive

Chapter 18. Popular Names for Asian Babies

In this chapter, we present the most popular names for Asian-American babies in the last five years (in states that break down this information by race). These eclectic choices, which reflect the amazing history and culture of China, Japan, and Korea, are intriguing options for parents who seek distinctive first and middle names from a traditional part of the world.

In reading this chapter, please note the source of the data, which prevents us from projecting it to a national level. By design, the Social Security Administration does not break down this information by race; they simply publish the number of times that a name is used across all racial and ethnic groups. Only five states report the information by race: Virginia, Colorado, Arkansas, Texas, and New York. For that reason, we are presenting the top names strictly from those states, in alphabetical order (rather than by popularity). Depending upon where you live - and the level of diversity in your community, these names may (or may not) be particularly common. They do, however, show the amazing range of names that are popular in Asian-American families in five distinctly different parts of the country.

Popular Chinese Names for Boys

An: (Chinese): peaceful
Chung: (Chinese): intelligent

Dai: (Chinese): sword technique
Fa: (Chinese): setting off

Fai: (Chinese): beginning to fly
Feng: (Chinese): sharp blade

Gan: (Chinese): dare, adventure
Geming: (Chinese): revolution

Gen: (Chinese): root
Guang: (Chinese): light

He: (Chinese): yellow river
Heng: (Chinese): eternal

Hong: (Chinese): wild swan
Hop: (Chinese): agreeable

Huan: (Chinese): happiness
Hung: (Chinese): brave

Jiang: (Chinese): fire
Jin: (Chinese): gold

Lei: (Chinese): thunder
Li: (Chinese): having great strength

Liang: (Chinese): good man
Liu: (Chinese): one who is quiet and peaceful

Park: (Chinese): the cypress tree
Ping: (Chinese): stable

Qiang: (Chinese): strong
Qiu: (Chinese): autumn

Shan: (Chinese): mountain
Shen: (Chinese): deep spiritual thought

Xiu: (Chinese): cultivated
You: (Chinese): friend

Zhen: (Chinese): astonished
Zian: (Chinese): peace

Popular Chinese Names for Girls

Bo: (Chinese): precious
Chun: (Chinese): springtime

Fang: (Chinese): fragrant
Far: (Chinese): flower

Hua: (Chinese): flower
Huan: (Chinese): happiness

Jia: (Chinese): beautiful
Jiao: (Chinese): dainty

Jing: (Chinese): stillness, luxurious
Lan: (Chinese): orchid

Li: (Chinese): upright
Lien: (Chinese): lotus

Lin: (Chinese): resembling jade
Ling: (Chinese): dainty

Meili: (Chinese): beautiful
Mingzhu: (Chinese): bright pearl

Nuo: (Chinese): graceful
Ping: (Chinese): peaceful

Qi: (Chinese): fine jade
Qiang: (Chinese): beautiful rose

Qing: (Chinese): dark blue
Rong: (Chinese): martial

Song: (Chinese): pine tree
Ting: (Chinese): graceful and slim

Xiang: (Chinese): pleasant fragrance
Xiu: (Chinese): grace

Wen: (Chinese): refinement
Yin: (Chinese): silver

Popular Japanese Names for Boys

Aki: (Japanese): autumn, bright
Amida: (Japanese): Buddha

Dai: (Japanese): sword technique
Daiki: (Japanese): of great value

Hiro: (Japanese): widespread
Hiromi: (Japanese): widespread beauty; wide-seeing

Isamu: (Japanese): courageous
Isas: (Japanese): meritorious

Jiro: (Japanese): second son
Jo: (Japanese): God will increase

Jun: (Japanese): truthful
Kiyoshi: (Japanese): quiet one

Kuo: (Japanese): approval
Kuro: (Japanese): ninth son

Naoki: (Japanese): honest tree
Naoko: (Japanese): honest

Nobu: (Japanese): faith
Norio: (Japanese): man of principles

Raiden: (Japanese): god of thunder and lightning
Ringo: (Japanese): peace be with you

Ronin: (Japanese): samurai without a master
Shin: (Japanese): truth

Shiro: (Japanese): fourth-born son
Tama: (Japanese): jewel

Popular Japanese Names for Girls

Aika: (Japanese): love song
Aki: (Japanese): born in autumn

Ame: (Japanese): rain, heaven
Anka: (Japanese): color of the dawn

Fujita: (Japanese): field
Fuyu: (Japanese): born in winter

Hachi: (Japanese): eight, good luck
Haya: (Japanese): quick, light

Kama: (Japanese): one who loves and is loved
Kana: (Japanese): dexterity and skill

Kayo: (Japanese): beautiful
Kenja: (Japanese): a sage

Kin: (Japanese): golden
Kita: (Japanese): north

Ko: (Japanese): filial piety
Kono: (Japanese): dexterity and skill

Kosame: (Japanese): fine rain
Kuma: (Japanese): bear, mouse

Mako: (Japanese): truth, grateful
Mana: (Japanese): truth

Midori: (Japanese): green
Mizuki: (Japanese): beautiful moon

Nami: (Japanese): wave
Naoki: (Japanese): honest tree

Nishi: (Japanese): west
Noriko: (Japanese): child of principles

Raeden: (Japanese): thunder and lightning
Rippina: (Japanese): brilliant light

Sada: (Japanese): pure
Sato: (Japanese): sugar

Sayo: (Japanese): born at night
Shima: (Japanese): true intention

Taka: (Japanese): borrowed
Tama: (Japanese): precious stone

Tomiko: (Japanese): wealthy
Tomoko: (Japanese): two friends

Yukiko: (Japanese): happy child
Yumiko: (Japanese): beautiful and helpful child

Popular Korean Names for Boys

Bae: (Korean): inspiration
Chin: (Korean): precious

Cho: (Korean): beautiful
Dae: (Korean): great

Dong: (Korean): the east
Eui: (Korean): righteousness

Eun: (Korean): silver
Hea: (Korean): grace

Hee: (Korean): brightness
Hyo: (Korean): filial duty

Hyun: (Korean): wisdom
Joo: (Korean): jewel

Ki: (Korean): arise
Kwan: (Korean): bold character

Kyong: (Korean): brightness
Kyu: (Korean): standard

Mee: (Korean): beauty
Min: (Korean): cleverness

Nam: (Korean): south
Soo: (Korean): excellent, long life

Yeo: (Korean): mildness
Young: (Korean): forever, unchanging

Popular Korean Names for Girls

Hae: (Korean): ocean
Hye: (Korean): graceful

Ja: (Korean): attractive, fiery
Ki: (Korean): arisen

Yeo: (Korean): mild
Yon: (Korean): lotus blossom

Chapter 19. Top 10 Names for Babies in Other Countries

Throughout this book, we have focused exclusively on names for babies in the United States. For readers with a global perspective, this chapter presents the most popular baby names in *other* countries across the globe. In all cases, the data are taken directly from government statistics for that nation (in the last year that data were available). All names are presented in the order of popularity.

Canada (2012) - Boys

1. **Ethan:** (Hebrew & Biblical): firm, strong
2. **Liam**: (Irish & Gaelic): determined protector
3. **Lucas:** (Gaelic, English & Latin America): light
4. **Mason:** (French & English): stone worker
5. **Logan:** (Irish): small cove; (Scottish): Finnian's servant; (Gaelic): from the hollow
6. **Noah:** (Biblical): rest, peace; (Hebrew): comfort, long-lived
7. **Alexander:** (Greek): protector of mankind
8. **Benjamin:** (English, Hebrew & Biblical): son of my right hand
9. **Jacob**: (Biblical): supplanter; (Hebrew): he grasps the heel
10. **Jack:** (English): God is gracious; (Hebrew): supplanter

Canada (2012) - Girls

1. **Olivia:** (Spanish & Italian): olive; (Biblical): peace of the olive tree
2. **Emma:** (English, Danish & German): whole, complete, universal
3. **Sophia:** (Greek & Biblical): wisdom
4. **Emily:** (Latin America): admiring
5. **Ava:** (Latin America): like a bird
6. **Ella:** (English); beautiful fairy; (Spanish): she
7. **Chloe:** (Greek): verdant, blooming
8. **Isabella:** (Hebrew): devoted to God; (Spanish): God is bountiful; (Biblical): consecrated to God
9. **Avery:** (English): counselor, sage, wise
10. **Hannah: (**English & Hebrew): favor, grace; (Biblical): grace of God

Australia (2012) - Boys

1. **William:** (English, German & French): protector
2. **Lucas:** (Gaelic, English & Latin America): light
3. **Oliver:** (French, English, Danish & Latin America): the olive tree; (German): elf army
4. **Noah:** (Biblical): rest, peace; (Hebrew): comfort, long-lived
5. **Jack:** (English): God is gracious; (Hebrew): supplanter
6. **Ethan:** (Hebrew & Biblical): firm, strong
7. **Lachian:** (Gaelic): war-like
8. **Thomas:** (Hebrew, Greek & Dutch): twin
9 **Joshua:** (Hebrew & Biblical): Jehovah saves
10. **James:** (English): supplant, replace; (Israel): supplanter

Australia (2012) - Girls

1. **Ruby:** (English & French): a precious jewel, a ruby
2. **Charlotte:** (French): feminine
3. **Emily:** (Latin America): admiring
4. **Olivia:** (Spanish & Italian): olive; (Biblical): peace of the olive tree
5. **Chloe:** (Greek): verdant, blooming
6. **Amelia:** (English & Latin America): industrious, striving
7. **Mia:** (Italian): my; (Biblical): mine

8. **Sophie:** (Greek & Biblical): wisdom
9. **Isabella:** (Hebrew): devoted to God; (Spanish): God is bountiful; (Biblical): consecrated to God
10. **Ava:** (Latin America): like a bird

Italy (2011) - Boys

1. **Francesco:** (Italian): a man from France
2. **Alessandro:** (Greek): defender of man
3. **Andrea:** (Italian): brave
4. **Lorenzo:** (Italian & Spanish): crowned with laurel
5. **Matteo:** (Italian): gift of God
6. **Gabriele:** (Israel): hero of God; (Hebrew): man of God; (Spanish): God is my strength
7. **Mattia:** (Italian): gift of God
8. **Leonardo:** (German): brave as a lion
9. **Davide:** (Hebrew, Scottish & Welsh): beloved
10. **Ricardo:** (Spanish & Italian): strong and powerful ruler

Italy (2011) - Girls

1. **Sofia:** (Greek & Biblical): wisdom
2. **Giulia:** (Italian): youthful; (Latin America): soft-haired, youthful
3. **Martina:** (Latin America): warlike
4. **Giorgia:** (Italian, Greek & German): farmer
5. **Sara(h):** (Hebrew, Spanish & Biblical): princess
6. **Emma:** (English, Danish & German): whole, complete, universal
7. **Aurora:** (Latin): dawn
8. **Chiara:** (Italian): daughter of the light
9. **Alice:** (Spanish): of the nobility
10. **Alessia:** (Greek): honest

England & Wales (2011) - Boys

1. **Harry:** (German): home or house ruler
2. **Oliver:** (French, English, Danish & Latin America): the olive tree; (German): elf army
3. **Jack:** (English): God is gracious; (Hebrew): supplanter
4. **Alfie:** (English): a diminutive form of Alfred, which means elf counselor
5. **Charlie:** (English): a diminutive form of Charles, which means strong, manly
6. **Thomas:** (Hebrew, Greek & Dutch): twin
7. **Jacob:** (Biblical): supplanter; (Hebrew): he grasps the heel
8. **James:** (English): supplant, replace; (Israel): supplanter
9. **Joshua:** (Hebrew & Biblical): Jehovah saves
10. **William:** (English, German & French): protector

England & Wales (2011) - Girls

1. **Amelia:** (English & Latin America): industrious, striving
2. **Olivia:** (Spanish & Italian): olive; (Biblical): peace of the olive tree
3. **Lily/Lilly:** (Hebrew, English & Latin America): lily, blossoming flower
4. **Jessica:** (Israel): God is watching; (Hebrew): rich, God beholds
5. **Emily:** (Latin America): admiring
6. **Sophie:** (Greek & Biblical): wisdom
7. **Ruby:** (English & French): a precious jewel, a ruby
8. **Grace:** (Latin America): grace of God; (American): land of grace
9. **Ava:** (Latin America): like a bird
10. **Isabella:** (Hebrew): devoted to God; (Spanish): God is bountiful; (Biblical): consecrated to God

France (2010) - Boys

1. **Lucas**: (Gaelic, English & Latin America): light
2. **Enzo**: (Italian): ruler of the estate
3. **Leo:** (Italian & English): a lion
4. **Louis:** (French): famous warrior
5. **Hugo:** (English): intelligent
6. **Gabriel:** (Israel): hero of God; (Hebrew): man of God; (Spanish): God is my strength
7. **Ethan:** (Hebrew & Biblical): firm, strong
8. **Mathis**: (English & Greek): a diminutive form of Matthias, which means gift of God
9. **Jules**: (French): youthful, downy-haired
10. **Raphael**: (Spanish): one who is healed by God

France (2010) - Girls

1. **Emma:** (English, Danish & German): whole, complete, universal
2. **Lea**: (Hebrew): weary
3. **Chloe**: (Greek): verdant, blooming
4. **Manon**: (French): bitter
5. **Ines**: (Spanish): a form of Agnes, which means pure
6. **Lola**: (Spanish): woman of sorrow
7. **Jade**: (Spanish): jewel, green gemstone
8. **Camille**: (Italian): a noble virgin, a ceremonial attendant
9. **Sara(h):** (Hebrew, Spanish & Biblical): princess
10. **Louise**: (German): famous warrior

Spain (2010) - Boys

1. **Alejandro**: (Spanish): defender of mankind
2. **Daniel: (**Hebrew & Biblical): God is my judge; (Irish & Welsh): attractive
3. **Pablo**: (Spanish): a form of Paul, which means small
4. **Hugo**: (English): intelligent
5. **Alvaro**: (Spanish & German): truth-speaker or guardian
6. **Adrian:** (German, Spanish & Italian): dark; (Greek): rich
7. **David:** (Hebrew, Scottish & Welsh): beloved
8. **Diego**: (Spanish): Saint James
9. **Javier**: (Spanish): owner of a new house
10. **Mario**: (Hebrew): bitter, king-ruler

Spain (2010) - Girls

1. **Lucia:** (Latin America): bringer of light
2. **Paula:** (Latin America): small
3. **Maria:** (Latin): bitter
4. **Sara(h):** (Hebrew, Spanish & Biblical): princess
5. **Daniela:** (Hebrew & Spanish): God is my judge
6. **Carla:** (Portuguese & Latin America): strong one
7. **Sofia:** (Greek & Biblical): wisdom
8. **Alba:** (Spanish & Italian): from the city of Alba
9. **Claudia:** (Spanish & Latin America): lame
10. **Martina:** (Latin America): warlike

Ireland (2011) - Boys

1. **Jack:** (English): God is gracious; (Hebrew): supplanter
2. **James:** (English): supplant, replace; (Israel): supplanter

3. **Sean:** (Irish): God is gracious
4. **Daniel:** (Hebrew & Biblical): God is my judge; (Irish & Welsh): attractive
5. **Conor:** (Irish): strong willed, much wanted
6. **Ryan:** (Gaelic): little king; (Irish): kindly, young royalty
7. **Adam:** (Hebrew): red; (Israel): man of the earth; (English): of the red earth
8. **Harry:** (German): home or house ruler
9. **Michael:** (Biblical & Hebrew): like God
10. **Alex:** (Greek): protector of mankind

Ireland (2011) - Girls

1. **Emily:** (Latin America): admiring
2. **Sophie:** (Greek & Biblical): wisdom
3. **Emma:** (English, Danish & German): whole, complete, universal
4. **Grace:** (Latin America): grace of God; (American): land of grace
5. **Lily/Lilly:** (Hebrew, English & Latin America): lily, blossoming flower
6. **Sara(h):** (Hebrew, Spanish & Biblical): princess
7. **Lucy:** (Latin America): bringer of light
8. **Ava:** (Latin America): like a bird
9. **Chloe:** (Greek): verdant, blooming
10. **Katie:** (Irish, English & French): diminutive of Katherine, which means pure, virginal

Norway (2012) - Boys

1. **Emil**: (Latin): eager, industrious
2. **Jonas:** (Hebrew): gift from God; (Spanish): dove; (Israel): accomplishing
3. **William:** (English, German & French): protector
4. **Mathias:** (Spanish & Hebrew): gift of God
5. **Magnus:** (Latin): great
6. **Oliver:** (French, English, Danish & Latin America): the olive tree; (German): elf army
7. **Henrik:** (German): ruler of the home
8. **Elias:** (Latin & Hebrew): the Lord is my God
9. **Liam**: (Irish & Gaelic): determined protector
10. **Adrian:** (German, Spanish & Italian): dark; (Greek): rich

Norway (2012) - Girls

1. **Emma:** (English, Danish & German): whole, complete, universal
2. **Nora:** (Hebrew): light
3. **Sofie:** (Greek & Biblical): wisdom
4. **Emilie:** (Latin America): admiring
5. **Ingrid:** (Scandinavian): having the beauty of God
6. **Linnea:** (Denmark): lime tree
7. **Thea:** (Greek): gift of God
8. **Anna:** (Hebrew): favor or grace; (Native American): mother; (Israel): gracious
9. **Amalie:** (French & Latin America): industrious; hard working
10. **Ida**: (English): hardworking

Chapter 20. Names with Similar Meanings

Throughout this book, we have listed the meaning of every name we have presented; we have also provided the same information for each of the 3,000 names in the appendix.

In this chapter, we have summarized a portion of that information for readers who are trying to select a name with a specific meaning. Bear in mind, translations vary widely among languages, which is why we encourage readers to further investigate their top choices, if meanings are important to them. With that in mind, these tables are a general guide to groupings of names that have similar - if not identical - meanings.

Boys Names That Mean "Strong"

Amos	Armstrong	Arnold	Barrett	Bernard	Bogart
Bjorn	Bryan	Carl	Charles	Carlo	Connor
Cornelius	Edward	Ethan	Everett	Harvey	Hartman
Kale	Ken	Jarrett	Malin	Pedro	Ricardo
Quinlan	Richard	Rico	Taurean	Valentino	Virgil

Boys Names That Mean "Brave"

Amos	Andre	Andrew	Bryan	Baldwin	Brendan
Conrad	Devlin	Dixon	Dre	Emerson	Everett
Garcia	Harding	Hardwin	Hillard	Hung	Kurt
Polo	Prewitt				

Boys Names That Mean "Warrior"

Aloysius	Boris	Clancy	Cole	Duncan	Dustin
Gideon	Gunther	Hillard	Keelan	Kane	Keith
Kelly	Lewis	Ludwig	Luigi	Luis	Polo
Mackinley	Malin	Marcel	Murphy	Owen	Sloan

Boys Names That Mean "Noble"

Adolph	Albert	Alan	Alvin	Alphonso	Ansel
Brian	Elgin	Dolph	Earl	Ellsworth	Elmer
Kareen	Knight	Grady	Nolan	Hirum	Odwin
Malloy	Patrick				

Boys Names That Mean "Bright"

Akiko	Albert	Bertram	Colbert	Delbert	Elbert
Englebert	Fulbright	Robert	Robin	Samson	Sheridan
Wilbur	Xavier	Zavier	Minh		

Boys Names That Mean "Dark"

Adrian	Blackwell	Black	Brown	Cole	Dwayne
Delaney	Dolan	Delano	Donal	Douglas	Doyal
Duff	Dugan	Finias	Kerry	Kerwin	Kieran
Maurice	Morrell	Morris	Sullivan		

Boys Names That Mean "Fiery"

Aiden	Dobbs	Egan	Reese	Ignacious	Kagen

Boys Names That Mean "Light"

Abner	Akiko	Alvin	Ashton	Barak	Bertram
Finian	Izod	Lambert	Lucian	Luke	Lux
Lucas	Luka	Orly	Uri		

Boys Names That Mean "Enlightened or Wise"

Aaron	Aryn	Aldo	Alvin	Aldrich	Avery
Cato	Cornelius	Dallas	Reynold	Eldridge	Elvis
Hakin	Rashad	Raymond	Thaddeus	Sage	Socrates

Boys Names That Mean "Beautiful or Handsome"

Adonis	Beauregard	Kane	Keefe	Kevin	Kenneth
Naveen	Jamal	Alan	Bellamy	Hasani	Hussein
Jamar	Japheth	Cullem	Kitoko	McKenna	Teagen

Boys Names That Mean "Peace"

Armani	Axel	Geoffrey	Godfrey	Frederick	Humphrey
Ingram	Jefferson	Pax	Pace	Jeffrey	Manfred
Liu	Noah	Paxton	Salem	Shiloh	Siegfried
Solomon	Wilfred	Zigfred	Ziggy		

Boys Names That Mean "Red"

Adam	Clancy	Derry	Flynn	Flann	Redford
Ridley	Reed	Roden	Rooney	Rory	Rowan
Rufus	Russell	Rusty	Monroe		

Boys Names That Mean "Gift from God"

Hans	Ian	Hansel	Jonas	Johann	Jonathan
Juan	Matteo	Lathan	Nathan	Matthew	Mitchell
Nathaniel	Theodore	Shane	Shiloh	Thierry	Zane

Boys Names That Mean "(God is) Gracious"

Chan	Hans	Elian	Giovanni	Hansel	Jenson
Ioan	Ivan	Jackson	Johann	Jan	Jean
Jock	John	Juan	Yan	Nino	Terrance
Sean	Shane				

Boys Names That Mean "Protector"

Alexander	Alistair	Edmund	Elmo	Fremont	Guillermo
Lex	Liam	Odon	Ramon	Raymond	Zander
Sacha	Sigmund	Warren	William		

Boys Names That Mean "Champion or Victorious"

Carlin	Carroll	Kendrick	Neal	Nigel	Roark
Ajay	Vijay	Kinsey	Nicholas	Niles	Nicolai
Seigfried	Sigmund	Victor	Vincent	Zigfred	Ziggy

Boys Names That Mean "Joy or Happy"

Alaire	Asher	Winston	Denton	Felix	Sayed

Boys Names That Mean "Sun"

Apollo	Helio	Ravi	Samson

Boys Names That Mean "Supplanter"

Coby	Jack	Iago	Jacques	Jacob	Jamie
James	Kobe	Kemo	Seamus		

Boys Names That Mean Defender

Alejandro	Azim	Eli	Hero	Titus	Onofrio
Warner	Zander				

Boys Names That Mean Intelligent

Akira	Chung	Hakin	Hewitt	Hugh	Keene
Hobart	Hubert	Fulbright	Akilah	Tomo	Trang

Boys Names Relating "To The Sea"

Hurley	Lamar	Marlon	Marvin	Merlin	Merrick
Merrill	Morgan	Mortimer	Murdoch	Murphy	Neptune
Ocean	Seaman	Seaton	Zale		

Girls Names That Mean "Beautiful or Handsome"

Adina	Alaina	Alanna	Ayanna	Annabella	Arabella
Belinda	Bella	Callie	Calla	Calliope	Calista
Carolina	Carrington	Ella	Inga	Jacinta	Jaffa
Kaelyn	Keely	Lydia	Mabel	Maribel	Maybelline
Meadow	Miyo	Naveen	Neena	Rosalind	Sapphire
Shaina	Shakila	Siri	Serlina	Zaynah	

Girls Names That Mean "Light"

Aileen	Chiara	Eileen	Elaine	Elena	Elani
Ellen	Evelyn	Helen	Helena	Helene	Ilene
Kenzie	Lucile	Lacretia	Letitia	Lucile	Lucinda
Lucy	Ming	Neriah	Nirel	Noor	Nora
Olena	Orle	Rhonwyn	Uriel	Yalena	Yelena
Yitta	Zia	Luka			

Girls Names That Mean "Bitter"

Annmarie	Magdalena	Marianna	Mali	Mara	Maria
Mariah	Marianne	Mariel	Marina	Marissa	Marlie
Marita	Marlene	Maureen	Mary	Meli	Minnie
Mitzi	Moira	Molly	Polly	Romy	

Girls Names That Mean "Strong"

Abira	Allison	Andres	Bree	Brianna	Bridget
Carla	Costanza	Carly	Drew	Ever	Isana
Mahogany	Miriam	Maude	Mena	Megan	Nina
Ondrea	Osita	Plato	Richelle	Valerie	Viveca

Girls Names That Mean "Peace"

Dove	Erin	Fia	Frida	Concordia	Fredericka
Irena	Lana	Malia	Irene	Olivia	Tully
Peace	Ping	Saloma	Serena	Serenity	Shiloh
Winetta	Xerena				

Girls Names That Mean "Noble"

Ada	Adelaide	Adele	Akela	Alberta	Alicia
Alison	Audrey	Camille	Della	Earlene	Elmira
Elsa	Ethyl	Heidi	Trisha	Lyra	Lecia
Marquis	Patricia				

Girls Names That Mean "Bright"

Alanis	Alberta	Candy	Clara	Claire	Clarise
Claudette	Bertha	Electra	Phoebe	Sheridan	Shula
Shirley	Roberta	Ziva	Zahara		

Girls Names That Mean "Brave"

Casey	Tracy	Emerson	Bernadette	Valentina	Valerie
Sloan					

Girls Names That Mean "Warrior"

Eloise	Fiana	Gertrude	Imelda	Katniss	Kimball
Kelly	Murphy	Lois	Louise	Sloan	Trudy

Girls Names That Mean "Dark"

Blake	Bronwyn	Ciara	Maura	Darcy	Delaney
Ebony	Keara	Keri	Layla	Maura	Melanie
Adriana					

Girls Names That Mean "Enlightened or Wise"

Athena	Avery	Freda	Jada	Medora	Minerva
Monique	Ophelia	Rae	Rain	Ramona	Rayna
Sage	Ulima				

Girls Names That Mean "Red"

Auburn	Clancy	Crimson	Derry	Flynn	Flann
Flynn	Scarlett	Sienna	Reed	Rooney	Rory
Rowan	Omri	Phoenix			

Girls Names That Mean "Fiery"

Edana	Flame	Reese	Seraphina	Keegan	McKenna
McKayla					

Girls Names That Mean "Gift from God"

Dita	Dora	Dorothea	Eudora	Dorothy	Isadora
Jane	Joan	Janice	Janine	Joanna	Juanita
Neveah	Pheodora	Shea	Shane	Sheena	Shiloh
Shona	Shonda	Siobhan	Theodora		

Girls Names That Mean "(God is) Gracious"

Anais	Anita	Anna	Annette	Annika	Elisha
Gia	Gianna	Giovanna	Jeanette	Ivana	Ivanka
Jana	Janae	Janelle	Janessa	Janice	Jeanne
Jane	Jean	Jeannette	Joann	Jensen	Jonna
Nanette	Shana	Shane	Shawn	Sheena	Winola

Girls Names That Mean "Protector/Defender"

Alexandria	Alexis	Alexi	Alejandra	Liv	Meredith
Ramona	Sasha	Sandrine	Shura	Sandra	Xantata
Willa					

Girls Names That Mean "Champion or Victorious"

Kinsey	Brea	Jane	Tori	Nia	Neela
Nikita	Eunice	Victoria	Sigourney	Collette	

Girls Names That Mean "Joy or Happy"

Abigail	Beatrice	Joy	Bliss	Carolyn	Hillary
Edith	Jovi	Jovita	Jubilee	Lakeisha	Ranita
Merry	Rona	Tatum	Tisha	Olina	Rowena
Blythe	Bunny	Felicia	Jocelyn	Nara	Gay

Girls Names Relating "To The Sea"

Bela	Chelsea	Cordelia	Delores	Doris	Galilee
Ionia	Mariah	Mali	Marin	Mariana	Marietta
Marianne	Marika	Marina	Marissa	Maris	Maureen
Meredith	Muriel	Meryl	Morgan	Ula	Umiko
Narelle	Narissa	Pasha	Sula		

Girls Names That Mean "Sun"

Asia	Dawn	Eldora	Kalina	Helene	Kira
Liane	Roxanne	Oriana	Sunshine	Solana	Sorina
Surya	Zelene	Zelia	Zora		

Girls Names That Mean "Consecrated to God"

Bettina	Elizabeth	Isabella	Talisa	Lisa	Liza

Girls Names That Mean "Queen"

Cleopatra	Dionne	Juno	Latanya	Malika	Nala
Nefertiti	Quintana	Queen	Quinn	Raine	Rani
Regina	Reina	Reya	Thema	Tania	Tatiana
Thelma	Tonia	Quinn			

Girls Names That Mean "Star"

Astra	Danica	Vega	Estelle	Esther	Hester
Spica	Quarralia	Vespera	Star	Stella	

Chapter 21. Names that Sound Alike

Many times, parents disagree on a potential name for superficial reasons:

- it is too popular
- the initials don't work
- their sister, best friend, or cousin is planning to use the same name
- a bad connotation (i.e., the name elicits memories of a professional rival, childhood bully, or former romantic partner)

Often, the solution to this dilemma is choosing a name that *rhymes* with the original - it has a similar sound and feel, without the negative "baggage." This chapter presents several combinations of baby names that rhyme. If you like one - but you can't persuade your partner to choose it, see if (s)he likes the other........

Boys Names That Rhyme

Aaron: (Jewish & Hebrew): enlightened
Darren: (English, Irish & Gaelic): great

Alvin: (Germany): light skin, noble friend; (English): wise friend
Calvin: (English & Latin America): bald

Barrett: (English & German): strength of a bear
Garrett: (Irish): to watch

Bryan: (Irish): strong one; (Celtic): brave
Ryan: (Gaelic): little king; (Irish): kindly, young royalty

Chance: (English & French): good luck, keeper of records
Lance: (Germany): spear; (French): land

Cody: (Irish): helpful; (English): a cushion, helpful
Brody: (Irish): brother, from the muddy place; (Scottish): second son

Dustin: (English): fighter, warrior
Justin: (English & French): just, true; (Irish): judicious

Devon: (English & Irish): a poet, a county in England
Kevin: (Irish & Gaelic): handsome, beautiful; (Celtic): gentle
Evan: (English): God is good; (Welsh): young; (Celtic): young fighter

Donald: (Celtic & Gaelic): dark stranger; (Irish, English & Scottish): great leader
Arnold: (German): strong as an eagle
Ronald: (English, Gaelic & Scottish): rules with counsel

Eric: (Scandinavian): honorable ruler
Derek: (German & English): gifted ruler

Frank: (Latin America): free
Hank: (Dutch & German): rules his household

Hogan: (Irish & Gaelic): young, young at heart
Logan: (Irish): small cove; (Scottish): Finnian's servant; (Gaelic): from the hollow

Kyle: (Gaelic): young; (Irish): young at heart
Lyle: (French & English): from the island

Jason: (Greek): to heal
Mason: (French & English): stone worker

Sean/Shawn: (Irish): God is gracious
John: (Israel): God is gracious; Jehovah has been gracious

Taylor: (English & French): a tailor
Tyler: (English): tile maker

Barry: (English & Irish): fair-haired; (Celtic); marksman; (Gaelic): spear
Harry: (German): home or house ruler
Larry: (Dutch & Latin America): laurels

Jordan: (Hebrew): to flow down; (Israel): descendant
Aiden: (Irish, Celtic & Gaelic): fire, fiery
Hayden: (English): the rosy meadow
Cayden: (Scottish): fighter
Jayden: (American): God has heard

Girls Names That Rhyme

Anna/Ana: (Hebrew): favor or grace; (Native American): mother; (Israel): gracious
Hannah: (English & Hebrew): favor, grace; (Biblical): grace of God

Bella: (Hebrew): devoted to God; (Spanish & Latin America): beautiful
Ella: (English); beautiful fairy; (Spanish): she
Stella: (French, Italian & Greek): star

Darcy: (Irish & Celtic): dark one
Marcy: (Latin America): marital

Kayla: (Irish): pure and beloved
Jayla: (Arabia): charity; (African American): one who is special
Layla: (Indian): born at night; (Arabian): dark beauty
Shayla: (Irish): her gift

Cara: (Celtic): friend; (Italian & Dominican Republic): dear, beloved
Mara: (English, Italian, Hebrew & Israel): bitter
Sara(h): (Hebrew, Spanish & Biblical): princess
Tara: (Irish & Scottish): a hill where the kings meet; (Irish): tower, hillside

Carla: (Portuguese & Latin America): strong one
Marla: (Greek): high tower

Candy: (American): bright, sweet; (Hebrew): famous bearer
Mandy: (Latin America): worthy of love
Sandy: (English): a diminutive for of Sandra, which means unheeded prophetess

Chloe: (Greek): verdant, blooming
Zoe (or Zoey): (Greek): life, alive

Ellen: (Greek): light
Helen: (Greek): light

Kiley: (Irish): narrow land
Riley/Rylee: (Irish): a small stream

Flynn: (Irish): heir to the red-headed
Lynn(e): (English): waterfall
Quinn: (Celtic): wise; (Irish): fifth, counsel, intelligent

Jayne: (Indian): victorious; (Hebrew): gift from God; (English): Jehovah has been gracious
Rain/Raine: (American): blessings from above; (French & Latin): ruler; (English): lord, wise
Blaine: (Gaelic, Irish & Celtic): thin

Callie: (Greek): beautiful; (English); lark
Tally: (Irish): surname

Addison: (English): son of Adam
Madison: (English): son of Matthew

Minnie: (Irish): bitter; (Hebrew): wished for a child
Winnie: (Irish & Celtic): white, fair

Clarissa: (Spanish & Italian): clear; (Latin America): brilliant
Alyssa: (Greek): logical
Melissa: (Greek): honey bee
Marissa: (Latin America): of the sea; (Hebrew): rebellion, bitter

Marilyn: (Israel): descendants of Mary
Carolyn: (English): joy, song of happiness

Valerie: (French): brave, fierce one; (English): strong, valiant
Mallory: (French): unfortunate; ill-fated; (German): war counselor

Hailey/Hailee/Haley: (English): hero, field of hay
Kaylee: (American): pure
Bailey: (English): bailiff, steward, public official

Jess: (Israel): wealthy
Tess: (English): harvester
Bess: (Hebrew, English & Israel): oath of God, God is satisfaction

Molly: (Israel & English): bitter
Holly: (French, English & Germany): shrub
Polly: (Latin America): bitter
Dolly: (America): cute child

Sherry: (Israel): beloved; (French): dear one
Merry: (English): merry, joyous

Laura: (English, Spanish & Latin America): crowned with laurel, from the laurel tree
Maura: (Italian, Irish & French): dark
Dora: (Greek): gift

Tia: (Greek); princess; (Spanish): princess, aunt; (African American): aunt
Lia: (Greek): bearer of good news
Mia: (Italian): my; (Biblical): mine
Nia: (Irish): champion
Pia: (Italian): devout
Gia: (Italian): God is gracious

Nina: (Hebrew); grace; (Spanish): girl; (Native American): strong
Tina: (English): river
Gina: (Italian): garden; (African American): powerful mother of black people
Dina: (Hebrew & Israel): avenged, judged; (English): from the valley

Gay: (English): merry, happy
Rae: (Scottish): grace; (Germany): wise protection
Fay: (French): fairy; (Irish): raven; (English): faith, confidence
Kay: (Greek): rejoice; (Scottish & Welsh): fiery
May: (English): name of month; (Hebrew & Latin America): from Mary

Stacy: (English): productive, resurrection
Tracy: (English): brave
Casey: (Celtic & Gaelic): brave; (Irish): observant, alert, brave; (Spanish): honorable
Macy: (English): enduring; (American): stone worker
Lacy: (Irish): surname; (English): derived from lace
Gracie: (English & Latin America): grace

Irene: (Greek & Spanish): peaceful
Eileen: (Irish & French): light
Colleen: (Irish & Gaelic): girl
Darlene: (English & French): little darling
Marlene: (Germany): bitter; (Hebrew): from the tower
Sharlene: (English & French): manly, from the name Charles

Appendix A: Alphabetical List of Boys Names

Aaron: (Jewish): enlightened; (Hebrew): lofty, exalted
Abbott: (Hebrew): father
Abdul: (Arabic): servant of God
Abe: (Jewish): father of nations
Abel: (Hebrew & Biblical): breathe, son
Abner: (Israel & Hebrew): father is light, father of light
Abraham: (Hebrew & Biblical): exalted father
Abram: (Hebrew): high father; (Israel): father of nations
Abu: (African): father
Ace: (Latin): unity
Achilles: (Greek): hero of the Trojan War
Ackerly: (English): meadow of oak trees
Adair: (Scottish): oak tree ford
Adalius: (German) : noble
Adam: (Hebrew): red; (Israel): man of the earth; (English): of the red earth
Adamson: (English): the son of Adam
Addison: (English): son of Adam
Adler: (German): eagle
Adolf/Adolph: (German): noble wolf
Adonis: (Greek): beautiful
Adrian: (German, Spanish & Italian): dark; (Greek): rich
Adriel: (Hebrew): from God's flock
Agustin: (Spanish): majestic dignity
Ahmad: (Arabic): one who thanks God
Ahman: (Arabic): a derivative of Ahmad, which means one who thanks God
Ahmet: (Turkish): worthy of praise
Aidan/Aiden/Adan: (Irish, Celtic & Gaelic): fire, fiery
Aiken: (English): sturdy, made of oak
Ainsley: (Scottish): my own meadow
Ainsworth: (English): from Ann's estate
Ajax: (Greek): warrior
Ajay: (Punjabi): victorious, undefeatable
Ajit: (Indian): invincible
Akeem: (Hebrew): a form of Joachim, which means God will establish
Aki: (Japanese): autumn, bright
Akiko: (Japanese): surrounded by bright light
Akil: (Arabian): intelligent
Akira: (Japanese): intelligent
Aladdin: (Arabian): faithful
Alaire: (French): filled with joy
Alan/Allan/Allen: (English & Irish): handsome; (Celtic): harmony, stone or noble
Alastair: (Scottish): a form of Alexander, which means protector of mankind
Albert/Alberto: (English & German): noble, bright
Alden: (English): old, wise protector
Aldo: (German): old and wise
Aldrich: (English): wise counselor
Alejandro: (Spanish): defender of mankind
Alessandro: (Greek): defender of man
Alexander/Alex/Alek/Alexi/Alexis: (Greek): protector of mankind
Alfonso/Alfonzo: (Italian): ready for battle
Alfred: (English): elf counselor
Alfie: (English): a diminutive form of Alfred, which means elf counselor
Alistair/Allister: (English): a form of Alexander, which means protector of mankind
Alon: (Hebrew): of the oak tree

Alonzo: (Spanish & American): ready for battle
Aloysius: (German): famous warrior
Alpha: (Greek): first-born child
Alphonso/Alphonse: (Italian & German): noble and eager
Altair: (Greek): star
Alton: (English): from the old town
Alvaro: (Spanish & German): truth-speaker or guardian
Alvin: (German): light skin, noble friend; (English): wise friend
Amadeus: (Latin): loves God
Amal: (Hebrew): worker; (Arabic): hopeful
Amani: (African): peaceful
Amare: (African): handsome
Amber: (French): amber
Ambrose: (Greek): immortal
Amerigo: (Teutonic): industrious
Ames: (French): friend
Amida: (Japanese): Buddha
Amil: (Hindu): invaluable
Amir: (Arabic): prince
Amit: (Arabic): highly praised
Ammon: (Egyptian): god of a unified Egypt
Amory: (German): ruler
Amos: (Hebrew): strong, carried, brave: (Israel): troubled
An: (Chinese & Vietnamese): peaceful
Anders: (Scandinavian): a courageous, valiant man
Anderson: (Scottish): son of Andrew
Andre: (French): manly, brave
Andrea: (Italian): brave
Andrei: (Italian): manlike
Andres: (Spanish): manly, courageous
Andrew: (English, Scottish & Biblical): manly; brave
Anel: (Greek): messenger of God, angel
Angel: (Spanish & Greek): angelic
Angelo: (Italian): angel
Angus: (Irish): vigorous one
Anil: (Hindu): wind god
Ansel: (French): follower of a nobleman
Anson: (German): divine
AnthonyAntony: (English & Biblical): worthy of praise
Antoine/Anton: (French): a flourishing man
Antonio: (Italian & Spanish): a flourishing man, worthy of praise
Antwan/Antwaun/Antwoine/Antwon/Antwone: (Arabic): worthy of praise
Anwar: (Arabic): luminous
Apollo: (Latin): strength, sun god
Apollos: (Israel): one who destroys
Archer: (Latin): a skilled bowman
Archibald: (German): bold
Archimedes: (Greek): to think about first
Arden: (Latin): passionate
Ares: (Greek): god of war
Aristotle/Ari: (Greek): thinker with a great purpose
Arlen: (Irish): pledge
Arlo: (Spanish): barberry
Armand/Armando: (French): of the army
Armani/Armon: (Hebrew): high fortress
Armstrong: (English): strong arm

Arne/Arnie/Arnold: (German): strong as an eagle
Arroyo: (Spanish): irrigation channel
Arsenio: (Greek): masculine, virile
Arthur/Art/Artur/Arturo: (English): bear, stone
Ary: (Hebrew): lion of God
Aryn: (Hebrew & Arabic): a form of Aaron, which means enlightened
Asa: (Hebrew): physician; Japan: born at dawn
Asante: (African): thank you
Ash/Ashe: (English): tree
Ashby: (Scandinavian): ash tree farm
Asher: (Hebrew & Israel): happy, blessed
Ashley: (English & Biblical): lives in the ash tree
Ashton: (Hebrew): shining light; (English): ash tree settlement
Atlas: (Greek): lifted, carried
Atticus: (Latin): a man from Athens
Attila: (Gothic): little father
Atwell: (English): one who lives at the spring
Aubrey: (English): one who rules with elf-wisdom
Auburn: (Latin): reddish-brown
Augustine/August/Augie/Augustus: (German): revered
Aurelius: (Latin): golden
Austin/Austen: (English): from the name Augustin, which means revered
Avery: (English): wise ruler
Avi: (Hebrew): my God, father; (Latin America): Lord of mine
Axel/Axl: (German & Hebrew): father of peace; (German): source of all life
Azariah: (Hebrew & Israel): God helps
Azim: (Arabic): defender

Baden: (German): bather
Bae: (Korean): inspiration
Bailey: (French): bailiff, steward
Bain: (Irish): fair-haired
Bainbridge: (Irish): fair bridge
Baird: (Irish): traveling minstrel
Baldwin: (German): brave friend
Balthazar: (English): the comedy of errors a merchant
Bancroft: (English): from the bean field
Barak: (Hebrew & Israel): flash of lightening
Barclay: (Scottish & English): birch tree meadow
Barlow: (English): bare hillside
Barnabus: (Hebrew & Israel): comfort
Barnett: (English): of honorable birth
Barney: (English): comfort
Baron: (English): a title of nobility
Barr: (English): a lawyer
Barrett: (German): strong as a bear
Barrington: (English): fenced town
Barry: (English & Irish): fair-haired; (Celtic); marksman; (Gaelic): spear
Bart: (Hebrew): ploughman; (English): from the barley farm
Bartholomew: (English, Hebrew & Biblical): son of a farmer
Bartlett: (French): son of the father
Barton: (English): from the barley town
Basil: (Greek & Latin): royal, kingly
Bautista: (Italian): John the Baptist

126

Baxter: (English): baker
Bay: (Vietnamese): born on a Saturday; (American): a natural body of water
Beacan: (Irish): small
Beau: (French): handsome, beautiful
Beaufort: (French): beautiful fort
Beaumont: (French): beautiful mountain
Beauregard: (French): handsome, beautiful
Beck: (English): the brook
Becker: (German): baker
Beckett/Beck: (English) : brook
Beckham: (Englidh): from the Beck homestead
Beethoven: (German): music
Bellamy: (French): handsome
Ben: (English): son of my right hand
Benedict: (Latin): Blessed
Benito: (Italian): blessed
Benjamin: (English, Hebrew & Biblical): son of my right hand
Bennett: (English): one who is blessed
Benoit: (French): bland
Benson: (English): son of Benedict
Bentley: (English): from the bent grass meadow
Beowulf: (English): intelligent wolf
Beresford: (English): from the barley ford
Bergen: (German): hill lover
Berkeley: (English & Irish): from the birch meadow
Bernard: (German): strong as a bear
Bertram/Bert: (German & English): bright light
Bevis: (Teutonic): an archer
Bing: (German): kettle-shaped hollow
Birch: (English): white, shining
Birkitt: (English): birch-tree coast
Birney: (English): from the island with the brook
Bjorn: (Scandinavian): a form of Bernard, which means strong as a bear
Black: (English): dark-skinned
Blackwell: (English): from the dark spring
Blade: (English): wielding a sword or knife
Blaine: (Gaelic, Irish & Celtic): thin
Blair: (Irish): plain, field
Blaise: (French & English): stutter, stammer
Blake: (English): pale, fair
Blaze: (Latin): one who stammers; (English): flame
Bodhi: (Indian): awakens
Bogart: (French): strong with a bow
Bonaventure: (Latin): one who undertakes a blessed venture
Booker: (English): bible, book maker
Boone: (French): good
Boris: (Slavic): warrior
Boston: (English): the city Boston
Bowen: (Gaelic): small son; (Irish): archer
Bowie: (Celtic): yellow-haired
Boyd: (Celtic): blond-haired
Bracken: (English): resembling a large fern
Braden/Brayden/Braiden: (Irish & English): broad hillside; (Scottish): salmon
Braddock: (English); from the broadly spread oak
Bradford: (English): from the wide ford

Bradman: (English): the foreman of Brad
Brady: (Gaelic & Irish): spirit; (Irish): broad-shouldered
Brandon: (Irish): little raven
Branson/Bransen: (English): the son of Brandon
Brant/Brantley: (English): steep, tall
Braxton: (English): from Brock's town
Breck: (Irish): freckled
Brendan: (Irish): prince; (Gaelic): brave; (Celtic & Irish): raven; (German): flame
Brennan: (Gaelic): teardrop
Brent: (English): from the hill
Bret/Brett: (French, English & Celtic): a native of Brittany
Brian: (Gaelic): noble birth; (Celtic): great strength
Brice: (Welsh): alert, ambitious
Brigham: (English): covered bridge
Britt/Britton/Brittan: (Scottish): from Britain
Brock: (English): badger
Broderick: (English): from the wide ridge
Brody: (Irish): brother, from the muddy place; (Scottish): second son
Brogan: (Gaelic & Irish): from the ditch
Bronson: (English): son of Brown
Brooks: (English): running water, son of Brooke
Brown: (English): brown color, dark-skinned
Bruce: (French & English): woods, thick brush
Bruno: (German): brown-haired
Brutus: (Latin): course, stupid
Bryan: (Irish): strong one; (Celtic): brave
Bryce: (Scottish): speckled
Bryson: (American): son of a nobleman
Buck: (German & English): male deer
Buckley: (English): deer meadow
Bud: (English): brotherly
Budha: (Hindu): the planet Mercury
Buford: (English): ford near the castle
Burgess: (English): town dweller, shopkeeper
Burke: (German): birch tree
Burton: (English): from the fortified town
Butler: (English): keeper of the bottles
Byrd: (English): bird-like
Byron: (French & English): barn or cottage

Cade: (American): pure
Caden: (Welsh): spirit of battle
Caesar: (Latin): emperor
Caiden/Caden: (American): friend, companion
Cain: (Israel): craftsman; (Hebrew): spear; (Welsh): clear water; (Irish): archaic
Caleb: (Israel): faithful; (Hebrew): dog or bold
Callan/Callen: (Australian): sparrow hawk
Callum: (Gaelic): resembling a dove
Calvin: (English & Latin America): bald
Camden: (Irish, Scottish, English & Gaelic): from the winding valley
Cameron: (Irish & Gaelic): crooked nose
Campbell: (Gaelic): crooked mouth; (French): from the beautiful field
Carey: (Greek): pure
Carl/Carle: (English): man; (German): strong one
Carlin: (Irish, Gaelic & Scottish): little champion
Carlisle: (English): from the walled city

Carlo: (French): strong; (Italian): manly
Carlos: (Spanish): a free man
Carlsen: (Scandinavian): son of Carl
Carlton/Carleton: (English): town of Charles
Carlyle: (English): Carl's island
Carmelo: (Hebrew & Israel): fruit orchard
Carmine: (Latin): beautiful song
Carroll: (Irish): champion
Carson: (English): son who lives in the swamp
Carter: (English): cart driver
Carver: (English): sculptor
Cary: (Celtic): from the river; (Welsh): from the fort on the hill
Cash: (Latin): money
Casper: (Persian): treasurer; (German): imperial
Cassius: (Latin): empty, hollow, vain
Castor: (Greek): bereaved brother of Helen
Cato: (Latin): sagacious, wise one, good judgment
Caton: (Spanish): knowledgeable
Cayden: (Scotland): fighter
Ceasar/Caesar: (Latin): long-haired
Cecil: (Latin): blind
Cedric: (English): battle chieftain
Chad: (English): battle
Chadwick: (English): from Chad's dairy farm
Chai: (Hebrew): giver of life
Chan: (Spanish): God is gracious
Chance: (English & French): good luck, keeper of records
Chancellor/Chancelor/Chancey: (English): record keeper
Chandler: (French): candle maker
Channing: (French): church official; (English): resembling a young wolf
Charles: (English): strong, manly
Chase: (English): hunter
Chauncey: (Latin): chancellor
Chavez: (Spanish): a surname
Che: (Spanish): a derivative of Jose, which means God will add
Chen: (Chinese): great, dawn
Chester: (English): a rock fortress
Chevy: (French): a diminutive form of Chevalier, which means horseman, knight
Chico: (Spanish): boy
Chikae: (African American): God's power
Chin: (Korean): precious
Chip: (English): chipping sparrow
Cho: (Korean): beautiful
Christian: (English & Irish): follower of Christ
Christopher/Christoff: (Biblical): Christ-bearer; (English): he who holds Christ in his heart
Chun: (Chinese): spring
Chung: (Chinese): intelligent
Cicero: (Latin): chickpea
Ciro: (Italian): a diminutive form of Cyril, which means lordly
Cisco: (Spanish): a diminutive form of Francisco, which means free
Clancy/Clancey: (Celtic): son of the red-haired warrior
Clarence: (English & Latin America): clear, luminous
Clark: (English): cleric, scholar, clerk
Claud/Claude: (English): lame
Claudius: (English): lame
Claus: (Greek): people's victory

Clay: (English): clay maker, immortal
Clayborne: (English): brook near the clay pit
Clayton: (English): mortal
Cleavon: (English): cliff
Clement: (French): compassionate
Cleo: (Greek): to praise, acclaim
Cletus: (Greek): illustrious
Cliff/Clifford/Clifton: (English): from the ford near the cliff
Clinton: (English): town on a hill
Clive: (English): one who lives near the cliff
Clyde: (Irish): warm
Coburn: (English): meeting of streams
Coby: (English): supplanter
Cody: (Irish): helpful; (English): a cushion, helpful
Colbert: (French): famous and bright
Cole: (Irish): warrior; (English): having dark features
Colin/Collin: (Irish & Gaelic): young; (Scottish): young dog; (English): of a triumphant people
Colt: (American): baby horse; (English): from the dark town
Colton: (English): coal town, from the dark town
Columbus: (Greek): curious
Conan: (English): resembling a wolf; (Gaelic): high and mighty
Cong: (Chinese): clever
Conlan: (Irish): hero
Connery: (Scottish): daring
Connor/Conner: (Irish): strong willed, much wanted
Conrad: (German): brave counselor
Constantine: (Latin): steadfast, firm
Cooper: (English): barrel maker
Corbett: (French): resembling a young raven
Cordero: (Spanish): little lamb
Cornelius: (Irish): strong willed, wise; (Latin America): horn-colored
Cory/Corey: (English & Irish): hill, hollow
Cosimo: (Italian): the order of the universe
Cosmo: (Greek): the order of the universe
Covington: (English); from the town near the cave
Coy/Coye/Coyt: (English): woods
Craig: (Scottish): dwells at the crag; (Welsh): rock
Cramer: (English): full
Crandall: (English): from the valley of cranes
Crawford: (English): from the crow's ford
Creed: (English): belief, guiding principle
Creighton: (Scottish): from the border town
Crispin: (Latin): curly-haired
Cristobal: (Spanish): bearer
Cromwell: (English): winding spring
Crosby: (English): town crossing
Cruz: (Spanish): of the cross
Cuba: (Spanish): tub
Cullen: (Irish & Gaelic): handsome; (Celtic): cub; (English): city in Germany
Culley: (Irish): woods
Culver: (English): dove
Cunningham: (Gaelic): descendant of the chief
Curran/Curry: (Celtic): hero
Curtis: (Latin): enclosure
Cutter: (English): tailor
Cyrano: (Greek): from Cyrene

Cyril: (English & Greek): master, lord
Cyrus: (English): far-sighted

Dack: (English): from the French town of Dax
Dae: (Korean): great
Daegan: (Irish): black-haired
Dai: (Chinese): sword technique
Daiki: (Japanese): of great value
Dakota: (Native American): friend to all
Dale: (German): valley; (English): lives in the valley
Dallas: (Irish & Gaelic): wise; (Scottish & Celtic): from the waterfall
Dalton: (English): from the town in the valley
Damian: (Greek): one who tames others
Damon: (English): calm, tame
Dane: (Hebrew & Scandinavian): God will judge; (English): brook
Daniel: (Hebrew & Biblical): God is my judge; (Irish & Welsh): attractive
Dante: (Latin): enduring, everlasting
Darian: (Irish): from the name Darren, which means great
Dario: (Spanish): affluent
Darius: (Greek): kingly, wealthy; (American): pharaoh
Darnel/Darnell: (English): hidden
Darren/Darrin/Darin/Darron/Darryn: (English, Irish & Gaelic): great
Darvell: (French): from the eagle town
Darwin/Derwin: (English): dear friend
Daryl/Darrell: (French): darling, beloved
Dashawn: (English): God is willing
Dashiell: (French): page boy
David: (Hebrew, Scottish & Welsh): beloved
Davis: (English & Scottish): David's son
Dawayne/Dwayne: (Irish): dark, small
Dawson: (English): son of David
Dax: (English & French): water
De: (Chinese): virtuous
Deacon: (American): pastor; (English): dusty one, servant
Dean: (English): head, leader
Deangelo: (Italian): a combination of De and Angelo, which means little angel
Decker: (German): one who prays: (Hebrew): piercing
Declan: (Irish): saint
Dedrick: (German): ruler of the people
Deepak: (Hindu): little lamp
Deion/Dion/Deiondre: (Greek & French): mountain of Zeus
Delaney: (Irish): dark challenger
Delano: (English): nut tree; (Irish): dark
Delbert: (English): proud, bright as day
Dell: (English): from the small valley
Delroy: (French): belonging to the king
Demarco: (African American): of Mark: (South African): warlike
Demetrius: (Greek): goddess of fertility, one who loves the earth
Demond: (African American): of man
Dennis: (Greek): wild, frenzied
Dennison: (English): son of Dennis
Denton: (English): happy home
Denzel: (English): fort; (African): wild
Derby: (English): deer park; (Irish): from the village of dames
Derek: (German & English): gifted ruler
Dermot: (Irish): free from envy

Derry: (English, Irish, German & Gaelic): red-haired, from the oak grove|
Deshawn/Deshaun: (American): a combination of De and Shawn, which means God is gracious
Desi: (Latin): desiring
Desmond: (Gaelic): a man from South Munster
Destin: (French): fate
Devin/Devaughn/Devon: (Irish): poet
Devlin: (Gaelic): fierce bravery
Dewayne: (American): a combination of De and Wayne, which means wagon maker
Dewey: (Welsh): prized
DeWitt: Flemish: blond hair
Dexter: (Latin): right-handed, skillful; (Latin America): flexible
Diego: (Spanish): Saint James
Diego Alejandro: (Spanish): Saint James/defender of mankind
Dierks: (Danish): ruler of the people
Diesel: (American): having great strength
Dietrich: (German): ruler of the people
Dijon: (French): a city in France
Dimitri/Demetrius: (Russian): lover of the earth
Dino: (Italian): one who wields a great sword
Dirk: (German): a diminutive form of Derek, which means gifted ruler
Dixon: (English): power, brave ruler
Dobbs: (English): fiery
Dolan: (Irish): dark-haired
Dolph: (German): diminutive form of Adolph, which means noble wolf
Domingo: (Spanish): born on a Sunday
Dominic: (Spanish): born on a Sunday
Donal/Donald: (Celtic & Gaelic): dark stranger; (Irish, English & Scottish): great leader
Dong: (Korean): the east
Donovan: (Irish): brown-haired chief
Doug/Dougal/Douglas: (Scottish): dark river
Doyle: (Irish): dark river
Drake: (English): male duck, dragon
Draper: (English): fabric maker
Dre: (American): a diminutive form of Andre, which means manly, brave
Drew/Dru: (English): courageous, valiant
Driscoll: (Celtic): mediator
Drummond: (Scottish): one who lives near the ridge
Drury: (French): loving
Dryden: (English): dry valley
Duane: (Gaelic): a dark and swarthy man
Dudley: (English): common field
Duff: (Scottish): dark
Dugan: (Irish): dark
Duke: (English): leader
Duncan/Dunn: (Scottish): brown warrior
Dustin/Dusty: (English): fighter, warrior
Dwayne: (Irish): dark
Dwight: (English): a diminutive form of DeWitt, which means blond hair
Dylan/Dillon/Dilan: (English & Welsh): born from the ocean, son of the wave; (Gaelic): faithful

Eagle: (Native American): resembling the bird
Eamon: (Irish): blessed guardian
Earl: (Irish): pledge; (English): nobleman
Earnest: (English): industrious

Eastman: (English): a man from the east
Easton: (English): from east town
Eben: (Hebrew): rock
Ebenezer: (Hebrew & Israel): rock of help
Edgar: (English): powerful and wealthy spearman
Edison: (English): son of Edward
Edmund/Edmond: (English): wealthy protector
Eduardo: (Spanish): wealthy protector or guardian
Edward: (English): wealthy guardian; (German): strong as a boar
Edwin: (English): wealthy friend
Efrain/Ephraim: (Hebrew): fruitful
Egan/Egin/Egen/Egyn: (Irish): ardent, fiery
Elan: (Hebrew): tree
Elbert: (English): a well-born man; (German): a bright man
Eldon: (English): from the sacred hill
Eldridge: (German & English): wise ruler
Elgin: (English) & Celtic): noble, white
Eli/Ely: (Hebrew): ascended, uplifted, high; (Greek): defender of man
Elian: (Spanish): consecrated to the gracious God
Elias: (Latin & Hebrew): the Lord is my God
Elijah: (Biblical): the Lord is my God; (Hebrew): Jehovah is God
Elliott: (Israel): close to God; (English): the Lord is my God
Ellis: (English & Hebrew): my God is Jehovah
Ellison: (English): son of Elias
Ellory/Ellery: (Cornish): resembling a swan
Ellsworth: (English): from the nobleman's estate
Elmer: (English): famous, noble
Elmo: (English): protector; (Latin): amiable
Elmore: (English): moor where the elm trees grow
Elon: (Biblical & African American): spirit, God loves me
Elroy: (French, English & African American): king; (Irish): red-haired youth
Elton: (English): old town
Elvin: (Irish): friend of elves
Elvis: (Scandinavian): wise
Elwood: (English): old forest
Emerson: (English): brave, powerful
Emery: (German): industrious leader
Emil/Emile: (Latin): eager, industrious
Emiliano: (Italian & Latin): rival, industrious
Emilio: (Spanish): flattering
Emmanuel: (Hebrew): God with us
Emmett/Emmitt: (English): whole, universal
Engelbert: (German): bright as an angel
Ennis: (Irish): island; (Gaelic): the only choice; (Greek): mine
Enoch: (Hebrew): dedicated, consecrated
Enos: (Hebrew): man
Enrique: (Spanish): ruler of the estate
Enzo: (Italian): ruler of the estate
Ephraim: (Hebrew & Israel): fruitful
Eric/Erik/Erich: (Scandinavian): honorable ruler
Ernest: (German): serious, determined, truth
Errol: (Latin): wanderer
Esau: (Hebrew): hairy, famous bearer; (Israel): he that acts or finishes
Esme: (French): esteemed
Esteban: (Spanish): crowned in victory

Ethan: (Hebrew & Biblical): firm, strong
Eugene: (Greek): well-born man
Eui: (Korean): righteousness
Eun: (Korean): silver
Evan: (English): God is good; (Welsh): young; (Celtic): young fighter
Evander: (Greek): benevolent ruler
Everett: (English): hardy, brave, strong
Ewan: (Celtic, Scotch & Irish): young
Ezekiel: (Hebrew & Israel): strength of God
Ezra: (Hebrew & Israel): helper

Fa: (Chinese): setting off
Fabian/Faber/Fabio: (Latin): bean grower
Fabrizio/Fabrice: (Italian): craftsman
Facundo: (Spanish): significant, eloquent
Fagan/Fagin: (Gaelic): ardent; (Irish): eager
Fai: (Chinese): beginning to fly
Fairbanks: (English): from the bank along the path
Faisal: (Arabic): decisive
Falkner: (English): trainer of falcons
Fargo: (American): jaunty
Farley: (English): bull meadow
Farnell: (English): fern-covered hill
Farrell/Ferrell: (Irish): heroic, courageous
Farrow: (English): piglet
Faust: (Latin): fortunate
Felipe: (Spanish): one who loves horses
Felix: (Latin): happy and prosperous
Felton: (English): from the town near the field
Feng: (Chinese): sharp blade
Fenn: (English): from the marsh
Fenton: (English): from the farm on the fens
Ferdinand: (German): courageous voyager
Fergus: (Gaelic): first and supreme choice
Fernando: (Spanish): daring, adventurous
Ferris: (Irish): small rock
Fidel: (Latin) faithful
Fielding: (Irish): from the field
Filbert: (English): brilliant
Finch: (Irish): resembling the small bird
Fineas/Phineas: (Egyptian): dark-skinned
Finian/Phinian: (Irish): light-skinned, white
Finlay/Findlay/Finian/Finley: (Irish): blond-haired soldier
Finn: (English): blond
Finnegan: (Irish): fair-haired
Fisher: (English): fisherman
Fitch: (English): resembling an ermine
Fitzgerald: (English) the son of Gerald
Fitzpatrick: (English): son of Patrick
Flann: (Irish): redhead
Fleming: (English): from Denmark
Fletcher: (English): one who makes arrows
Flint: (English): stream, hard quartz rock
Flynn: (Irish): ruddy complexion; heir to the red-head
Fogarty: (Irish): exiled
Foley: (English): creative

Fontaine: (French): from the water source
Ford: (English): from the river crossing
Forrest: (English & French): from the woods
Forster: (American & French): from the woods
Foster: (English & French): one who keeps the forest
Fox: (English): fox
Francesco: (Italian): a man from France
Francis/Franco: (Latin): a man from France
Francisco: (Spanish): a man from France, free
Franco: (Spanish): frank, free
Frank/ Frankie/Franklin: (English): free man
Franz/Frantz: (German): a man from France
Fraser: (Scottish): strawberry flowers
Frasier: (French): strawberry, curly-haired
Fred: (German): peaceful ruler
Frederick/Frederique/Frederico/Freidrich: (German): peaceful ruler
Freeborn: (English): child of freedom
Freeman: (English): free
Fremont: (French): protector of freedom
Frey: (English): lord
Frick: (English): bold
Fulbright: (English): brilliant
Fuller/Fullerton: (English): from Fuller's town
Fyfe: (Scottish): a man from Fifeshire
Fynn: (Russian): the Offin River

Gabe: (English): strength of God
Gabriel: (Israel): hero of God; (Hebrew): man of God; (Spanish): God is my strength
Gaetan: (French & Italian): from Italy
Gage/Gaige: (French): a pledge or pawn
Galbraith: (Scottish): a foreigner
Gale/Galen: (Gaelic): tranquil; (English): festive party: (Greek): healer, calm
Galileo: (Hebrew): one who comes from Galilee
Gallagher: (Irish & Gaelic): eagle helper
Galt: (English): from the wooded land
Gan: (Chinese): dare, adventure
Gannon: (Irish & Gaelic): fair-skinned
Garcia: (Spanish): one who is brave in battle
Gared: (English): mighty with a spear
Garen/Garin/Garren/Garrin: (English): mighty spearman
Garfield: (English): battlefield
Garnet: (English): gem, armed with a spear; (French): keeper of grain
Garrett: (Irish): to watch
Garrick: (English): oak spear
Garrison: (French): prepared
Garroway: (English): spear fighter
Garry/Gary: (English): mighty spearman
Garson: (English): the son of Gar
Garth: (Scandinavian): keeper of the garden
Gaston: (French): a man from Gastony
Gavin: (English): little hawk; (Welsh): hawk of the battle
Gaylord: (French): merry lord, jailer
Geming: (Chinese): revolution
Gen: (Chinese): root
Gene: (English): a well-born man
Genovese/Geno: (Italian): from Genoa, Italy

Gentry: (English): gentleman
Geoffrey/Geffrey/Jeffrey/Geoff/Geff/Jeff: (English): a man of peace
George: (English): farmer
Gerald/Gerry: (German): one who rules with the spear
Gerard: (French): one who is mighty with the spear
Geronimo: (Greek & Italian): a famous chef
Gervaise: (French): honorable
Gibson: (English): son of Gilbert
Gideon: (Hebrew & Israel): great warrior
Gilbert/Gil: (French): bright promise: (English): trustworthy
Giles: (Greek): resembling a young goat
Gill: (Gaelic): servant
Gilmore: (Irish): devoted to the Virgin Mary
Gilroy: (Irish): devoted to the king
Gino: (Greek): a diminutive form of Eugene, which means well-born man
Giovanni/Gian: (Italian); God is gracious
Guiseppe: (Italian): God will add
Gizmo: (American): playful
Glade: (English): from the clearing in the woods
Glendon: (Scottish): fortress in the glen
Glenn: (Scottish): glen, valley
Glover: (English): one who makes gloves
Goddard: (German): divinely firm
Godfrey: (German): God is peace
Godric: (English): power of God
Goldwin: (English): a golden friend
Goliath: (Hebrew): exiled
Gomer: (Hebrew): completed, finished
Gomez: (Spanish): man
Gonzalo:(Spanish): wolf
Goode: (English): upstanding
Gordon: (Gaelic): from the great hill, hero
Grady: (Gaelic): famous, noble
Graham: (Scottish): from the gray home
Granger: (English): farmer
Grant: (Latin): great
Granville: (French): from the large village
Gray: (English): gray-haired
Grayson: (English): son of the bailiff
Gregory/Greg: (English & Greek): vigilant
Griffin: (Latin): prince, (Welsh): strong in faith
Griffith: (Welsh): mighty chief
Grover: (English): grove
Guang: (Chinese): light
Guido: (Italian): guide
Guillermo: (Spanish): a form of William, which means protector
Gunner/Gunther: (Scandinavian): warrior
Gus: (German): revered
Gustav: (Scandinavian): of the staff of the gods
Guthrie: (German): war hero
Guy: (French): guide; (Hebrew): valley; (Celtic): sensible; (Latin America): living spirit

Hackett/Hackman: (German & French): little wood cutter
Hadley: (English & Irish): from the heath covered meadow
Hagen: (Gaelic): youthful
Haig: (English): enclosed with hedges

Haim: (Hebrew): giver of life
Haines: (English): from the vine-covered cottage
Hakin: (Arabic): wise and intelligent
Hal: (English): ruler of the army
Hallan: (English): dweller at the hall
Halley: (English): from the hall near the meadow
Halliwell: (English): from the holy spring
Halsey: (English): Hal's island
Hamid: (Arabic): praised
Hamilton: (English): from the flat-topped hill
Hamlet: (English): home
Hammond: (English): village
Hancock: (English): one who owns a farm
Hanford: (English): from the high ford
Hank: (Dutch & German): rules his household
Hanley: (English): from the high meadow
Hannibal: (Phoenician): grace of god
Hans: (German & Hebrew): gift from God; (Scandinavian): God is gracious
Hansel: (Hebrew): gift from God; (Scandinavian): God is gracious
Harcourt: (French): fortified dwelling
Harding: (English): brave, manly
Hardwin: (English): brave friend
Harim: (Arabic): superior
Harlan: (English): hare's land
Harley: (English): hare's meadow
Harlow: (English): from the army on the hill
Harold: (Scandinavian): ruler of the army
Harper: (English): one who plays or makes harps
Harrington: (English): from the herring town
Harrison: (English): son of Harry
Harry/Harris: (German): home or house ruler
Hartford: (English): from the stag's ford
Hartley: (English): from the stage meadow
Hartman: (German): hard, strong
Hartwell: (English): deer well
Harvey: (English): strong, ready for battle
Hasam: (Turkish): reaper, harvester
Hasani: Swahili: handsome
Hasim: (Arabic): decisive
Hasin: (Hindu): laughing
Haven: (Dutch): safe harbor or port
Hawk: (English): hawk
Hawkins: (English): resembling a small hawk
Hawthorne: (English): from the hawthorn tree
Hayden: (English & Welsh): in the meadow or valley
Hayes: (English): from the hedged place
He: (Chinese): yellow river
Hea: (Korean): grace
Heath: (English): from the heath wasteland|
Heathcliff: (English): cliff near the heath
Heaton: (English): from the town on high ground
Hector: (Greek): steadfast, the prince of Troy
Hedley: (English): heather-filled meadow
Hee: (Korean): brightness
Heinrich: (German): a form of Henry, which means rules his household
Helio: (Greek): god of the sun

Henderson: (Scottish): son of Henry
Heng: (Chinese): eternal
Henley: (English): from the high meadow
Henrik: (German): ruler of the home
Henry: (English, German & French): rules his household
Herbert: (German): glorious soldier
Hercules: (Greek): son of Zeus
Herman: (German): soldier
Hermes: (Greek): stone pile
Hero: (Greek): great defender
Hershel: (Hebrew): resembling a deer
Hewitt: (English): little smart one
Hillard: (German): brave warrior
Hilton: (English): town on a hill
Hiro: (Japanese): widespread
Hiromi: (Japanese): widespread beauty; wide-seeing
Hirum: (Hebrew): noblest, exalted
Hobart: (American): having a shining intellect
Hobson: (English): son of Robert
Hoffman: (German): influential
Hogan: (Irish & Gaelic): young, young at heart
Holbrook: (English): brook in the hollow
Holcomb: (English): from the deep valley
Holden: (English): from a hollow in the valley
Holland: (American): from the Netherlands
Hollis: (English): from the holly tree
Holt: (English): wood, by the forest
Homer: (Greek & English): pledge, promise
Hong: (Chinese): wild swan
Hop: (Chinese): agreeable
Horace/Horatio: (French): hour, time
Horton: (English): garden estate
Houghton: (English): settlement on the headland
Houston: (Gaelic): from Hugh's town: (English): from the town on the hill
Howard: (English): guardian of the home
Howe: (German): high
Howell: (Welsh): remarkable
Hoyt: (Irish): mind, spirit
Hu: (Chinese): tiger
Huan: (Chinese): happiness
Hubert: (German): having a shining intellect
Hud: (Arabic): religion, a Muslim prophet
Hudson: (English): son of the hooded man
Hugh/Hugo: (English): intelligent
Humbert/Humberto: (German): brilliant strength
Humphrey: (German): peaceful strength
Hung: (Vietnamese): brave
Hunter: (English): one who hunts
Huntley: (English): hunter's meadow
Hurley: (Irish): sea tide
Hurst: (Irish): dense grove, thicket
Hussein: (Arabic): little, handsome
Hutton: (English): house on the jutting ledge
Huxley: (English): Hugh's meadow
Huy: (Vietnamese): glorious
Hy: (Vietnamese): hopeful

Hyatt: (English): high gate
Hyde: (English): animal hide
Hyo: (Korean): filial duty
Hyun: (Korean): wisdom

Iago: (Welsh & Spanish): supplanter
Ian: (Scottish): gift from God
Ibsen: (German): archer's son
Ichabod: (Hebrew): the glory has gone
Ignacio: (Italian): fiery
Ignatius/Iggy: (Latin): fiery
Igor: (Scandinavian): hero; (Russian): soldier
Ike: (Hebrew): full of laughter
Iker: (Spanish): visitation
Ilias: (Greek): form of Elijah, which means the Lord is my God
Indiana: (English): from the land of the Indians, the state of Indiana
Ingo: (Scandinavian): lord; (Danish): from the meadow
Ingram: (Scandinavian): a raven of peace
Ioan: (Greek, Bulgarian & Romanian): a form of John, which means God is gracious
Ira: (Hebrew & Israel): watchful
Irv/Irvin/Irving: (Irish): handsome
Irwin: (English): friend of the wild boar
Isaac: (Biblical): he will laugh
Isaiah: (Hebrew): the Lord is generous; (Israel): salvation by God
Isamu: (Japanese): courageous
Isas: (Japanese): meritorious
Isham: (English): from the iron one's estate
Ishmael: (Hebrew, Israel & Spanish): God listens, God will hear
Isidore: (Greek): a gift of Isis
Israel: (Israel): prince of God; (Hebrew): may God prevail
Ivan: (Slavic): God is gracious
Ives: (Scandinavian): the archer's bow
Izod: (Irish): light haired
Jabari: (African): valiant
Jabbar: (Indian): one who consoles others
Jabin: (Hebrew): God has built
Jabo: (American): feisty
Jacinto: (Spanish): resembling a hyacinth
Jack: (English): God is gracious; (Hebrew): supplanter
Jackson: (English): son of Jack; (Scottish): God has been gracious
Jacob: (Biblical): supplanter; (Hebrew): he grasps the heel
Jacobo: (Spanish): supplanter
Jacques: (French): supplanter
Jaden: (American): God has heard
Jafar: (Hindu): little stream
Jagger: (English): a carter, to carry
Jai: (Tai): heart
Jaime/Jamie: (Spanish): supplanter
Jake: (Hebrew): he grasps the heel
Jaleel/Jalen: (American): one who heals others
Jamal/Jamaal/Jamall/Jamaul: (Arabic): handsome
Jamar: (American): handsome
James: (English): supplant, replace; (Israel): supplanter
Jameson/Jamieson: (English): son of James
Jan: (Dutch): a form of John, which means God is gracious
Janus: (Latin American): god of beginnings

Janson/Jansen: (Dutch): son of Jan

Japheth: (Hebrew): handsome

Jared: (Hebrew): descending

Jarek: (Slavic): born in January

Jaron: (Hebrew): he will sing

Jarrett/Jerritt: (English): one who is strong with a spear

Jarvis: (German): skilled with a spear

Jasdeep: (Sikh): the lamp radiating Gods' glories

Jason: (Greek): to heal

Jasper/Jaspar: (Hebrew, French & English): precious stone

Javier/Xavier: (Spanish): owner of a new house

Jax: (American): son of Jack

Jaxon: (American): son of Jack

Jay: (German): swift; (French): blue jay; (English): to rejoice; (Latin America): a crow

Jayce/Jace: (American): God is my salvation

Jayden: (American): God has heard

Jaylen: (English); to rejoice

Jazz: (American): jazz

Jean: (French): a form of John, which means God is gracious

Jeb/Jed/Jebidiah/Jedidiah: (Hebrew): one who is loved by God

Jefferson: (English): son of Jeffrey, which means divine peace

Jeffrey: (French, German & English): divine peace

Jensen: (Scandinavian): God is gracious

Jerald: (English): one who rules with the spear

Jeremiah: (Hebrew): may Jehovah exalt; (Israel): sent by God

Jeremy: (Israel): God will uplift

Jericho: (Arabic): city of the moon

Jermaine: (French): a man from Germany; (Latin): brotherly

Jerome: (Greek): of the sacred name

Jess: (Israel): wealthy

Jesse: (Hebrew): wealthy; (Israel): God exists; (English): Jehovah exists

Jesus: (Hebrew): God is my salvation

Jethro: (Hebrew & Israel): excellence

Jett: (English): resembling the black gemstone

Jiang: (Chinese): fire

Jim: (English): supplanter

Jin: (Chinese): gold

Jiro: (Japanese): second son

Jo: (Japanese): God will increase

Joab: (Israel): paternity, voluntary

Joachim/Joaquin: (Hebrew): God will establish

Job/Jobe: (Hebrew): afflicted

Jock: (Scottish): God is gracious

Jody: (Hebrew): a diminutive form of Joseph, which means God will increase

Joel: (Hebrew): Jehovah is God; (Israel): God is willing

Johann: (German): God's gracious gift

John: (Israel): God is gracious; Jehovah has been gracious

Johnnie: (French, English & Hebrew): diminutive of John, which means God is gracious

Johnson: (Scottish & English): son of John

Jonah: (Hebrew & Israel): a dove

Jonas: (Hebrew): gift from God; (Spanish): dove; (Israel): accomplishing

Jonathan: (Hebrew): Jehovah has given: (Israel): gift of God

Joo: (Korean): jewel

Jordan: (Hebrew): to flow down; (Israel): descendant

Jorell: (American): he saves

Jorge: (Spanish): farmer

Jose: (Spanish): God will add

Joseph/Josef/Jozef: (Biblical): God will increase; (Hebrew): may Jehovah add/give

Joshua: (Hebrew & Biblical): Jehovah saves

Josiah: (Hebrew): Jehovah has healed; (Israel): God has healed

Josue: (Spanish & Hebrew): God is salvation

Journey: (American): one who likes to travel

Jovan: (Latin): majestic

Juan: (Hebrew): gift from God; (Spanish): God is gracious

Juan David: (Spanish): God is gracious/beloved

Juan Diego: (Spanish): God is gracious/Saint James

Juan Esteban: (Spanish): God is gracious/crowned in victory

Juan Felipe: (Spanish): God is gracious/one who loves horses

Juan Ignacio: (Spanish): God is gracious/fiery

Juan Jose: (Spanish): God is gracious/God shall add

Juan Manuel: (Spanish): God is gracious/like God

Juan Pablo: (Spanish): God is gracious/borrowed

Juan Sebastian: (Spanish & Greek): God is gracious/the revered

Judah/Judas/Jude/Judd: (Hebrew & Israel): praised

Jules: (French): youthful, downy-haired

Julian/Julius/Julio: (Spanish, French & Greek): youthful

Jun: (Chinese): truthful; (Japanese): obedient, pure

Jung: (Korean): a righteous man

Justice/Justus: (English): fair and moral

Justin: (English & French): just, true; (Irish): judicious

Kacey: (Irish): vigilant

Kadeem: (Arabic): servant

Kaden/Kade/Kadin/Caden: (Arabic): beloved companion

Kagen: (Irish): fiery

Kai: (American): ocean; (Welsh): keeper of the keys; (Scottish): fire

Kale: (English): manly and strong

Kaleb/Caleb: (Hebrew): resembling an aggressive dog

Kalil/Khalil/Kali: (Arabic): friend

Kamil/Kamal: (Arabic & Hindu): lotus

Kana: (Japanese): powerful

Kane: (Welsh): beautiful; (Gaelic): little warrior

Kang: (Korean): healthy

Kano: (Japanese): powerful

Kareem: (Arabic): noble, distinguished

Karl: (English & Icelandic): man; (French): strong, masculine; (Danish): one who is free

Kavi: (Hindu): poet

Kayden: (American): fighter

Keanu: (Hawaiian): of the mountain breeze

Keaton: (English): from the town of hawks

Kedrick: (English): a form of Cedric, which means battle chieftain

Keefe: (Irish): handsome, loved

Keegan/Kaegan/Keigan: (Gaelic): small and fiery

Keelan/Keilan: (Irish): mighty warrior

Keenan: (Irish): little Keene

Keene: (German): bold, sharp; (English): smart

Keith: (Scottish): wood; (Irish): warrior descending; (Welsh): dwells in the woods

Kellen/Kallen: (Gaelic): slender; (German): from the swamp

Kelley/Kelly: (Celtic): warrior; (Gaelic): one who defends

Kelsey: (English): from the island of ships

Kelvin: (Irish): narrow river

Ken: (Welsh): clear water; (English): royal obligation; (Irish): handsome; (Japanese): strong

Kendall: (English & Celtic): from the bright valley
Kendrick: (English): royal ruler; (Gaelic): champion
Kenley: (English): from the king's meadow
Kennedy: (Scottish): ugly head; (Irish & Gaelic): helmeted
Kenneth: (Celtic, Scottish & Irish): handsome; (English): royal obligation
Kent: (English & Welsh): white; (Celtic): chief
Kenton: (English): from the king's town
Kenyon: (Gaelic): blond-haired
Kermit: (Irish): free from envy
Kerrick: (English): king's rule
Kerry: (Irish): dark-haired
Kerwin: (Irish): little, dark
Kesler: (American): energetic and independent
Keung: (Chinese): a universal spirit
Kevin: (Irish & Gaelic): handsome, beautiful; (Celtic): gentle
Khouri: (Arabic): spiritual, a priest
Ki: (Korean): arise
Kidd: (English): resembling a young goat
Kiefer: (German): one who makes barrels
Kieran: (Gaelic): the little dark one
Kiley/Kile: (Gaelic): young; (Irish): young at heart
Kim: (Vietnamese): as precious as gold; (Welsh): leader
Kimball: (Greek): hollow vessel
Kimo: (Hawaiian): a form of James, which means supplant
Kin: (Japanese): golden
Kincaid: (Celtic): the leader during a battle
King: (English): royal ruler
Kingsley: (English): from the king's meadow
Kingston: (English): from the king's village
Kinsey: (English): victorious prince
Kioshi: (Japanese): quiet
Kip/Kipp: (English): from the small pointed hill
Kirby: (Scandinavian): church village
Kirk: (Norse): a man of the church
Kirkland: (English): from the church's land
Kirkley: (English): from the church's meadow
Kit: (English): one who bears Christ inside
Kitoko: (African): handsome
Kiyoshi: (Japanese): quiet one
Knight: (English): noble soldier
Knox: (English): from the hills
Kobe/Kobi/Koby: (African): supplanter; (American): from California
Kode: (English): helpful
Kojo: (African): born on a Monday
Kong: (Chinese): glorious, sky
Kramer: (German): shopkeeper
Kris/Kristian/Kristoff/Kristopher: (Swedish): Christ-bearer
Krishna: (Hindu): delightful, pleasurable
Kuo: (Japanese): approval
Kuro: (Japanese): ninth son
Kurt: (German): brave counselor
Kwame: (Akan): born on a Saturday
Kwan: (Korean): bold character
Kyle: (Gaelic): young; (Irish): young at heart
Kyong: (Korean): brightness
Kyu: (Korean): standard

Lachian: (Gaelic): war-like

Lafayette: (Israel): to God to the mighty

Laine/Lane: (English): narrow road

Laird: (Scottish): lord; (Irish): head of household

Laken: (American): man from the lake

Lamar: (German): famous land; (French): of the sea

Lambert: (Scandinavian): the light of the land

Lamont: (Scandinavian): lawyer

Lance: (German): spear; (French): land

Lancelot: (English & French): servant

Landon: (English): grassy plain; from the long hill

Langley: (English): long meadow

Langston: (English): from the tall man's town

Lanier: (French): one who works with wool

Larkin: (Irish): tough, fierce

Lars/Larry: (Dutch & Latin America): laurels

Larson: (Scandinavian): the son of Lars

LaSalle: (French): from the hall

Lashaun: (American): enthusiastic

Lathan: (American): gift from God

Latimer: (English): an interpreter

Laurent/Laurence: (French & African American): crowned with laurel

Lautaro: (Spanish): crowned with laurel

Lawford: (English): from the ford near the hill

Lawrence/Lawry: (Latin America): crowned with laurel

Lawson: (English): son of Lawrence, which means crowned with laurel

Lazarus/Lazaro: (Hebrew & Israel): God will help

Leander: (Greek): man of lions

Lear: (English): Shakespearean king

Leavitt: (English): a baker

Lee/Leigh: (English): meadow

Legend: (American): memorable

Lei: (Chinese): thunder

Leib: (Yiddish): roaring lion

Leif: (Scandinavian): beloved descendent

Leighton: (English): from the town near the meadow

Leland: (English): meadow land

Len: (Native American): one who plays the flute

Lenard: (French & German): lion, bold

Lenin: (Russian): one who belongs to the river Lena

Lennon: (English): son of love

Lennox: (Scottish): one who owns many elm trees

Leo: (Italian & English): a lion

Leon/Leonard: (Spanish, German, French & Latin America): lion

Leonardo: (German): brave as a lion

Leron: (French): round, circle

Leroy: (French): king

Les/Leslie/Lester: (Scottish): gray fortress

Levi/Levin: (Hebrew & Israel): attached, united as one

Levon: (Armenian): lion

Lew/Lewis: (German): famous warrior

Lewellyn: (Welsh): resembling a lion

Lex/Lexus: (English): a diminutive form of Alexander, which means protector of mankind

Li: (Chinese): having great strength

Liam: (Irish & Gaelic): determined protector

Liang : (Chinese): good man

Lilo: (Hawaiian): generous

Linc/Lincoln: (English): Roman colony at the pool; (Latin America): village

Lindberg: (German): mountain where linden grow

Linden/Lyndon: (English): linden hill

Lindley: (English): from the meadow of linden trees

Linley: (English): flax meadow

Linus: (Latin America): flaxen

Linwood: (English): flax wood

Lionel: (French): lion cub

Liu: (Asian); one who is quiet and peaceful

Livingston: (English): Leif's town

Lloyd: (Celtic, Welsh & English): gray

Locke: (English): forest

Logan: (Irish): small cove; (Scottish): Finnian's servant; (Gaelic): from the hollow

Loki: (Scandinavian): trickster god

Lombard: (Latin): long-bearded

Lon/Lonnie: (Irish): fierce

London: (English): fortress of the moon

Lonzo: (Spanish): ready for battle

Lorcan: (Irish): the small fierce one

Lorenzo: (Italian & Spanish): crowned with laurel

Lot: (Hebrew): hidden covered

Loudon: (German): low valley

Louis: (French): famous warrior

Lovell/Lowell: (French & English): young wolf

Loyal: (English): faithful, loyal

Luc/Luca/Lucian/Lucius: (Latin): surrounded by light

Lucas: (Gaelic, English & Latin America): light

Luciano: (Spanish): light

Lucifer: (Israel): bringing light

Ludwig: (German): famous warrior

Luigi: (Italian): famous warrior

Luis: (Spanish): famous warrior

Luka: (Latin America): light; (Russian): of Luciana

Luke: (Greek & Latin America): light

Luther: (German): soldier of the people

Lux: (Latin): man of the light

Lyle: (French & English): from the island

Lyman: (English): meadow

Lynch: (Irish): mariner

Lyndon: (English): flexible

Lynn: (English): waterfall

Lysander: (Greek): liberator

Mac: (Gaelic): the son of Macarthur or Mackinley

Macallister: (Gaelic): the son of/ Alistair

Macarthur: (Gaelic): the son of Arthur

Macauley: (Scottish): son of righteousness

Macbride: (Scottish): son of a follower of Saint Brigid

Macdonald: (Scottish): son of Donald

Macdougall: (Scottish): son of Dougal

Macintosh: (Gaelic): the son of the thane

Mack/Mac: (Scottish): son

Mackenzie: (Scottish): son of Kenzie

Mackinley: (Gaelic): the son of the white warrior

Maclean: (Irish): son of Leander

Macon: (English): to make
Madden: (Pakistani): well organized
Maddox: (English): son of the Lord; (Celtic): beneficent
Magnus: (Latin): great
Maguire: (Gaelic): the son of the beige one
Mahmud/Mahmoud: (Arabic): one who is praiseworthy
Maitland: (English): from the meadow land
Major: (Latin): greater, military rank
Malachi/Malachy: (Hebrew): angel of God
Malcolm: (Gaelic): follower of St. Columbus
Malik: (African & Arabic): king, master
Malin: (English): strong, warrior
Mallory: (German): army counselor
Malloy: (Irish): noble chief
Manfred: (English): man of peace
Manley: (English): hero's meadow
Mann: (German): man
Manu: (African): the second-born child
Manuel: (Spanish): God is with us
Marcel: (French): little warrior
Marcelo: (Italian & Latin): hammer
Marcos: (Spanish): of mars; (Portuguese): the god of war
Marcus/Marcellus/Marco: (Gaelic): hammer; (Latin America): warlike
Mario: (Hebrew): bitter, king-ruler
Mark/Marc: (Latin): dedicated to Mars, the god of war
Marlon: (French): falcon, of the sea fortress
Marlowe: (English): from the hill by the lake
Marquis: (French): nobleman
Marshall: (French): caretaker of horses; (English): a steward
Marston: (English): from the town near the marsh
Martin: (Latin): dedicated to Mars, the god of war
Marvin: (Welsh): friend of the sea
Mason: (French & English): stone worker
Matias: (Spanish & Hebrew): gift of God
Mathis: (English & Greek): a diminutive form of Matthias, which means gift of God
Matisse: (French): one who is gifted
Matlock: (American): rancher
Matteo: (Italian): gift of God
Matthew: (Hebrew & Biblical): gift of the Lord
Matthias: (English & Greek): gift of God
Maurice: (Latin): dark-skinned
Mauricio: (Spanish): moorish; (Portuguese): dark-skinned
Maverick: (American): independent
Max: (English): greatest
Maximilian: (Latin): greatest
Maximiliano: (Italian): greatest
Maximo (Italian): greatest
Maximus: (Greek): greatest
Maxwell: (English): capable, great spring
Maynard: (English): powerful, brave
McKenna: (Gaelic): the son of Kenna, to ascend; (English): handsome, fiery
McKenzie: (Irish): fair, favored one
McKinley: (English): offspring of the fair hero
Mead: (English): meadow
Mee: (Korean): beauty
Melton/Melville: (English): from the mill town

Melvin: (English): a friend who offers counsel
Mendel: (English): repairman
Mercer: (English): storekeeper
Meredith: (Welsh): guardian from the sea
Merle: (French): blackbird; (English): falcon
Merlin: (Welsh): of the sea fortress
Merrick: (English): ruler of the sea
Merrill: (English): falcon, shining sea
Meyer: (Jewish & Hebrew): shining
Micah: (Israel): like God
Michael: (Biblical & Hebrew): like God
Michelangelo: (Italian): a combination of Michael and Angelo
Mickey: (Irish, English & Hebrew): diminutive of Michael, which means like God
Miguel: (Portuguese & Spanish): who is like God
Mika/Micah: (Finnish): like God; (Japanese): new moon
Mikhail: (Greek & Russian): a form of Michael, which means like God
Miles: (German): merciful; (Latin): a soldier
Milford: (English): from the mill's forge
Miller: (English): one who works at the mill
Milo: (English): soldier
Milton: (English): mill town
Min: (Korean): cleverness
Minh: (Vietnamese): bright
Mitchell: (Hebrew): gift from God
Mohammed/Muhammad: (Arabic): one who is greatly praised
Monroe: (Gaelic): from the red swamp; (Scottish): from the river; (Irish): near the river roe
Montel: (Italian): mountain
Montgomery/Monty/Monte: (French): rich man's mountain
Mooney: (Irish): a wealthy man
Moore: (French): dark-skinned; (Irish & French): surname
Moran: (Irish): a great man
Morell: (French): dark
Morgan: (Celtic): lives by the sea; (Welsh): bright sea
Morley: (English): from the meadow on the moor
Moroccan: (African): one from Morocco
Morris: (Latin America): dark skinned; (English): son of More
Mortimer: (French): of the dead sea
Moses: (Hebrew & Biblical): saved from the water
Muir: (Scottish): moor
Murdoch: (Scottish): from the sea
Murphy: (Gaelic): warrior of the sea
Murray: (Scottish): sailor
Myles: (Latin): soldier
Myron: (Greek): fragrant oil

Nam: (Korean): south
Namir: (Hebrew): leopard
Naoki: (Japanese): honest tree
Naoko: (Japanese): honest
Napier: (French): a mover; (Spanish): new city
Napoleon: (French): fierce one
Narcissus: (Greek): self-love
Naresh: (Indian): king
Nash: (American): adventurer
Nathan/Nathaniel/Nate: (Hebrew & Israel): gift of God
Navarro: (Spanish): from the plains

Naveed: (Persian): our best wishes
Naveen: (Hindu): new; (Irish): beautiful, pleasant
Neal/Neil: (Irish, English & Celtic): a champion
Ned: (English & French): diminutive of Edward, which means wealthy guardian
Nehemiah: (Hebrew): compassion of Jehovah
Nelson: (English, Celtic, Irish & Gaelic): son of Neil
Nemo: (Greek): glen, glade
Neo: (Greek & American): new
Neptune: (Latin): sea ruler
Nero: (Latin & Spanish): stern
Nesbit: (English): nose-shaped bend in a river
Nevada: (Spanish): covered in snow
Neville: (French): from the new village
Nevin: (Irish): worshipper of the saint
Newman: (English): a newcomer
Newton: (English): new town
Ngu/Nguyen: (Vietnamese): sleep
Nicholas/Nico/Nicco: (Greek): victorious people
Nicol: (Scottish & English): victorious
Nicolai: Russian: victorious
Nigel: (English, Gaelic & Irish): champion; (American): ahead
Nikola: (Greek): victorious
Niles: (English): champion
Nino: (Italian): God is gracious; (Spanish): a young boy
Nixon: (English): son of Nick
Noah: (Biblical): rest, peace; (Hebrew): comfort, long-lived
Nobu: (Japanese): faith
Noel: (French): Christmas
Nolan: (Irish & Gaelic): famous; (Celtic): noble
Norbert/Norberto: (Scandinavian): brilliant hero
Norio: (Japanese): man of principles
Norris: (French): northerner
North: (English): from the north
Northcliff: (English): from the northern cliff
Norward: (English): guardian of the north
Noshi: (Native American): fatherly
Nuriel: (Hebrew): God's light
Nye: (English): one who lives on the island

O'Neal/O'Neil: (Irish): Son of Neil
O'Shea/O'Shay: (Irish): son of Shea
Oberon: (German): bear heart
Ocean/Oceanus: (Greek): a titan who rules the sea
Octavio/Octavius: (Latin): eighth
Oden/Odin: (Scandinavian): ruler
Odon: (Hungarian): wealthy protector
Odwin: (German): noble friend
Odysseus: (Greek): wrathful
Ogden: (English): oak valley
Oki: (Japanese): from the center of the ocean
Olaf/Olav/Ole: (Scandinavian): the remaining of the ancestors
Oleg: (Russian): one who is holy
Oliver/Olivier: (French, English, Danish & Latin America): the olive tree; (German): elf army
Olney: (English): from the loner's field
Omar: (Arabian): ultimate devotee; (Hebrew): eloquent speaker
Omega: (Greek): the last great one

Onofrio: (Italian): a defender of peace
Onslow: (Arabic): from the hill of the enthusiast
Oral: (Latin): verbal, speaker
Oram: (English): from the enclosure near the river bank
Ordell: (Latin): of the beginning
Ordway: (Anglo-Saxon): a fighter armed with a spear
Oren: (Hebrew): from the pine tree; (Gaelic): fair-skinned
Orion: (Greek): a hunter in Greek mythology
Orland: (English): from the pointed hill; (Spanish & German): renowned in the land
Orlando: (Spanish): land of gold: (German): famous throughout the land
Orly: (Hebrew): surrounded by light
Ormond: (English): one who defends with a spear
Orpheus: (Greek): an excellent musician
Orrin: (English): river
Orson: (Latin): resembling a bear
Orton: (English): from the settlement by the shore
Orville: (French): golden city; (English): spear-strength
Orwell: (Welsh): of the horizon
Osborn/Osbourne: (Norse): a bear of God
Oscar: (English): a spear of the gods; (Gaelic): a friend of deer
Oswald: (English): the power of God
Oswin: (English): a friend of God
Othello: (Spanish): rich
Otis: (German & Greek): wealthy
Otto: (German): wealthy or prosperous
Ovid: (Latin): a shepherd, egg
Owen: (English, Welsh & Celtic); young warrior; (Irish): born to nobility
Oz: (Hebrew): having great strength
Ozzy: (English): divine ruler

Pablo: (Spanish): a form of Paul, which means small
Pace: (English): a peaceful man
Paco: (Spanish): a man from France
Page/Paige: (French): youthful assistant
Paine/Payne: (Latin): a peasant
Palmer: (English): a pilgrim bearing a palm branch
Pan: (Greek): god of flocks
Pancho: (Spanish): diminutive form of Francisco, which means free
Panya: (African): resembling a mouse
Panyin: (African): the first-born twin
Paolo: (Italian): a form of Paul, which means small
Paris: (Greek): downfall; (French): the capital city of France
Park: (Chinese): the cypress tree
Parker: (English): keeper of the park or forest
Parnell: (French): little Peter
Parry: (Welsh): the son of Harry
Pascal: (French): born at Easter
Patricio: (Spanish): patrician, noble
Patrick: (Latin): a nobleman
Patton: (English): from the town of warriors
Paul: (English & French): small, apostle in the Bible
Pax: (English): peaceful
Paxton: (English): from the peaceful farm; (Latin America): town of peace
Pearce/Pierce: (English): a form of Peter, which means small rock
Pearson: (English): son of Peter
Pedro: (Spanish): solid and strong as a rock

Peeta/Peetamber: (Indian): yellow silk cloth
Pegasus: (Greek): winged horse
Peli: (Latin): happy
Pell: (English): a clerk
Pelton: (English): from the town by the lake
Pembroke: (Welsh): headland
Penley: (English): from the enclosed meadow
Penn: (Latin): pen, quill
Pepe: (Spanish): a diminutive form of Jose, which means God will add
Pepin: (German): determined
Percival: (French): one who can pierce the vale
Percy: (English): piercing the valley
Perez: (Hebrew): to break through
Perry: (English): a familiar form of Peter, which means a small stone or rock
Peter: (Greek & English): a small stone or rock, apostle in the Bible
Peterson: (English): son of Peter
Peyton: (English): from the village of warriors
Pharell/Pharrell: (American): of proven courage
Philip: (French, Greek & English): lover of horses
Phinean/Finian: (Irish): light-skinned, white
Phineas/ Phinneaus/Fineas: (Hebrew): oracle; (Israel): loudmouth; (Egyptian): dark-skinned
Phong: (Vietnamese): of the wind
Pierce: (English): rock
Pierre: (French): a rock
Ping: (Chinese): stable
Placido: (Spanish): serene
Plato: (Greek): broad-shouldered
Platt: (French): flatland
Pollock: (Greek): crown; (English): little rock
Pollux: (Latin American): brother of Helen
Polo: (Tibetan): brave warrior
Ponce: (Spanish): fifth
Porter: (French): gate keeper; (Latin America): door guard
Powell: (English): alert
Prentice: (English): a student
Prescott: (English): from the priest's cottage
Presley: (English): priest's land
Preston: (English): from the priest's farm
Prewitt: (French): brave little one
Primo: (Italian): first, premier quality
Prince: (Latin): chief, prince
Pryor: (Latin): head of the monastery
Puck: (English): elf
Pullman: (English): one who works on a train
Purnam: (English): dweller by the pond
Purvis: (French & English): providing food

Qiang: (Chinese): strong
Qiu: (Chinese): autumn
Quade: (Latin): fourth
Quiad: (Irish): the commander of the army
Quain: (French): clever
Quashawn: (American): tenacious
Quentin: (Latin): fifth
Quigley: (Irish): maternal side
Quillan: (Gaelic): resembling a cub

Quimby: (Scandinavian): woman's estate
Quincy: (English): fifth-born child; (French): estate belonging to Quintus
Quinlan: (Gaelic): strong and healthy man
Quinn: (Celtic): queenly; (Gaelic): one who provides counsel
Quinton/Quinten/Quintin: (Latin): from the queen's town

Radcliff/Radcliffe: (English): red cliff
Rafael/Raphael: (Spanish): one who is healed by God
Rafe: (Irish): a tough man
Rafferty: (Irish): prosperous
Raiden: (Japanese): god of thunder and lightning
Rain/Raine: (American): blessings from above; (Latin): ruler; (English): lord, wise
Rainer: (German): counsel
Raj/Rajan/Rajah: (Hindu): king
Raleigh/Rawley: (English): deer meadow
Ralph: (English): wolf counsel
Ram: (Hindu): god, god-like
Ramon: (Spanish): a wise or mighty protector
Ramsey: (Scottish): island of ravens
Rand/Randy/Randall/Randolph: (German): the wolf shield
Raoul: (French): wolf counsel
Rashad: (Arabic): wise counselor
Raul: (French): a form of Ralph, which means wolf counsel
Ravi: (Hindu): from the sun
Ray: (French): regal: (Scottish): grace; (English): wise protector
Rayburn: (English): deer brook
Raymond: (German): wise protector
Razi: (Aramaic): my secret
Rebel: (American): outlaw
Redford: (English): over the red river, from the reedy ford
Redmond: (German): protecting counselor
Reece/Reese: (English &Welsh): ardent, fiery, enthusiastic
Reed/Reid: (English & French): red-haired
Reeve: (English): a bailiff
Regan/Reagan: (Gaelic): born into royalty
Reginald/Reggie: (Latin): the king's advisor
Regis: (Latin): regal; (Latin America): rules
Reilly: (Gaelic): outgoing
Reinhart/Reynard/Reynold/Renaldo/Rey: (French): wise, bold, courageous
Remi/Remy: (French): oarsman or rower, from Rheims
Remington: (English): from the town of the raven's family
Rene/Renee: (French): reborn
Reuben/Ruben: (Hebrew): behold, a son
Rex: (Latin): king
Rhett: (English): stream
Rhodes: (Greek): where roses grow
Rhys: (Welsh): enthusiasm for life
Ricardo: (Spanish): strong and powerful ruler
Richard: (English, French & German): a strong and powerful ruler
Rico: (German): glory; (Spanish & Cuban): strong ruler
Ridge: (English): from the ridge
Ridley: (English): from the red meadow
Rigby: (English): ruler's valley
Riley: (English): from the rye clearing; (Irish): a small stream
Ringo: (Japanese): peace be with you
Rio: (Spanish & Portuguese): river

Ripley: (English): from the noisy meadow
Rishi: (Hindu): sage
River: (Latin & French): stream, water
Roan: (English): from the Rowan tree
Roark: (Gaelic): champion
Robert: (English, French, German & Scottish): famed, bright, shining
Robin: (English): a diminutive form of Robert, which means famed, bright, shining
Robinson: (English): son of Robin
Rocco: (Italian & German) rest
Rocket/Rockett/Rockitt: (English): fast
Rockford: (English): from the rocky ford
Rockwell: (English): rocky spring
Roden: (English): red valley
Roderick: (German): famous ruler
Rodney: (English): land near the water, island of reeds
Rodrigo: (Spanish): famous ruler
Roger: (German): renowned spearman
Roland/Rollo/Rolle: (French, German & English): renowned in the land
Rolf: (German): wolf counsel
Roman: (Spanish & Latin America): from Rome
Romeo: (Italian, Spanish, Latin America & African American): from Rome
Romulus: (Latin): citizen of Rome
Ronald: (English, Gaelic & Scottish): rules with counsel
Ronan: (Gaelic): resembling a little seal
Ronin: (Japanese): samurai without a master
Rooney: (Gaelic): red-haired
Roosevelt: (Danish): from the field of roses
Rory: (Irish): famous brilliance, famous ruler; (Gaelic): red-haired
Roscoe: (Norwegian): deer forest
Ross: (Scottish): from the peninsula
Roswell: (English): fascinating
Rowan: (Irish): red-haired; (English & Gaelic): from the rowan tree
Roy: (Irish & French): king, regal; (Scottish, Gaelic & Scottish): red, red-haired
Royce: (English): royal, son of the king: (German): famous
Rudolph: (German): a famous wolf
Rufus: (Latin America): redhead
Ruiz: (Spanish): a good friend
Rupert: (German): bright fame
Russell/Russ/Rush: (French): a little red-haired boy
Rusty: (English): one who has red hair or a ruddy complexion
Rutherford: (English): from the cattle's ford
Ryan: (Gaelic): little king; (Irish): kindly, young royalty
Ryder: (English): knight
Ryker: (Danish): a powerful ruler
Rylan/Ryland: (English): the place where rye is grown

Saber: (French): man of the sword
Sacha: (French): protector of mankind
Said/Sa'id/Sayed: (Arabic): happy
Saige/Sage: (English & French): wise one; (English): from the spice
Sailor: (American): sailor
Salem: (Hebrew): peace
Salisbury: (English): fort at the willow pool
Salmon: (Czech): a form of Solomon, which means peaceful
Salvador/Salvatore: (Spanish & Italian): savior
Samson/Sampson: (Hebrew & Israel): bright as the sun

Samuel: (Israel): God hears; (Hebrew): name of God
Sanborn: (English): sandy brook
Sandburg: (English): from the sandy village
Sandeep: (Punjabi): enlightened
Sanford: (English): from the sandy crossing
Sanjay: (American): a combination of Sanford and Jay
Santana: (Spanish): saintly
Santiago: (Spanish): named for Saint James
Santino: (Italian): little angel
Santo: (Italian): a holy man
Sargent: (French): army officer
Satchel: (French): Saturn
Saturn: (Latin): the god of agriculture
Saul: (Israel): borrowed: (Hebrew & Spanish): asked for
Sawyer: (English): one who works with wood
Saxon/Sax: (English): a swordsman
Sayid: (African): lord and master
Schaffer/Schaeffer: (German): a steward
Schuman: (German): shoemaker
Scott: (Scottish): wanderer
Scout: (French): scout
Scully: (Irish): herald; (Gaelic): town crier
Seaman: (English): a mariner
Seamus: (Irish): a form of James, which means supplant
Sean/Shawn: (Irish): God is gracious
Sebastian: (Greek): the revered one
Sergio/Sergei/Serge: (Latin, Italian & Russian): a servant
Seth: (Hebrew): anointed; (Israel): appointed
Seton/Seaton: (English): from the farm by the sea
Seung: (Korean): a victorious successor
Seven: (American): the number seven
Sexton: (English): church custodian
Seymour: (French): from the town of Saint Maur
Shade: (English): secretive
Shan: (Chinese): mountain
Shane: (Hebrew): gift from God; (Irish): God is gracious
Shannon: (Gaelic): having ancient wisdom
Sharif: (Arabic): noble
Shaw: (English): from the woodland
Shawn: (Irish): a form of Sean, which means God is gracious
Shea: (Irish): majestic, fairy place
Sheffield: (English): from the crooked field
Sheldon: (English): from the steep valley
Shelton: (English): from the farm on the ledge
Shen: (Chinese): deep spiritual thought
Shepherd: (English): one who herds sheep
Sheridan: (Irish, English & Celtic): untamed; (Gaelic): bright, a seeker
Sherlock: (English): fair-haired
Sherman: (English): one who cuts wool cloth
Sherwin: (English): swift runner
Shiloh: (Hebrew): he who was sent, God's gift, the one to whom it belongs; (Israel): peaceful
Shin: (Japanese): truth
Shiro: (Japanese): fourth-born son
Sidney: (English): wide island
Siddhartha: (Hindu): the original name of Buddha
Siegfried: (German): victorious peace

Sierra: (Spanish): from the jagged mountain range
Sigmund: (German): victorious protector
Silas: (Latin America): man of the forest
Silver: (English): precious metal, the color silver
Simba: (African): lion
Simmons: (Hebrew): the son of Simon
Simon: (Israel): it is heard
Simpson: (Hebrew): son of Simon
Sinclair: (English): man from Saint Clair
Singh: (Hindu): lion
Skelly: (Irish): storyteller
Skylar/Schuyler: (Dutch): sheltering
Slade: (English): child of the valley
Slater: (English): one who works with slate
Sloan: (English): raid; (Irish, Celtic, Scottish & Gaelic): fighter, warrior
Smith: (English): artisan, tradesman
Socrates: (Greek): wise, learning
Solomon: (Hebrew & Israel): peaceful
Soo: (Korean): excellent, long life
Spalding: (English): divided field
Speck: (German): bacon
Spence/Spencer: (English): dispenser, provider
Stanford: (English): from the stony ford
Stanley: (English): stony meadow
Stanton: (English): from the stony ford
Stavros: (Greek): one who is crowned
Steadman: (English): one who lives at the farm
Stefan: (German, Polish & Swedish): a form of Steven, which means crowned one
Stefano/Stephano: (Italian): a form of Steven, which means crowned one
Stephen/Steven: (English & Greek): crowned one
Sterling: (English): valuable
Stern: (English): austere
Stone/Stony: (English): stone
Storm/Stormy: (English): tempest; (American): impetuous nature
Striker: (American): aggressive
Stuart: (Scottish): steward; (English): bailiff; (Irish): keeper of the estate
Sullivan: (Gaelic): dark eyes
Sully: (English): from the southern meadow
Sven: (Scandinavian): youth
Sydney: (English): wide island
Sylvester/Sly: (Latin): man from the forest

Taft: (French): from the homestead
Taggart: (Gaelic): son of a priest
Tai: (Chinese): large; (Vietnamese): prosperous, talented
Taj: (Indian): one who is crowned
Tam: (Vietnamese): having heart, the number eight
Tama: (Japanese): jewel
Tanner: (English & German): leather worker
Tannon: (German): from the fir tree
Tao: (Chinese): one who has a long life
Tarek/Tarik/Tariq: (Arabic): conqueror
Tate/Tatum: (English): cheerful
Taurean: (Latin): strong
Tavor/Tavarus/Tavaris: (Aramaic): misfortune
Taye: (Ethiopian): *one who has been seen*

Taylor: (English & French): a tailor
Teagan: (Gaelic): handsome, attractive
Ted/Teddy: (English): a gift from God
Teller/Telly: (English & Greek): storyteller
Tennessee: (Native American): from the state of Tennessee
Tennyson: (English): a form of Dennison, which means son of Dennis
Terrell: (German): thunder ruler
Terrence/Terrance: (Latin America): tender, gracious
Tex: (English): of Texas
Texas: (Native American): one of many friends, from the state of Texas
Thaddeus: (Hebrew): valiant, wise: (Greek): praise, one who has courage
Thang: (Vietnamese): victorious
Thanh: (Vietnamese): finished
Thatcher: (English): one who repairs roofs
Theodore: (Greek): divine gift
Thiago: (Spanish, Portuguese & Brazilian): Saint James
Thierry: (French): a dorm of Theodore, which means divine gift
Thomas: (Hebrew, Greek & Dutch): twin
Thor: (Norse): god of thunder
Thorne: (English): from the thorn bush
Thurmond: (English): defended by Thor
Thurston: (English): Thor's town
Tien: (Chinese): heaven
Tiernan: (Gaelic): lord of the manor
Tiger: (English): powerful cat
Tilden: (English): tilled valley
Tilford: (English): prosperous ford
Timon: (Hebrew): honor
Timothy: (Greek & English): to honor God
Tito: (Italian): honor
Titus: (Greek): of the giants; (Latin): great defender
Tobias: (Hebrew & Israel): God is good
Toby: (English): God is good
Todd: (Scottish): fox
Tolbert: (English): tax collector
Tomas: (German): a form of Thomas, which means twin
Tong: (Vietnamese): fragrant
Torin: (Irish): chief
Torrence: (Irish): knolls
Travis: (French): to cross over
Trent: (Welsh): dwells near the rapid stream
Trenton: (English): town of Trent
Trevor: (Welsh): from the large village
Trey/Treat: (English & Latin): third-born child
Treyvon: (American): a form of Trevon, which is a combination of Trey and Von
Trigg: (Norse): truthful
Tripp: (English): traveler
Tristan: (English, Celtic & French): outcry, tumult; (Welsh): noisy; (Irish): bold
Trong: (Vietnamese): respected
Troy: (French): curly haired; (Irish): foot soldier
True: (English): loyal
Twain: (English): divided in two
Tybalt: (Latin): he who sees the truth
Tye/Ty: (English): from the fenced-in pasture
Tyler: (English): maker of tiles
Tyr: (Norway): god of war

154

Tyrell: (American & English): thunder ruler
Tyrone/Tyronne: (French): from Owen's land
Tyson: (French): explosive; (English): son of Tye

Udell: (English): from the valley of yew trees
Udi: (Hebrew): one who carries a torch
Ugo: (Italian): a great thinker
Ulmer: (German): having the fame of a wolf
Ulrich: (German): wolf ruler
Ulysses: (Latin): hateful
Unique: (Latin): only one; (American): unlike others
Unity: (English): unity, togetherness
Upton: (English): upper town
Uranus: (Greek): mythical father of the titans
Urban: (Latin): city dweller, courteous
Uri: (Hebrew): God is my light
Usher: (Latin): from the mouth of the river; (English): doorkeeper
Utah: (Native American): people of the mountains, the state of Utah
Uzi: (Hebrew): having great power
Uziel: (Hebrew): God is my strength

Vadim: (Russian): god looking
Valentine/Val: (Latin): strong and healthy
Valentino: (Italian): brave or strong; (Latin America): health or love
Vance: (English): windmill dweller
Vandyke: (Danish): from the dike
Vardon: (French): from the green hill
Varick: (German): a protective ruler
Vaughn: (Celtic): small
Vernon/Vern: (Latin): youthful, young at heart; (French & English): alder tree grove
Verrill: (German): masculine; (French): loyal
Vicente: (Spanish): a form of Vincent, which means winner
Victor: (Spanish & Latin America): winner
Vijay: (Hindu): victorious
Vikram: (Hindu): valorous
Vincent: (English & Latin America): conquering, victorious
Vicente: (Spanish): conquering, victorious
Vinson: (English): son of Vincent
Virgil/Vergil: (English): flourishing; (Latin America): strong
Vito: (Latin): one who gives life
Vladimir: (Slavic): a famous prince
Vulcan: (Latin): the god of fire

Wade: (English): ford, cross the river
Wadley: (English): from the meadow near the ford
Wadsworth: (English): from the estate near the ford
Wagner: (German): wagoner
Wainwright: (English): one who builds wagons
Waite: (English): watchman
Walden: (English): wooded valley
Walker: (English): one who trods the cloth
Wallace: (Scottish): a man from the south
Walter: (German): the commander of the army
Walton: (English): walled town
Wane/Wayne: (English): craftsman, wagon maker
Wang: (Chinese): hope, wish

Warden: (English): guard
Wardell: (English): from the guardian's hill
Warner/Werner: (German & English): defender
Warren: (English): to preserve; (German): protector, loyal
Warrick: (English): a protective ruler
Washington: (English): town near water
Watson: (English): the son of Walter
Waverly: (English): quaking aspen
Wayan: (Indonesian): first son
Waylon: (English): land by the road
Wayne/Wane: (English): craftsman, wagon maker
Webb: (English): weaver
Webster: (English): a weaver
Wei: (Chinese): a brilliant man, great strength
Weiss: (German): white
Welborne: (English): spring-fed stream
Wendall/Wendell: (German): a wanderer
Wentworth: (English): village, from the white one's estate
Wesley: (English & German): from the west meadow
West: (English): from the west
Weston: (English): west town
Wheatley: (English): wheat field
Whit: (English): white-skinned
Whitby: (English): from the white farm
Whitfield: (English): from the white field
Whitley/Whit: (English): from the white meadow
Whitman: (English): white-haired
Whitmore: (English): white moor
Whitney: (English): white island
Wickley: (English): village meadow
Wilbur: (English): bright willows, fortification
Wilder: (English): wilderness
Wiley: (English): crafty
Wilford: (English): from the willow ford
Wilfred: (German): determined peacemaker
William/Willem: (English, German & French): protector
Willis: (English): son of Willie, which is a diminutive form of William
Wilmer: (German): determined and famous
Wilson: (English & German): son of William
Windsor: (English): riverbank with a winch
Winston: (English): joy stone
Winter: (American): the season
Winthrop: (English): from the friendly village
Winton: (English): from the enclosed pastureland
Wolf: (English): the animal, wolf
Wolfgang: (German): wolf quarrel
Woodley: (English): wooded meadow
Woodrow: (English): forester, row of houses
Wyatt: (English): guide, wide, wood, famous bearer; (French): son of the forest guide
Wyndham: (English): from the windy village

Xander: (Greek): a diminutive form of Alexander, which means protector of mankind
Xannon: (American): from an ancient family
Xavier: (Basque): owner of a new house; (Arabic): one who is bright
Xiu: (Chinese): cultivated
Xoan: (Gaelic): God is gracious

Xue: (Chinese): studious

Yale: (Welsh): from the fertile upland
Yan/Yann: (Russian): a form of John, which means God is gracious
Yancy: (Native American): Englishman
Yang: (Chinese): people of goat tongue
Yao: (Ewe): born on a Tuesday
Yaphet: (Hebrew): handsome
Yardley: (English): from the fenced-in meadow
Yasir: (Arabic): well-off financially
Yeo: (Korean): mildness
Yeoman: (English): a man-servant
Yitzchak: (Hebrew): a form of Isaac, which means he will laugh
Yo: (Cambodian): honest
Yohan: (German): God is gracious
Yong: (Korean): courageous
York: (Celtic, English & Latin America): from the yew tree
Yosef: (Hebrew): a form of Joseph, which means God will increase
Yoshi: (Japanese): adopted son
You: (Chinese): friend
Young: (Korean): forever, unchanging
Yul/Yule: (English): born at Christmas
Yuri: (Russian & Ukrainian): a form of George, which means farmer
Yves: (French): a young archer

Zachariah/Zacarias/Zachary: (Hebrew): Jehovah has remembered; (Israel): remembered by the Lord
Zaden/Zayden: (Arabic & Dutch): a sower of seeds
Zale: (Greek): having the strength of the sea
Zander: (Slavic): helper and defender of mankind
Zane/Zain: (Hebrew): gift from God; (Arabian): beloved
Zared: (Hebrew): one who is trapped
Zarek: (Polish): may God protect the king
Zavier: (Arabic): a form of Xavier, which means bright
Zebulun/Zebulon/Zeb: (Hebrew & Israel): habitation
Zedekiah/Zed: (Hebrew): God is mighty and just
Zeke: (English): strengthened by God
Zeno: (Greek): cart, harness
Zephyr: (Greek): west wind
Zeus: (Greek): powerful one
Zhen: (Chinese): astonished
Zia: (Hebrew): trembling
Zian: (Chinese): peace
Zigfrid/Ziggy: (Latvian & Russian): a form of Siegfried, which means victorious peace
Zion: (Hebrew): from the citadel
Zoltan: (Hungarian): kingly

Appendix B: Alphabetical List of Girls Names

Aaliyah/Aliyah: (Arabic): an ascender; (Muslim): exalted; (American): immigrant to a new home
Abby/Abbey/Abby: (Hebrew): diminutive form of Abigail, which means father rejoiced
Abena: (African): born on a Tuesday
Abiela: (Hebrew): my father is Lord
Abigail: (Hebrew): father rejoiced; (Biblical): source of joy
Abira: (Hebrew): strong
Abra: (Hebrew): mother of many nations
Abril: (Spanish): April
Ada: (English): wealthy; (Hebrew): ornament; (German): noble; (African): first daughter
Addison: (English): son of Adam
Adelaide: (French & German): noble, kind
Adelina/Adeline: (French & Spanish): of the nobility
Adell/Adele: (German & French): noble, kind
Adina: (Israel): beautiful; (Hebrew): slender
Adriana/Adrianna: (Spanish, Greek & Italian): woman with dark and rich features
Afra: (Hebrew): young doe
Afton: (English): from the Afton River
Agatha: (Latin & Greek): pure, virtuous, good
Agnes: (Greek): pure
Agustina: (Latin America): majestic, grand
Aika: (Japanese): love song
Aileen: (Irish): light bearer, from the green meadow
Ainsley: (Scottish): one own's meadow
Aisha/Aiesha: (African): womanly, lively; (Muslim): life, lively
Aiyanna/Aiyana/Aianna: (Native American): forever flowering
Aja: (Indian): goat
Akela: (Hawaiian): noble
Aki: (Japanese): born in autumn
Akilah: (Arabic): intelligent
Akira: (Scottish): anchor
Alaina: (French): dear child, beautiful and fair woman
Alana: (Irish): beautiful, peaceful
Alanis: (English): attractive and bright
Alba: (Spanish & Italian): from the city of Alba
Alberta: (German & French): noble and bright
Alejandra: (Spanish): defender of mankind
Alessia: (Greek): honest
Alexandria/Alessandra/Alexa/Alexandra: (Greek, English & Latin America): defender of mankind
Alexi: (English): helper, defender
Alexis: (English): helper, defender; (Biblical): protector of mankind
Ali: (Arabian): noble, sublime
Alice/Alyce: (Spanish): of the nobility
Alicia/Alysha: (English): of noble birth; (Spanish & German): sweet
Aline: (Dutch): alone; (Celtic & Irish): fair, good looking
Allegra: (Latin): cheerful
Allison/Alison: (English): noble, truthful, strong character
Alma: (Latin & Italian): nurturing, kind
Almira: (Arabic): aristocratic
Alpha: (Greek): first-born
Althea: (Greek): wholesome, healer
Alyssa: (Greek): logical
Amalia/Amalie: (French & Latin America): industrious; hard working
Amanda: (Latin): much loved

Amaranth: (Greek): an unfading flower
Amaya: (Japanese & Arabic): night rain
Amber: (Arabic): precious jewel, yellow-brown color
Ambra: (French): jewel; (Italian): Amber color
Ambrosia: (Greek): immortal
Ame: (Japanese): rain, heaven
Amelia: (English & Latin America): industrious, striving
America: (English): ruler of the home
Amethyst: (Greek): wine, a purple gemstone
Amira: (Arabic): princess
Amrita: (Hindu): nectar of eternal immortality
Amy/Aimee: (English, French & Latin America): beloved
Anais: (Hebrew): gracious
Anastasia: (Greek): resurrection
Anat: (Hebrew & Israel): a singer
Andrea: (Greek & Latin): courageous, strong
Andrina: (English): courageous, valiant
Angel: (Spanish & Greek): angelic
Angela: (Spanish, French, Italian & Latin America): angel
Angelina: (Italian): little angel
Angelique: (Greek): heavenly messenger
Anita: (Italian, Hebrew & Latin America): gracious
Aniyah: (Polish & Hebrew): God has shown favor
Anja: (Russia): grace of God
Anjelica: (Greek): a diminutive form of Angela, which means angel
Anka: (Japanese): color of the dawn
Anna/Ana: (Hebrew): favor or grace; (Native American): mother; (Israel): gracious
Annabel/Annabelle: (Italian): graceful and beautiful
Annabeth: (English): graced with God's bounty
Annalynn: (English): from the graceful lake
Anne: (Hebrew & Israel): favor or grace
Annette: (French & Hebrew): gracious
Annika: (Dutch): gracious
Annmarie: (English): filled with bitter grace
Anona: (English): pineapple
Antonia: (Greek): flourishing or flowering
Antonella: (Latin America): praiseworthy
Antoinette: (French): flowering; (Latin): praiseworthy
Anya: (Russian): graced with God's favor
Anyssa/Anissa: (English): a form of Agnes, which means pure
Aphrodite: (Greek): beauty, love goddess
Apollonia: (Greek): strength
Apple: (America): sweet fruit
April: (English): opening buds of spring; (Latin America): opening, fourth month
Arabella: (Latin): answered prayer, beautiful altar
Arden: (English): passionate, enthusiastic, valley of the eagle
Aretha: (Greek): virtuous
Aria: (Italian): melody
Arianna/Ariana: (Greek & Italian): holy
Ariel/Arial: (Hebrew): lioness of God
Arista: (Latin): harvest
Arizona: (Native American): from the little spring, from the state of Arizona
Arlene/Arleen: (Irish): pledge
Artemis: (Greek): goddess of the moon

Ashanti: (African): great African woman
Ashley: (English & Biblical): lives in the ash tree
Ashlyn: (American): combination of Ashley and Lynn
Asia: (Greek & English): resurrection, rising sun
Aspen: (English): from the aspen tree
Astra: (Latin): of the stars
Astraea: (Greek): justice
Astrid: (Scandinavian & German): divine strength
Athena: (Greek): wise, goddess of wisdom and war
Aubrey: (English): one who rules with elf-wisdom
Audrey: (English): noble strength
Audrina: (English): nobility, strength
Augusta: (Latin): venerable, majestic
Aura: (Greek): soft breeze: Latin: golden
Aurora: (Latin): dawn
Autumn: (English & Latin America): the fall season
Ava: (Latin America): like a bird
Avalon: (Latin): island
Avery: (English): counselor, sage, wise
Avril: (English); born in April
Ayanna: (Hindi & African): innocent, resembling a beautiful flower
Azura/Azure: (Persian): a blue, semi-precious stone

Babette: (French & German): a diminutive form of Barbara, which means stranger
Bailey: (English): bailiff, steward, public official
Bambi: (Italian): child
Barbara: (Latin America): stranger
Bathsheba: (Hebrew): oath, voluptuous, famous bearer; (Biblical): seventh daughter
Bea: (American): blessed
Beatrice: (Italian): blessed; (French): bringer of joy
Bebe: (Spanish): a diminutive form of Barbara, which means stranger
Becca: (Hebrew): a diminutive form of Rebecca, which means tied or bound
Bela: (Slovakian): she of fair skin; (Indian): sea shore; (Hebrew): destruction
Belinda: (English): beautiful and tender woman
Belisama: (Celtic): goddess of rivers and lakes
Bella: (Hebrew): devoted to God; (Spanish & Latin America): beautiful
Belle: (French): beautiful
Bernadette: (French): brave as a bear
Bernadine: (English & German): brave as a bear
Bernice: (French & Greek): one who brings victory
Bertha: (Germany): bright
Beryl: (Greek & English): green jewel
Bess: (English): my God is bountiful
Beth: (Scottish): lively
Bethany: (Hebrew & Israel): a life-town near Jerusalem
Bettina: (English): consecrated to God
Beulah: (Hebrew & Israel): married
Beverly: (English): beaver field
Beyonce: (American): one who surpasses others
Bianca: (Italian): white, fair
Bibi: (Latin): lively
Bijou: (French): as precious as a jewel
Billie: (English): desire to protect
Blaine: (Gaelic, Irish & Celtic): thin
Blair: (Irish & Celtic): from the plain, (Gaelic): child of the fields; (Scottish): peat moss
Blake: (English): pale blond or dark; (Scottish): dark-haired

Bliss: (English): joy, happiness
Blossom: (English): fresh, flowerlike
Blue: (English): the color blue
Blythe: (English): happy
Bo: (Chinese): precious
Bonnie: (English): good; (French): sweet; (Scottish): pretty, charming
Brady: (Irish): a large-breasted woman
Brande/Brandy/Brandie: (English): a woman wielding a sword, an alcoholic drink
Branwen: (Welsh): raven
Brea: (French): champion
Bree: (Celtic): broth; (Irish): hill, strong one
Brenda: (Gaelic): little raven; (Scandinavian): sword
Brenna: (Welsh): like a raven
Brianna/Breanna: (Irish): strong; (Celtic & English): she ascends
Brice/Bryce: (Welsh): alert, ambitious
Bridget/Brigid: (Irish): strong and protective
Brie: (French): from the northern region of France
Bristol: (English): bridge
Britt/Britta: (Swedish): high goddess
Brittany: (English & Celtic): from Britain
Bronte: (Greek): thunder
Bronwyn: (Welsh): dark and pure; (English): white-skinned
Brooke: (English): lives by the stream
Brooklyn: (English): water, stream
Brynn: (Welsh): hill
Buffy: (American): buffalo, from the plains
Bunny: (Greek): a diminutive form of Beatrice, which means blessed, happy
Burgundy: (French): a region of France that is famous for its wine

Caden: (English): battle maiden
Cadence: (Latin): rhythmic and melodious
Cady: (American): happiness
Cairo: (African): the Egyptian city
Caitlyn/Kaitlyn: (Irish): pure
Caledonia: (Latin): woman of Scotland
Callie/Cally: (Greek): beautiful; (English); lark
Calliope: (Greek): beautiful voice
Calista: (Greek): most beautiful
Calla: (Greek): resembling a lily, beautiful
Cambria: (Latin): woman of Wales
Camdyn: (English): of the enclosed valley
Cameo: (Italian): sculptured jewel; (English & Latin America): a shadow or carved gem portrait
Cameron/Camryn: (Irish & Gaelic): crooked nose
Camila/Camilla/Camille: (Italian): a noble virgin, a ceremonial attendant
Campbell: (Scottish): crooked mouth
Candace: (English): pure, glittering white
Candida: (Latin): white-skinned
Candy/Candi: (American): bright, sweet; (Hebrew): famous bearer
Canisa: (Greek): much-loved
Cantrelle: (French): song
Caprice: (Italian): fanciful
Caprina: (Italian): from the island Capri
Cara: (Celtic): friend; (Italian & Dominican Republic): dear, beloved
Carey: (Irish): pure; (Celtic): from the fortress
Cari: (Latin America): beloved

Carina: (Latin): little darling
Carissa/Caressa: (Greek): woman of grace
Carla: (Portuguese & Latin America): strong one
Carleen/Carlene: (English): derivative of Caroline, which means song of happiness
Carlessa: (American): restless
Carlie/Carly: (American): strong one; (Latin America): little, womanly
Carlotta: (Italian): a derivative of Charlotte, which means feminine
Carmel: (Hebrew): garden; (Israel): woodland; (Celtic): from the vineyard
Carmela/Carmella: (Hebrew & Israel): golden; (Spanish): garden
Carmen: (English): garden; (Spanish & Latin America): song
Carnie: (Latin): vocal
Carol: (French): melody, song
Carolina/Caroline: (Mexican): beautiful woman; (French & English): song of happiness
Carolyn: (English): joy, song of happiness
Carrie: (American): melody, song
Carrington: (English): beautiful
Carys: (Welsh): one who loves and is loved
Casey/Cacie/Kasey: (Celtic & Gaelic): brave; (Irish): observant, brave; (Spanish): honorable
Casia: (English): alert, vigorous
Cassandra: (Greek): prophet of doom
Cassidy: (Irish): curly-haired
Catalina: (Spanish): pure
Cate: (English): blessed, pure, holy
Catherine: (English): pure, virginal
Cathleen/Kathleen: (Irish): a form of Catherine/Katherine, which means pure, virginal
Cayenne: (French): hot and spicy
Cayla: (American): crowned with laurel
Caylee: (American): crowned with laurel
Ceara: (Irish): a derivation of Ciara, which means dark-skinned
Cecilia: (Latin): blind
Cecily/Cicely: (Latin): a form of Cecilia, which means blind
Celeste: (Latin): heavenly daughter
Celia: (Italian): heavenly
Celina/Celine: (Latin): of the heavens
Cera: (French): colorful woman
Cerise: (French): cherry
Chai: (Israel & Hebrew): life
Chakra: (Arabic): center of spiritual energy
Chalice: (French): goblet
Chambray: (French): a lightweight fabric
Chanda: (Sanskrit): enemy of evil
Chandelle: (French): candle
Chandra: (Hindi): of the moon
Chanel: (French): from the canal, a channel
Chantal/Chantel: (French): song
Chantrise: (French): a singer
Charisma: (Greek): grace
Charity: (English): kindness, generous, goodwill
Charlaine: (English): feminine form of Charles, which mean manly
Charlize: (French): manly
Charlotte: (French): feminine
Charmaine: (English): song; (French): beautiful orchard
Chastity: (Latin): pure
Chelsea: (English): seaport
Chen: (China): great, dawn
Cher: (English): beloved

Cherise/Cherice/Cherisse: (French): cherry, dear one
Cherish: (English): to be held dear, values
Cherry: (French): dear one; America: cherry
Cheryl/Sheryl: (English): beloved
Chesney: (English): one who promotes peace
Cheyenne: (French): dog; (Native American): an Algonquin tribe
Chiara: (Italian): daughter of the light
China: (Chinese): fine porcelain
Chiquita: (Spanish): little one
Chloe: (Greek): verdant, blooming
Christina/Christine/Christal/Christa/Chrissy: (English): follower of Christ
Chun: (Chinese): springtime
Ciara: (Irish): dark beauty
Cierra: (Spanish): dark-skinned
Cilla: (Latin): sturdy, vision
Cinderella: (French & English): of the ashes
Cinnamon: (American): reddish-brown spice
Clancy/Clancey: (American): light-hearted
Clara: (French & Catalonia): clear, bright
Clarabelle: (French & Catalonia): clear, bright/(French): beauty
Clare/Clair/Claire: (English): clear; (French): bright
Clarice: (French): famously bright
Clarissa: (Spanish & Italian): clear; (Latin America): brilliant
Claudia/Claudine: (Spanish & Latin America): lame
Claudette: (Spanish): a form of Clara, which means clear, bright
Clementine: (French): merciful
Cleo/Clio: (English); father's glory
Cleopatra: (Greek): glory to the father; (African American): queen
Cloris: (Greek): goddess of flowers
Clove: (German): spice
Clover: (English): meadow flower
Coby: (Hebrew): supplanter
Cody: (English): cushion
Colleen: (Irish & Gaelic): girl
Collette: (English): victorious people
Concordia: (Latin): peace
Constanza/Constance/Connie: (American): strong-willed
Consuela: (Spanish): provides consolation
Contessa: (Italian): a countess
Cora: (Greek & English): maiden; (Scottish): seething pool
Coral: (English): a reef formation
Corazon: (Spanish): of the heart
Cordelia: (English, Welsh & Celtic): of the sea
Coretta: (Greek): a form of Cora, which means maiden
Corey/Cory: (Irish): from the hollow, of the churning waters
Corina: (Latin): spear-wielding woman
Corinthia: (Greek): woman of Clorinth
Cornelia: (Latin): horn
Cota: (Spanish): lively
Cote: (French): from the riverbank
Courtney: (English): courteous
Cree: (Native American): name of tribe
Cressida: (Greek): golden girl
Crimson: (English): deep red color
Crystal/Krystal: (English): jewel; (Latin America): a clear brilliant glass

Cyan: (American): light blue or green
Cylee: (American): darling daughter
Cynthia: (Greek): moon
Cyrene: (Greek): maiden huntress

Dagmar: (Scandinavian): born on a glorious gay
Dahlia: (Swedish): from the valley, resembling the flower
Daisy: (English); day's eve; (American): daisy flower
Dakota: (Native American): friend, ally, tribal name
Dale: (English): valley
Dalia/Dahlia: (Hebrew): tree branch
Dana: (English, Danish, Irish & Hebrew): a person from Denmark
Dania: (English, Hebrew & Denmark): God is my judge
Danica: (Slavic): the morning star
Daniela: (Hebrew & Spanish): God is my judge
Danielle: (Hebrew): God is my judge
Danna: (Indian): gift
Daphne: (Greek): of the laurel tree
Dara: (Hebrew): compassionate
Darby: (Irish & Gaelic): free man; (English): deer park
Darcy: (Irish & Celtic): dark one
Daria: (Greek): wealthy
Darlene: (English & French): little darling
Davena/Davina: (Scottish): feminine form of David, which means beloved one
Davon: (English): river
Dawn: (English): aurora; (Greek): sunrise
Dea: (Greek): resembling a goddess
Deana/Deanna: (English & Latin America): from the valley
Deborah: (Hebrew & Israel): honey bee
Deidre: (Gaelic): a raging or broken-hearted woman
Dekla: (Latvian): a trinity goddess
Dela/Della: (German, Greek & English): noble
Delaney: (Irish): dark challenger; (French): from the elder-grove tree
Delia: (Greek): visible
Delilah: (Hebrew): a seductive woman
Delora/Delores/Deloris: (Latin America): of the seashore; (English): sorrow
Delta: (Greek): from the mouth of the river, the fourth letter of the Greek alphabet
Demeter: (Greek): lover of the earth
Demi: (Greek): a petite woman; (French): half
Dena: (Hebrew & Israel): vindicated; (Native American): valley
Denali: (Indian): a superior woman
Dendara: (Egyptian): from the town on the river
Denise: (French): a follower of Dionysus
Deondra/Deandra: (American): a combination of Dee and Andrea
Derry: (English, Irish, German & Gaelic): red-haired, from the oak grove
Desiree: (French): desired
Destiny: (English): fate
Deva: (Hindi): divine
Devin/Devon: (Irish): poet
Dextra: (Latin): skillful
Dharma: (Indian): ultimate law of all things
Diamond: (English): bridge protector: (Greek): unbreakable
Diana: (Greek): divine, goddess of the moon and the hunt
Diane: (Latin America): hunter
Dina: (Hebrew & Israel): avenged, judged; (English): from the valley
Dinah: (Hebrew & Israel): judgment

Dionne: (Greek): divine queen
Dita: (Spanish): a form of Edith, which means gift
Dixie: (American): woman of the south
Dolly: (American): cute child
Dolores: (Spanish): woman of sorrow
Dominique: (French): belonging to God
Donna: (Italian): lady
Dora/Dori/Dory: (Greek): gift
Doreen: (French): golden one; (Gaelic): brooding
Doris: (Greek): sea
Dorothea: (Dutch): gift of God
Dorothy (Greek): gift of God
Dove: (American): bird of peace
Drucilla/Drusilla: (Biblical): fruitful, dewy-eyed; (Latin America): mighty
Drew: (Greek): courageous, strong
Drury: (French): greatly loved
Dulce: (Latin): very sweet

Earlene: (Irish): pledge; (English): noble
Eartha: (English): earthy
Easter: (American): from the holiday or Christian festival
Easton: (American): wholesome
Ebony: (American): dark strength
Echo: (Greek): sound returned
Edana: (Irish): fiery
Eden: (Hebrew): delight; (Israel): paradise
Edie: (English): blessed
Edith: (English): joyous, a treasure
Edna: (Celtic): fire; (Hebrew): rejuvenation; (Israel): spirit renewed
Edwina: (English): prosperous friend
Effie: (Greek): melodious talk
Eileen: (Irish & French): light
Elaine: (French): light
Elana: (Hebrew): from the oak tree
Elata: (Latin): high spirited
Eldora: (Spanish): golden, blond, gift of the sun
Eleanor/Elinor: (English): torch
Electra: (Greek): bright, the shining one
Elena: (Spanish): the shining light
Eleni: (Greek): light
Eliana: (Hebrew): the Lord answers our prayers
Elisa/Elise: (Hebrew): my God is bountiful
Elisha: (Hebrew): God is salvation; (Israel): God is gracious
Eliza: (French): consecrated to God
Elizabeth: (English): my God is bountiful; (Hebrew & Biblical): consecrated to God
Ella: (English); beautiful fairy; (Spanish): she
Elle: (English): torch
Ellen/Ellyn: (Greek): light
Ellery: (English): cheerful
Ellie: (English): a diminutive form of Ellen, which means light
Elliott: (Israel): close to God; (English): the Lord is my God
Ellis: (English & Hebrew): my God is Jehovah
Elma: (German): having God's protection
Elmira: (English): noble
Eloisa/Eloise: (Latin): famous warrior
Elrica: (German): great ruler

Elsa: (German): noble
Elsie: (English): my God is bountiful
Elvira: (Latin): truthful, trusted
Emerald: (English, Spanish & French): a bright green gem
Emerson: (English): brave, powerful
Emery: (German): industrious
Emilia: (Spanish): flattering
Emily: (Latin America): admiring
Emma: (English, Danish & German): whole, complete, universal
Emmanuelle: (Hebrew): God is with us
Emme: (Latin America): industrious, striving
Emmylou: (American): universal ruler
Enid: (Welsh): life, spirit
Enya: (Scottish): jewel, blazing
Epiphany: (Greek): manifestation
Erica: (Denmark): honorable ruler
Erin: (Irish): peace
Ernestina/Ernestine: (German): determined, serious
Esme: (French): esteemed
Esmeralda: (Spanish): resembling a prized emerald
Essence: (English): scent
Estelle: (French & Latin America): star
Esther: (Hebrew & Africa): star
Estrella: (Spanish): star
Ethyl: (English): noble
Etta: (German): little
Eudora: (Greek): honored gift
Eugenia: (Greek): well-born
Eunice: (Greek): happy, victorious
Eva: (Hebrew, Israel, Indian & Spanish): one who gives life
Evangeline: (Greek): like an angel
Eve: (Hebrew): to breathe
Evelyn: (Celtic): light; (English & Hebrew): life, hazelnut
Ever: (English): strong as a boar
Evita: (Spanish): a derivative of Eve, which means to breathe

Fabiana: (Latin): bean grower
Faith: (English): faithful; (Latin America): to trust
Faline: (Irish): in charge
Fallon: (Irish): a commanding woman
Fang: (Chinese): fragrant
Far: (Chinese): flower
Fantasia: (Latin): from a fantasy land
Farren: (English): wanderer
Fatima: (Arabic): the perfect woman
Fauna: (French): fawn, a young deer
Fawn: (French & English): young deer
Fay/Faye: (French): fairy; (Irish): raven; (English): faith, confidence
Felicia/Felice/Phylicia: (French & Latin America): happiness
Felicity: (French, English & Latin America): happiness
Fern: (English): the fern plant
Fernanda: (Spanish): adventurous
Fia: (Portuguese): weaver; (Italian): from the flickering fire; (Scottish): from the dark of peace
Fiana: (Irish): warrior huntress
Fidelity/Fidealia: (Latin): faithful, true
Filipa: (Spanish): friend of horses

Fina: (English): God will add
Finley: (Gaelic): fair-haired, heroine
Fiona: (Gaelic): fair, a white-shouldered woman
Fiorella: (Italian): little flower
Flair: (English): natural talent
Flame: (American): passionate, fiery
Fleta: (English): swift
Fleur: (French): flower
Flora: (English): flower: (Latin): flowering
Florence: (English): flowering; (Latin America): prosperous
Florencia: (Spanish): flowering, blooming
Flynn: (Irish): heir to the red-head; ruddy complexion
Fortuna: (Latin): fortunate
Fran/Francine: (Latin America): free
Frances: (Latin America): free
Francesca: (Italian): one who is free
Freda/Freida: (German): wise judge
Frederica: (German): peaceful ruler
Freira: (Spanish): sister
Freya: (Norse): lady
Frida: (German): peaceful
Fujita: (Japanese): field
Fuschia: (Latin): resembling the color
Fury: (Greek): an enraged woman
Fuyu: (Japanese): born in winter

Gabriella: (Israel & Hebrew): God gives strength; (Italian): woman of God
Gabrielle: (French): strength of God
Gail/Gale/Gayle: (English): merry, lively
Galiana: (Arabic): a Moorish princess
Galilee: (Hebrew): from the sacred sea
Gardenia: (English): a sweet-smelling flower
Garnet: (English): gem, armed with a spear; (French): keeper of grain
Gay: (English): merry, happy
Gemma: (French & Italian): jewel
Genesis: (Hebrew): origin, birth; (Israel): beginning
Geneva: (French): juniper berry: (German): of the race of woman
Genevieve: (French): white-skinned
Genia/Genie: (Greek): well-born
Gentry: (English): gentleman
Georgette/Georgeann/Georgeanna/Georgina: (French): farmer
Georgia: (Greek & German): farmer
Geraldine: (English): mighty with a spear
Germaine: (French): from Germany
Gertrude: (German): adored warrior
Gia: (Italian): God is gracious
Giada: (Italian): jade
Gianna: (Italian): diminutive form of Giovanna, which means God is gracious
Gillian/Jillian: (English): child of the gods; (Irish): young at heart
Gina/Geena: (Italian): garden; (African American): powerful mother of black people
Ginger: (English): the spice
Giovanna: (Italian): God is gracious
Giselle: (French): pledge
Gita: (Hindi): beautiful song; (Hebrew): good woman
Gitana: (Spanish): gypsy

Giulia/Giuliana: (Italian):youthful
Gladys: (Welsh): lame
Glenna: (Gaelic): from the valley between the hills
Gloria: (Latin): renowned, highly praised
Glynnis: (Welsh): from the valley between the hills
Golda/Goldie: (English): resembling the precious metal
Grace/Gracie: (Latin America): grace of God; (American): land of grace
Greer: (Scottish): alert, watchful
Greta: (German): pearl
Gretchen: (German): a form of Margaret, which means pearl
Gretel: (German & Scandinavian): pearl
Guadalupe: (Spanish): from the valley of wolves
Guinevere: (Celtic): white lady; (English): white wave
Gwen: (Celtic): mythical son of Gwastad
Gwendolyn: (Welsh): fair
Gwyneth: (Welsh): blessed with happiness
Gypsy: (English): wanderer

Hachi: (Japanese): eight, good luck
Hadley: (English): from the field of heather
Hae: (Korean): ocean
Hagan: (Irish): youthful
Hagar: (Hebrew): forsaken, flight, famous bearer; (Israel): flight
Hailey/Hailee/Haley/Haylee: (English): hero, field of hay
Haimi: (Hawaiian): one who searches for the truth
Hallie/Halle: (English): hay meadow
Halsey: (American): playful
Hana: (Japanese): flower; (Arabic): blissful
Hannah: (English & Hebrew): favor, grace; (Biblical): grace of God
Hara: (Hebrew): from the mountainous land
Harley: (English): from the meadow of the hares
Harlow: (American): impetuous
Harmony: (Latin America): a beautiful blending
Harper: (English): musician, harp player
Harriet: (English & German): rules the home
Hattie: (English): a form of Harriet, which means rules the home
Haven: (English): safe place
Haya: (Japanese): quick, light
Hayden: (English): from the hedged valley
Haylee: (English): from the hay meadow, hero
Hazel: (English & Irish): the hazel tree
Heather: (English): a flowering plant
Heaven: (American): from the heavens
Hedda/Hedy: (German): battler
Heidi: (German): noble, serene
Helen: (Greek): light
Helena: (Greek): light
Helene: (French): in the light of the sun
Helga: (German): wealthy, blessed
Heloise: (French): famous in battle
Henrietta: (German): ruler of the house
Hera: (Greek): Goddess of marriage
Hermione: (Greek): earthly
Hermona: (Hebrew): from the mountain peak
Herra: (Greek): daughter of the earth
Hester: (Greek): star

Hestia: (Greek): goddess of the hearth
Hilary/Hillary: (English & Greek): joyous, cheerful
Hilda: (German): battle maiden
Hoda: (Indian): child of God
Holly: (French, English & Germany): shrub
Honey: (English): sweet
Honor: (Spanish & Irish): honor; (Latin America): integrity
Hope: (English): trust, faith
Hua: (Chinese): flower
Huan: (Chinese): happiness
Hunter: (English): hunter
Hye: (Korean): graceful

Ida: (English): hardworking
Idona: (Scandinavian): fresh-faced
Ilaina/Ilana: (Hebrew): tree
Ileana: (Roman): torch; (Greek): from the city of lion
Ilene: (Irish): a form of Helen, which means light
Ilia: (Greek): from the ancient city
Ilsa: (German): abbreviation of Elizabeth, which means God is bountiful
Imala: (Native American): one who disciplines others
Iman: (Arabic): having great faith
Imani: (Kenya): faith
Imari: (Japanese): daughter of today
Imelda: (Italian): warrior
Imogene: (Latin): image, likeness
Ina: (Polynesian): moon goddess
Inara: (Arabic): heaven-sent daughter
Inari: (Finnish): successful, woman from the lake
Inca: (Indian): adventurer
India: (English): from India
Indigo: (Latin America): dark blue
Indira: (Hindi): splendid
Ineesha: (American): sparkling
Inez/Ines: (Spanish): a form of Agnes, which means pure
Inga: (Danish & Swedish): beautiful daughter
Ingrid: (Scandinavian): having the beauty of God
Inis: (Irish): woman from Ennis
Iona: (Greek): woman from the island
Ionanna: (Hebrew): filled with grace
Ionia: (Greek): of the sea and islands
Ipsa: (Indian): desired
Ireland: (Irish): country of the Irish
Irena: (Greek): peace
Irene: (Greek & Spanish): peaceful
Iris: (Greek): colorful, rainbow; (Hebrew & English): the flower
Irma: (German): whole, universal
Isabel: (Hebrew): devoted to God; (Spanish & Biblical): consecrated to God
Isabella: (Hebrew): devoted to God; (Spanish): God is bountiful; (Biblical): consecrated to God
Isadore/Isadora: (Greek): gift from the goddess Isis
Isana: (German): strong willed
Ishtar: (Arabic): mythical goddess of love and fertility
Isidora: (Spanish): gifted with many ideas
Isis: (Egyptian): most powerful goddess
Isla: (Greek & Irish): from the island
Isra: (Arabic): one who travels in the evening

Ivana: (Slavic): God is gracious

Ivanka: (Slavic): God is gracious

Ivette/Yvette: (French): a form of Yvette, which means young archer

Ivory: (English & Latin America): white, pure

Ivy/Ivey: (English): vine

Ja: (Korean): attractive, fiery

Jacey/Jacy/Jacie: (American): resembling the hyacinth

Jacinda: (Greek): beautiful

Jacinta: (Spanish): resembling the hyacinth

Jacqueline: (French): to protect

Jada/Jayda: (Israel): wise

Jade: (Spanish): jewel, green gemstone

Jae: (English): resembling a jaybird

Jael: (Hebrew): mountain goat, climber

Jaffa: (Hebrew): beautiful

Jai: (Tai): heart

Jaiden: (Spanish): a form of Jade, which means jewel

Jailyn: (American): a combination of Jae and Lynn

Jalila: (Arabic): important

Jalisa: (American): a combination of Jae and Lisa

Jamaica: (American): from the island of springs

Jamie/Jayme: (Hebrew): supplanter

Jamielee: (American): a combination of Jamie and Lee

Jamielynn: (American): a combination of Jamie and Lynn

Jana: (Slovakian): God is gracious

Janae: (American): a form of Jane, which means gracious

Jane: (Hebrew): gift from God; (English): gracious, merciful

Janelle/Jeanelle: (French): a form of Jane, which means gracious

Janesha/Janessa: (American): a form of Jane, which means gracious

Janet: (Hebrew & English): gift from God

Janice/Janis: (Hebrew): gift from God; (Israel): God is gracious

Janine: (Hebrew): gift from God

January: (American): the first month of the year

Jasmine: (Persian): a climbing plant; (English): a fragrant flower

Javiera/Xaviera: (Spanish): owner of a new house

Jayla: (Arabia): charity; (African American): one who is special

Jayne: (Indian): victorious; (Hebrew): gift from God; (English): Jehovah has been gracious

Jazmin: (Japanese): the flower

Jean: (Hebrew): God is gracious

Jeanette: (French): a derivative of Jean, which means God is gracious

Jeanne: (Scottish): a form of Jean, which means God is gracious

Jemima: (Hebrew): our little dove

Jemma: (English): as precious as a jewel

Jena/Jenna: (Arabic): our little bird

Jennifer: (English & Welsh): fair one; (English & Celtic): white wave

Jensen: (Scandinavian): God is gracious

Jeri/Jerri/Jerrie: (American): diminutive forms of Geraldine, which means mighty with a spear

Jerica: (American): a combination of Jeri and Erica

Jermaine: (French): woman from Germany

Jessica: (Israel): God is watching; (Hebrew): rich, God beholds

Jetta: (Danish): resembling the gemstone

Jewel/Jewelle: (English & French): precious gem

Jezebel: (Hebrew): one who is not exalted

Jia: (Chinese): beautiful

Jiao: (Chinese): dainty

Jiera: (Lithuanian): lively
Jill: (English): girl, sweetheart
Jillian/Gillian: (English): child of the gods; (Irish): young at heart
Jinelle: (Welsh): fair skin
Jing: (Chinese): stillness, luxurious
Jiselle: (American): one who offers her pledge
Jo: (English): God will add
Joan: (Hebrew): gift from God; (English): God is gracious
Joann: (English & Hebrew): God is gracious
Joanna: (Hebrew & French): gift from God
Joba/Joby: (Hebrew): afflicted
Jobeth: (American): a combination of Jo and Beth
Jocelyn/Josslyn/Josselin: (Latin): cheerful, happy
Joda: (Hebrew): an ancestor of Christ
Jody: (Hebrew): praised
Joelle: (Hebrew): God is willing
Jolene/Joleen/Joline: (English): God will add
Jolie: (French): pretty young woman
Jonna/Johnna: (Danish): God is gracious
Jordan/Jordana: (Hebrew): to flow down; (Israel): descendant
Jorja: (English): farmer
Josephina/Josefina: (Hebrew): God will add
Josephine: (French): God will add
Josette: (French): a form of Josephine, which means God will add
Journey: (American): one who likes to travel
Jovana/Jovanna: (Spanish): daughter of the sky
Jovi/Jovita: (Spanish): joyful
Joy: (French, English & Latin America): rejoicing
Joyce: (English & Latin America): cheerful, merry
Juana/Juanita: (Spanish): a form of Jane, which means gift from God
Jubilee: (Latin): joyous celebration
Judith/Judy/Judi: (Hebrew): praised; (Israel): from Judah
Julia/Julie: (French): youthful; (Latin America): soft-haired, youthful
Juliana: (Spanish): soft-haired
Juliet/Juliette: (French): youthful, soft-haired
Julietta/Julieta: (French): youthful, young at heart
June: (Dominican Republic): born in June
Juno: (Roman): mythical queen of the heavens
Justina: (Greek): just
Justine: (English): just, upright; (Latin America): fairness

Kacey/Casey: (Irish): brave
Kacia: (Greek): the adoptive mother of Romulus and Remus
Kady/Katy: (American): a diminutive form of Katherine, which means pure or virginal
Kaelin/Kaylin/Kaelyn: (American): a combination of Kay and Lynn; (Irish): beautiful girl from the meadow
Kaia: (Greek): earth
Kailani: (Hawaiian): sky
Kaitlyn/Caitlyn/Katelyn/Catelyn: (Irish): pure
Kala: (Hawaiian): princess
Kalina/Kaleena/Kalena: (Indian): of the sun
Kallan: (Slavic): stream, river
Kama: (Indian & Japanese): one who loves and is loved
Kamala: (Hawaiian, Hindu & Indian): lotus; (Arabic): perfection
Kami: (Hindu): loving; (Japanese): divine aura
Kamila: (Czechoslovakian): young ceremonial attendant
Kana: (Japanese): dexterity and skill

Kanda: (Native American): a magical woman
Kara: (Greek): pure; (Italian): dearly loved; (Gaelic): a good friend
Karen: (Greek): pure
Kari: (Norwegian): blessed, pure, holy
Karina/Kareena/Karena/Carina/Carena/Careena: (Scandinavian & Russian): dear one, pure
Karisma/Charisma: (English): blessed with charm
Karissa: (Greek): grace, kindness
Karla: (German): a small and strong woman
Karmel: (Latin): of the fruitful orchard
Kasia: (English): alert, vigorous
Kate: (Irish, English & French): diminutive of Katherine, which means pure, virginal
Katherine/Kathryn: (Irish): clear; (English): pure; (Greek): pure, virginal
Kathleen/Kathy: (English, Irish & French): diminutive of Katherine, which means pure
Katniss: (American): female warrior
Katrina: (German): a form of Katherine, which means pure
Kay: (Greek): rejoice; (Scottish & Welsh): fiery
Kayden: (French, English & Arabic): round, gentle; companion
Kayla: (Irish & Greek): pure and beloved
Kaylee/Kayleen/Kaylene: (American): pure
Kayo: (Japanese): beautiful
Keagan/Keegan: (Irish): little, fiery
Keara: (Irish): dark, black
Kearney: (Irish): the winner
Keaton: (English): from a shed town
Keely/Keeley: (Irish): beautiful
Keilani: (Hawaiian): glorious chef
Keira: (Celtic): black-haired
Keisha/Keesha: (African): favorite
Kelly/Kelli/Kelleigh/Kellee: (Gaelic & Irish): warrior; (Scottish): wood
Kelsey: (English): from the island of ships
Kendall: (English & Celtic): from the bright valley
Kendra: (English): having royal power
Kenja: (Japanese): a sage
Kennedy: (Gaelic): a helmeted chief
Kent: (English & Welsh): white; (Celtic): chief
Kenya: (Israel): animal horn
Kenzie: (Scottish): light-skinned; (American): diminutive of McKenzie
Keri/Kerry: (Irish): dusky, dark
Ki: (Korean): arisen
Kiara: (Irish): small and dark
Kiera: (Irish): dusky
Kiley: (Irish): narrow land
Kim: (Vietnamese): as precious as gold; (Welsh): leader
Kimball: (English): chief of warriors
Kimberlin/Kimberlyn: (English): a form of Kimberly, which means ruler
Kimberly: (English): ruler
Kimora: (American): royal
Kin: (Japanese): golden
Kina: (Hawaiian): woman of China
Kinley: (American): diminutive of McKinley
Kinsey: (English): the king's victory
Kira: (Russian): sun
Kirby: (Scandinavian): church village
Kirsten: (Greek): Christian, annointed
Kismet: (English): fate
Kita: (Japanese): north

Kitty: (Greek): a diminutive form of Katherine, which means pure, virginal
Ko: (Japanese): filial piety
Kobe/Kobi/Koby: (African): supplanter; (American): from California
Komala: (Indian): tender and delicate
Kona: (Hawaiian): girly
Kono: (Japanese): dexterity and skill
Kosame: (Japanese): fine rain
Kris/Kristen/Kristi/Krista: (Irish): Christ-bearer
Kristina/Kristine: (English): follower of Christ
Krystal: (American): clear, brilliant glass
Kuma: (Japanese): bear, mouse
Kyla: (English): from the narrow channel
Kyle: (Irish): attractive
Kylee: (Celtic): a straight and narrow channel
Kylie: (Australian): a boomerang
Kyra: (Greek): noble

Lacrecia/Lacresha/Lucretia: (Latin): bringer of light
Lacy/Lacey: (Irish): surname; (English): derived from lace
Laila/Leila/Leyla: (Arabic): beauty of the night
Laine/Lane/Lainey/Laney/Lanie: (English): narrow road, from the long meadow
Lake/Laken/Lakin/Lakyn: (American): body of water, from the lake
Lakeisha: (American): joyful, happy
Lalita: (Indian): playful and charming
Lan: (Chinese): orchid
Lana: (Latin): wooly; (Irish): attractive, peaceful
Lanassa: (Russian): cheerful, lighthearted
Landon: (English): from the long hill
Lani: (Hawaiian): from the sky, heavenly
Laquita: (American): fifth-born child
Lara: (Greek): cheerful; (Latin): shining, famous
Laramie: (French): shedding tears of love
Larissa/Laryssa/Laurissa: (Greek): cheerful
Lark: (English): a lark; (American): songbird
Larue: (American): a medicinal herb
Lashawna: (American): filled with happiness
Lata: (Indian): of the lovely wine
Latanya: (American): daughter of the fairy queen
Latisha/Leticia/Letitia: (Latin): a form of Lucretia, which means bringer of light
Latoya: (American): a combination of La and Toya
Laura: (English, Spanish & Latin America): crowned with laurel, from the laurel tree
Laurel: (English & French): crowned with laurel, from the laurel tree
Lauren/Laryn/Lauryn: (French): crowned with laurel
Laurie/Lori: (English): crowned with laurels
Lavender: (English): a purple flowering plant
Laverne: (French): woodland, like the spring
Lavina/Lavinia: (Latin): purified
Layla/Leila(h): (Indian): born at night; (Arabian): dark beauty
Layne: (English): path, roadway
Leah/Leia: (Hebrew): weary
Leann: (English): gracious meadow
Lecia: (English): noble, truthful
Leda: (Greek): mother creator
Leeza: (Hebrew & English): a form of Lisa, which means devoted to God
Leigh: (English): from the meadow
Leighton: (English): herb garden, town by the meadow

Leila/Leyla: (Persian): night, dark beauty
Leilani: (Hawaiian): heavenly flower, heavenly child
Lena: (Israel): illustrious
Lenora/Lenore/Leora: (Greek & Russian): a form of Eleanor, which means torch
Leona: (Latin): strength of a lion
Leslie/Lesley: (Gaelic): from the holly garden
Leta: (Latin): glad
Leticia: (Spanish): joy, gladness
Levin: (Hebrew): heart; (English): dear friend
Levona: (Hebrew): spice, incense
Lexa/Lexia: (Czech): defender of mankind
Li: (Chinese): upright
Lia: (Greek): bearer of good news
Liane/Liana: (English): daughter of the sun
Libby: (English): my God is bountiful
Liberty: (English): free, independent
Libra: (Latin): balanced, the seventh sign of the zodiac
Lien: (Chinese): lotus
Lila: (Arabia): night
Lilac: (Latin America): bluish purple; (American): a flowering bluish purple shrub
Lilith: (Babylonian): woman of the night
Lillian: (Latin): resembling the lily
Lilo: (American): generous one
Lily/Lilly: (Hebrew, English & Latin America): lily, blossoming flower
Lin: (Chinese): resembling jade
Lina: (Arabic): tender
Linda: (Spanish): pretty; (English): lime tree; (German): snake, lime tree
Linden: (English): from linden hill
Lindley: (English): from the pasture land
Lindsay/Lindsey/Lyndsay/Lyndsey: (English): from the land of linden trees
Linette/Lynette: (Welsh): idol; (French): bird
Ling: (Chinese): dainty
Linnea: (Denmark): lime tree
Lisa: (German): devoted to God; (Israel): consecrated to God
Lisette/Lissettte/Lizette: (French): derivation of Elizabeth, which means my God is bountiful
Liv: (Norwegian): protector
Livia: (English): life
Liza: (Hebrew): consecrated to God
Lois: (Israel): good; (German): famous warrior
Loki: (Norse): a trickster god in mythology
Lola: (Spanish): woman of sorrow
Lolita: (Spanish): sorrowful
Lona/Loni: (English): ready for battle
London/Londyn: (English): capital of England; fortress of the moon
Lora: (Latin): crowned with laurel
Lorelei: (German): from the rocky cliff
Loretta: (Italian): crowned with laurel
Lori: (English) the laurel tree; (Latin America): crowned with laurel
Lorita: (Latin America): laurel
Lorraine: (French): from the kingdom of Lothair
Lotus: (Greek): the flower
Louise/Louisa: (German): famous warrior
Love: (English): full of affection
Luana/Luann: (Hawaiian): contented
Lucile: (English): a form of Lucy, which means bringer of light
Lucinda: (Latin): a form of Lucy, which means bringer of light

Lucrecia: (Spanish): brings light
Lucy/Lucia/Luciana: (Latin America): bringer of light
Luka: (Latin America): bright
Lulu: (Arabic): pearl; (English): soothing
Luna: (Latin & Latin America): the moon
Lupe/Lupa/Lupita: (Latin): wolf
Lurleen/Lurlene: (Scandinavian): war horn
Lydia: (Greek): beautiful maiden
Lyla/Lila: (Arabic): born at night
Lynn(e): (English): waterfall
Lyric: (Greek): melodic word; (French): of the lyre
Lysandra: (Greek): liberator
Mabel: (English): lovable, beautiful
Mackenna: (Gaelic): daughter of the handsome man
Mackenzie/Mackinsey: (Irish & Scottish): fair, favored one
Macy: (English): enduring; (American): stone worker
Maddox: (English): born into prosperity
Madeline/Madelyn: (Greek): high tower
Madge: (English): pearl
Madison: (English): son of Matthew
Madonna: (Italian): my lady
Maeve: (Irish): intoxicating, joyous
Magdalena: (Hebrew): from the tower; (Spanish): bitter
Maggie: (English): resembling a pearl
Magnolia: (French): resembling the flower
Mahogany/Mahogony: (Spanish): rich, strong
Maia: (French): May; (Greek): mother
Maisie: (Scottish): resembling a pearl
Maite: (Spanish): loved
Makala: (English): princess; (Hawaiian): resembling myrtle
Makayla: (English & Irish): like God
Makena: (African): filled with happiness
Mako: (Japanese): truth, grateful
Mali: (Thai): resembling a flower; (Welsh): from the sea of bitterness
Malia: (American): calm, peaceful
Malika: (African): queen, princess
Mallory/Malerie: (French): unfortunate; ill-fated; (German): war counselor
Mamie: (American): a diminutive form of Margaret, which means pearl
Mana: (Japanese): truth
Mandy: (Latin America): worthy of love
Manon: (French): bitter
Manuela: (Spanish): God is with us
Mara: (English, Italian, Hebrew & Israel): bitter
Marcela/Marcella: (Spanish): warring
Marcia/Marsha: (Latin): dedicated to Mars
Marcy: (Latin America): marital
Maren/Marin: (Latin): sea
Margaret: (Greek & Latin America): a pearl
Mari: (Finnish): bitter
Maria/Marie: (Latin): bitter
Mariah: (English): bitter; (Latin): star of the seas
Mariana/Marian: (Spanish): star of the sea; (French): bitter
Marianne/Marian: (French): bitter; (Spanish): star of the sea
Maribel: (French): beautiful
Mariel: (Hebrew): bitter
Marietta: (French): star of the sea

Marika: (Danish): star of the sea
Marjorie/Margery: (English): resembling a pearl
Marlie/Marley/Marleigh/Marly: (American): bitter
Marlo: (English): one who resembles driftwood
Marilyn/Marlyn: (Israel): descendants of Mary
Marina: (Greek, Italian & Slovakian): from the sea
Maris: (Latin): sea
Marissa: (Latin America): of the sea; (Hebrew): rebellion, bitter
Marita: (Dutch): bitter
Marla: (Greek): high tower
Marlene: (German): bitter; (Hebrew): from the tower
Marlowe: (English): from the hill by the lake
Marnie/Marny: (Hebrew): rejoice
Marquesa: (Spanish): she who works with a hammer
Marquise: (French): noble woman
Marsala: (Italian): from the place of sweet wine
Martha: (Israel): lady
Martina: (Latin America): warlike
Mary: (Biblical, English & Slovakian): bitter
Matilda: (German): powerful battler
Maude: (French): strong in war; (Irish): strong battle maiden
Maura: (Italian, Irish & French): dark
Maureen: (Irish): star of the sea, from the sea of bitterness
Mauve: (American): purplish color
Maven: (English): having great knowledge
Mavis: (French): resembling a songbird
Maximiliana: (Latin): eldest
Maxine/Maxie: (Latin): greatest
May/Mae: (English): name of month; (Hebrew & Latin America): from Mary
Maya/Mya: (Indian): an illusion or dream; (Hebrew): woman of the water
Maybelline: (Latin): a form of Mabel, which means lovable, beautiful
McKayla: (Gaelic): fiery
McKenzie: (Irish): fair, favored one
McKinley: (English): offspring of the fair hero
Meadow: (American): beautiful field
Meagan/Megan: (Irish): soft and gentle; (Greek): strong and mighty
Medea: (Greek): cunning ruler
Medina: (Arabic): the site of Muhammad's tomb
Medora: (Greek): wise ruler
Medusa: (Greek): a Gorgon with snakes for hair
Megara: (Greek): wife of Hercules
Meili: (Chinese): beautiful
Melanie: (Greek): dark-skinned beauty
Melba: (Greek): slender, thin-skinned
Meli: (Native American): bitter
Melia: (German): industrious
Melika: (Greek): as sweet as honey
Melina: (German): industrious, striving
Melinda: (Latin): sweet and gentle
Melissa: (Greek): honey bee
Melita: (Greek), a form of Melissa, which means honey bee
Melody: (Greek): beautiful song
Melora: (Greek): golden apple
Mena: (German & Dutch): strong
Mercedes: (Latin): reward, payment; (Spanish): merciful
Mercy: (English): compassion; (French): merciful

Meredith: (Welsh): great ruler, protector of the sea
Merrilee: (American): a combination of Merry and Lee
Merry: (English): joyful, mirthful
Meryl: (German): famous; (Irish): shining sea
Mia: (Italian): my; (Biblical): mine
Michaela: (Celtic, Hebrew, English, Gaelic & Irish): who is like God
Michelle: (French & Hebrew): like God, close to God
Midori: (Japanese): green
Mika/Micah: (Finnish): like God; (Japanese): new moon
Mikala/Mikaela: (Hawaiian): who is like God
Mila: (Russian): dear one; (Serbian): favor, glory
Mildred: (English): gentle counselor
Miley: (American): virtuous
Millicent: (English): industrious
Mimi: (French): a diminutive form of Miriam, which means rebellious
Mindy: (English): sweet and gentle
Minerva: (Latin): wise
Ming: (Chinese): brilliant light
Mingzhu: (Chinese): bright pearl
Minka: (Teutonic): great strength
Minnie: (Irish): bitter; (Hebrew): wished for a child
Mira: (Hindu): prosperous
Mirabel: (Spanish): of uncommon beauty
Miranda: (Latin): worthy of admiration
Miriam: (Hebrew): rebellious; (Israel): strong-willed
Mischa: (Russian): like God
Misty: (English): shrouded by mist
Mitzy/Mitzi: (German): diminutive form of Mary, which means bitter
Miya: (Japanese): from the sacred temple
Miyo: (Japanese): beautiful daughter
Mizuki: (Japanese): beautiful moon
Moesha: (American): drawn from the water
Moira: (Irish): bitter
Molly: (Israel & English): bitter
Mona: (Gaelic): born into nobility
Monica: (Greek & Spanish): advisor
Monique: (French): one who provides wise counsel
Monroe: (Gaelic): from the red swamp; (Scottish): from the river; (Irish): near the river roe
Monserrat: (Latin): jagged mountain
Montana: (Latin America): mountainous
Morgan: (Celtic): lives by the sea; (Welsh): bright sea
Morgana: (Welsh & Celtic): dweller of the sea
Mulan: (Chinese): magnolia blossom
Muriel: (Arabian): myth; (Celtic): shining sea
Murphy: (Irish): sea warrior
Mya: (American): emerald
Myka: (Hebrew): who is like God
Myra: (Greek): fragrant
Myrina: (Latin): an amazon in mythology
Myrtle: (Greek): the tree, victory; (English): the flowering shrub

Nadia: (Slovakian): hopeful
Nadine: (French): hopeful; (German): the courage of a bear
Nadira: (Arabic): rare, precious
Nailah/Naila: (Arabic): successful
Nala: (African): successful; (Tanzanian): queen

Nami: (Japanese): wave
Nan: (English): gracious
Nana: (Hawaiian): born in the spring
Nancy: (Hebrew & English): grace
Nandita: (Indian): delightful daughter
Nanette: (English): favor; (French & Hebrew): gracious
Naoki: (Japanese): honest tree
Naomi: (Hebrew & Israel): pleasant
Nara: (Greek): happy; (English): north; (Japanese): oak
Narella: (Greek): intelligent
Narelle: (Australian): woman from the sea
Nari: (Japanese): thunder
Narissa/Narcissa: (Greek): dafodil
Natalia/Natalie: (French): to be born at Christmas; (Slovakian): to be born
Natasha: (Greek): rebirth
Naveen: (Hindu): new; (Irish): beautiful, pleasant
Navida: (Iranian): brings good news
Nazareth: (Hebrew): religion
Neda: (Slovakian): Sunday's child; (English): wealthy guardian
Neena: (Hindi): beautiful eyes
Nefertiti: (Egyptian): queenly
Neila/Neela/Neely: (Irish): champion
Nelle/Nelly: (English): torch
Nena: (English): girl
Neriah: (Israel): light lamp of the Lord
Nerissa: (Italian): black-haired beauty; (Greek): sea nymph
Nessa: (Hebrew): miracle child; (Greek): pure, chaste
Neta: (Hebrew): plant, shrub
Neva: (Spanish): covered with snow
Nevada: (English): covered in snow
Nevaeh: (American): gift from God, heaven spelled backwards
Neve: (Irish): radiant; (Hebrew): life
Nevena: (Irish): worshipper of the saint
Neylan: (Turkish): fulfilled wish
Nia: (Irish): champion; (African): purpose
Nicole: (French): victory of the people
Nicolette: (French): a form of Nicole, which means victory of the people
Nikita: (Russian): victorious people
Nila: (Indian): blue
Nina: (Hebrew); grace; (Spanish): girl; (Native American): strong
Nirel: (Hebrew): light of God
Nishi: (Japanese): west
Nissa: (Hebrew): sign, emblem
Nita: (Hebrew): planter; (Choctaw): bear
Noa: (Israel): movement
Noelle: (French): born at Christmastime
Nola: (Irish): champion
Nona: (English): ninth
Noor: (Aramaic): light
Nora/Norah: (Hebrew): light
Noriko: (Japanese): child of principles
Norleen: (Irish): honest
Norma: (Latin America): from the north
Nuala: (Irish): white, fair-shouldered
Nula: (Irish): white: shouldered

Nuna: (Native American): land
Nuo: (Chinese): graceful
Nyala: (African): resembling an antelope
Nyssa: (Greek): the beginning

O'Shea: (Irish): child of Shea
Oba: (Yoruba): chief, ruler
Ocean/Oceana: (Greek): ocean
Octavia: (Latin America): eighth; (Italian): born eighth
Odelia: (Greek): melodic
Odessa: (Latin America): the odyssey
Odette: (German & French): a form of Odelia, which means melodic
Odina: (Latin): from the mountain
Okalani: (Hawaiian): from the heavens
Oksana: (Russian): hospitality
Ola: (Nigerian): precious; Scandinavian: ancestor
Oleda: (English): resembling a winged creature
Olena: (Russian): a form of Helen, which means light
Olethea: (Latin): truthful
Olga: (Slovakian): holy
Oliana: (Polynesian): oleander
Olina: (Hawaiian): joyous
Oliva: (Latin): olive tree
Olive: (Irish): olive; (Latin America), olive branch, peace
Olivia: (Spanish & Italian): olive; (Biblical): peace of the olive tree
Olympia: (Greek): from Mount Olympus
Oma: (Hebrew): reverent
Omri: (Arabic): red-haired
Ona: (Hebrew): grace
Ondrea: (Slavic): courageous and strong
Onida/Oneida: (Native American): the one expected
Onyx: (Greek): the onyx stone
Oona: (Gaelic): pure, chaste
Opal: (English & Indian): precious gem
Ophelia: (Greek): useful, wise
Ophrah/Oprah: (Hebrew): resembling a fawn
Orabella: (Latin): a form of Arabella, which means answered prayer
Oriana: (Latin): born at sunrise
Orin: (Latin): dark-haired beauty
Orion: (Greek): huntress
Orla: (Irish): golden woman
Orli: (Hebrew): light
Orna/Ornice: (Irish): pale skinned
Ornat: (Irish): green
Ornella: (Italian): of the flowering ash tree
Orpah: (Israel): fawn
Osaka: (Japanese): from the city of industry
Osita: (Spanish) divinely strong
Overton: (English): from the upper side of town
Ozora: (Hebrew): wealthy

Padma: (Hindi): lotus
Paige: (French): assistant, attendant
Paloma: (Spanish): dove-like
Pamela: (Greek, English & Indian): honey
Pandora: (Greek): gifted and talented woman

Paola: (Italian): little
Parker: (English): keeper of the park
Paris: (Persian): angelic face; (Greek): downfall; (French): the capital city of France
Parthenia: (Greek): virginal
Pasha: (Greek): sea
Patience: (English): patient, enduring
Patricia: (Spanish & Latin America): noble
Patrina/Patrice: (American): born into nobility
Paula/Paulette: (Latin America): small
Pauline/Paulina: (Latin America): small
Peace: (English): peaceful
Peaches: (English): fruit
Pearl: (English): gemstone
Pembroke: (English): from the broken hill
Penelope: (Greek): weaver
Penny: (Greek): diminutive form of Penelope, which means weaver
Peony: (Greek): resembling the flower
Pepita: (Spanish): God will add
Perdita: (Latin): lost
Peri: (Persian): fairy; (English); from the pear tree
Perlita: (Italian): pearl
Peta: (Blackfoot): golden eagle
Petra/Petrina/Petrisse: (Greek & Latin): small rock
Petunia: (English): resembling the flower
Peyton: (English): village
Pheodora: (Greek): supreme gift
Phernita: (American): well-spoken
Phia: (Italian): saintly
Philana: (Greek): lover of mankind
Philippa/Pippa: (English): friend of horses
Philomena: (Greek): friend of strength
Phoebe: (Greek): bright, shining one
Phoenix: (Greek): dark-red color, an immortal bird
Phylicia/Felicia: (Latin): fortunate, happy
Phyllis: (Greek): green leaf
Pia: (Italian): devout
Pilar: (Spanish): pillar of strength
Ping: (Chinese): peaceful
Piper: (English): plays the flute
Pippi: (French): friend of horses; (English): blushing
Pita: (African): fourth daughter
Pixie: (English): mischievous fairy
Plato: (Greek): strong shoulders
Plena: (Latin): abundant, complete
Polina: (Russian): small
Polly: (Latin America): bitter
Pollyanna: (American): overly optimistic
Poloma: (Choctaw): bow
Pomona: (Latin): goddess of fruit trees
Poppy: (English & Latin America): the poppy flower
Portia/Porsha/Porscha/Porsche: (Latin): offering
Posy: (English): God will increase
Precious: (American): treasured
Presley: (English): priest's land
Prima: (Latin): first, beginning
Primrose: (English): the first rose, primrose flower

Princess: (English): born to royalty
Priscilla: (Latin): from an ancient family
Prudence: (English): prudent or cautious
Pua: (Hawaiian): flower
Pyria: (American): cherished
Pythia: (Greek): prophet

Qi: (Chinese): fine jade
Qiana/Quiana: (American): living with grace, heavenly
Qiang: (Chinese): beautiful rose
Qing: (Chinese): dark blue
Quana: (Native American): sweet
Quarralia: (Australian): star
Quartilla: (Latin): fourth
Queen/Queenie/Quenna: (English): queen
Querida: (Spanish): dearly loved
Queta: (Spanish): head of the household
Quilla: (Incan): goddess of the moon
Quincy: (English): fifth-born child; (French): estate belonging to Quintus
Quinn: (Celtic): queenly; (Gaelic): one who provides counsel
Quintana/Quinella: (Latin): the fifth girl; (English): the queen's lawn
Quintessa: (Latin): of the essence

Rachel: (Hebrew): ewe; (Israel): innocent lamb
Racine: (French): root
Rae: (Scottish): grace; (German): wise protection
Raeden: (Japanese): thunder and lightning
Raelene/Rayleen: (American): a combination of Rae and Lee
Raelynn: (American): a form of Raylene
Rafaela/Raphaela: (Hebrew): healed by God
Rafiki: (African): friend
Rain/Raine/Raina: (American): blessings from above; (French & Latin): ruler; (English): lord, wise
Rainbow: (English): rainbow
Raisa: (Russian): a form of Rose
Raja: (Arabic): filled with hope
Ramona: (Spanish): wise protector
Randi: (English): shielded by wolves
Rani: (Sanskrit): queen
Ranita: (Hebrew): song, joyful
Raquel: (Spanish): innocent lamb
Rasha: (Arabic): resembling a young gazelle
Rashida: (Swahili & Turkish): righteous
Raven: (English): to be black, blackbird
Rayna: (Hebrew): pure; (Scandinavian): wise counsel
Razi: (Aramaic): secretive
Reagan: (Celtic): regal; (Irish): son of the small ruler
Reba: (Hebrew): fourth
Rebecca: (Biblical): servant of God
Rebel: (American): outlaw
Reese/Reece: (English &Welsh): ardent, fiery, enthusiastic
Regina: (Italian, Spanish & Latin America): queen
Rein: (German); advisor, counselor
Reina: (French & Spanish): queen; (English): wise ruler
Remi/Remy: (French): oarsman or rower from Rheims
Rena: (Hebrew): song
Renata: (French): a form of Renee, which means reborn

Renee: (French): reborn
Reta: (African): shaken
Reva: (Hebrew): rain
Reya: (Spanish): queenly
Reza: (Hungarian): harvester
Rhea: (Greek): rivers
Rhianna: (English): goddess; (Welsh): nymph
Rhiannon: (Welsh): pure maiden
Rhoda: (Greek): roses
Rhonda: (Welsh): carrying a good spear
Rhonwyn: (Irish): a form of Bronwyn, which means light-skinned
Ria: (Spanish): from the river's mouth
Richelle: (French): feminine form of Richard, which means strong ruler
Ricki/Rickelle: (American): a form of Erica, which means honorable ruler
Rielle: (Hebrew): a feminine form of Gabriel, which means God is my strength
Riley: (English): from the rye clearing; (Irish): a small stream
Rio: (Spanish & Portuguese): river
Rippina: (Japanese): brilliant light
Risa: (Latin): one who laughs often
Rita: (Greek): precious pearl
Riva: (French): river bank
River: (Latin & French): stream, water
Roberta: (English): bright with fame
Robin/Robyn: (English): a small bird
Rochelle: (French): from the little rock
Roja: (Spanish): red-haired woman
Rolanda: (German): well-known
Romina: (Arabian): from the Christian land
Romy: (French): a form of Rosemary, which means bitter rose
Rona: (Hebrew): my joy
Rong: (Chinese): martial
Rory: (Irish): famous brilliance, famous ruler; (Gaelic): red-haired
Rosa: (Spanish): rose
Rosalind/Rosalee: (Spanish): beautiful one
Rosario: (Filipino & Spanish): rosary
Rose: (English, French & Scottish): flower, a rose; (German): horse, fame
Roseanne/Rosanna: (Greek): graceful rose
Rosemary: (English): bitter rose
Rosetta: (Italian): rose
Roshonda/Roshawna: (American): a combination of Rose & Shawna
Rosina/Rosita: (Celtic): little rose
Roslyn/Rossalyn: (Scottish): cape, promontory
Rowan: (Irish): red-haired; (English & Gaelic): from the rowan tree
Rowena: (Welsh): fair and slender: (German): happy and famous
Roxanne: (Persian): sunrise
Roz/Roza: (Polish): rose
Ruby: (English & French): a precious jewel, a ruby
Rue: (Greek): herb of grace
Rula: (Latin & English): ruler
Rumer: (English); gypsy
Ruth: (Hebrew & Israel): companion, friend
Rylan: (English): the place where rye is grown
Rylee/Rylie: (Irish): a form of Riley, which means a small stream

Sabine/Sabina: (Latin): a tribe in ancient Italy
Sable: (English): sleek

Sabrina: (English): legendary princess
Sada: (Japanese): pure
Sadie: (English): a lady
Saffron: (English): resembling the yellow flower
Sahara: (Arabian): wilderness
Saige/Sage: (English & French): wise one; (English): from the spice
Sailor: (American): sailor
Sakari: (Native American & Hindi): sweet girl
Salina: (French): solemn, dignified
Sally/Sallie: (English): princess
Saloma/Salome: (Hebrew): peace and tranquility
Samantha: (Hebrew & Biblical): listener of God
Samina: (Hindi): happiness
Samira: (Arabic): entertaining
Sandra: (Greek): helper of humanity; (English): unheeded prophetess
Sandrine: (Greek): defender of mankind
Saniya: (Indian): a moment in time preserved
Santana: (Spanish): saintly
Santina: (Spanish): little saint
Sapphira/Sapphire: (Hebrew): sapphire; (Israel): beautiful
Sara(h): (Hebrew, Spanish & Biblical): princess
Sarafina/Saraphina: (Greek): gentle wind
Sardinia: (Italian): from the mountainous island
Sasha: (English): defender of mankind
Sato: (Japanese): sugar
Savannah: (Spanish): open plain, field
Sayo: (Japanese): born at night
Scarlett: (English): red
Scout: (French): scout
Season: (Latin): a fertile woman
Sedona: (American): the American city
Sela(h): (Israel): pause and reflect
Selene/Selena/Seline/Selina: (Greek): of the moon
Selma: (Scandinavian): divinely protected
Sena: (Persian): blessed
Sequoia: (Cherokee): giant redwood tree
Seraphina: (Israel): burning fire; (Hebrew): fiery-ringed
Serefina: (Latin): a winged angel
Serena/Syrena/Sirena: (Latin): peaceful disposition; (African American): calm, tranquil
Serenity: (Latin & English): peaceful
Shaba: (Spanish): rose
Shada: (Native American): pelican
Shae/Shea/Shay/Shayla: (Celtic & Irish): gift
Shahina: (Arabic): falcon
Shaina: (Yiddish): beautiful
Shakila: (Arabic): beautiful one
Shakira: (Arabic): grateful
Shamara: (Arabic): ready for battle
Shana/Shanea/Shanae: (Hebrew): God is gracious
Shandy/Shandie/Shandi: (English): rambunctious
Shane: (Hebrew): gift from God; (Irish): God is gracious
Shanel/Shanell/Shanelle/Shannel: (American): a form of Chanel, which means from the canal
Shani: (African): marvelous
Shania: (Native American): on my way
Shanika: (American): a combination of Sha and Nika

Shannon/Shannen: (Gaelic): having ancient wisdom
Sharlene: (English & French): manly, from the name Charles
Sharon: (Hebrew & Israel): a flat clearing
Shasta: (Native American): from the triple-peaked mountain
Shawn: (Irish): a form of Sean, which means God is gracious
Shawnee: (Native American): name of tribe
Shawnda: (English): God is gracious
Shaylee: (Gaelic): fairy princess
Sheba: (Hebrew): an ancient country in Arabia
Sheena: (Gaelic): God's gracious gift
Sheila/Sheela: (English & Irish): blind; (Italian): music
Shelby: (English): from the willow farm
Shelley/Shelly/Shellie: (English): meadow on the ledge
Sheridan: (Irish, English & Celtic): untamed; (Gaelic): bright, a seeker
Sherry/Sheree/Sheri/Sherri: (Israel): beloved; (French): dear one
Sheryl/Cheryl: (English): beloved
Shiloh: (Hebrew): he who was sent, God's gift, the one to whom it belongs; (Israel): peaceful
Shilpa: (Indian): well proportioned
Shima: (Japanese): true intention
Shirley: (English): bright meadow
Shona/Shonda: (Irish): a form of Jane, which means gift from God
Shoshana: (Arabic): white lily
Shu: (Chinese): kind, gentle
Shula: (Arabic): flaming, bright
Shura: (Russian): defender of mankind
Sibley: (English): sibling, friendly
Sibyl/Sybil/Cybil: (English): a seer or prophetess
Sidney/Sydney: (French): from Saint Denis
Sienna: (Italian): reddish brown in color
Sierra: (Spanish): mountain; (Irish): dark
Signe/Signy: (Latin): sign
Signourney: (English): victorious conquerer
Silvia/Sylvia: (Latin): forest
Silver: (English): precious metal
Simone: (French): one who listens well
Sinead: (Irish): gift from God
Siobhan: (Irish): gift from God
Siri: (Scandinavian): beautiful victory
Skye: (English): sky
Skylar/Skyler: (English): a scholar
Sloan: (English): raid; (Irish, Celtic, Scottish & Gaelic): fighter, warrior
Snow: (American): frozen rain
Solana: (Latin): from the east; (Spanish): sunshine
Solange: (French): religious and dignified
Soledad: (Spanish): solitary
Solita: (Latin): solitary
Sondra: (Greek): defender of mankind
Song: (Chinese): pine tree
Sonja/Sonia/Sonya: (Scandinavian): wisdom
Sonora: (Spanish): pleasant sounding
Sophia/Sofia/Sophie: (Greek & Biblical): wisdom
Sophie: (Greek): wisdom
Sora: (Native American): chirping songbird
Sorina: (Romanian): sun
Spencer/Spenser: (English): dispenser of provisions
Spica: (Latin): ear of wheat, a star in the constellation Virgo

Spring: (English): the spring season
Stacy/Stacey: (English): productive, resurrection
Starr: (English & American): star
Stella: (French, Italian & Greek): star
Stephanie: (Greek): crowned in victory
Stevie: (English & American): from the name Steven, which means crowned one
Stormy: (English): tempest; (American): impetuous nature
Suki: (Japanese): loved one
Sula: (Icelandic): large sea bird
Summer: (English): the summer season
Suni: (Zuni): native, a member of our tribe
Sunshine: (English): brilliant rays from the sun
Suri: (Todas): pointy nose
Surya: (Sanskrit): a sun god
Susan/Suzanne/Susannah/Suzie: (Hebrew): graceful lily; (Israel): lily
Sybil: (Greek): prophet
Sydney: (English): wide island
Sylvia/Silvia: (Latin): forest
Tabitha/Tabatha/Tabbitha: (Hebrew): beauty, grace; (Israel): a gazelle
Tacita/Taci/Tacey: (Latin): silent
Taffline/Taffy: (Welsh): beloved
Tahira: (Arabic): virginal, pure
Tai: (Chinese): large; (Vietnamese): prosperous, talented
Taima: (Native American): clash of thunder
Taja/Tajah: (Hindi): crowned
Taka: (Japanese): borrowed
Takenya: (Hebrew): animal horn
Taki: (Japanese): waterfall
Takia: (Arabic): worshipper
Tala: (Native American): a stalking wolf
Talia/Tahlia: (Hebrew): morning dew from heaven; (Greek): blooming
Talisa/Talissa: (American): consecrated to God
Talisha: (American): damsel, innocent
Tallis: (French & English): forest
Tallulah: (Choctaw): leaping water
Tama: (Japanese): precious stone
Tamaka: (Japanese): bracelet
Tamara/Tamra/Tamyra/Tammy: (Hebrew): palm tree; (Israel): spice
Tameka: (Aramaic): twin
Tamika/Tamiko: (Japanese): child of the people
Tamira: (Hebrew): palm tree, spice
Tandy: (English): team
Tangia: (American): angel
Tani: (Japanese): valley
Tania/Tonya/Tanya: (Slovakian): a fairy queen
Tanisha: (English): worthy of praise
Tao: (Chinese & Vietnamese): peach
Tara/Tari/Tarin/Tarryn: (Irish & Scottish): a hill where the kings meet
Tasha: (Greek): born on Christmas day
Tatiana: (Slavic): fairy queen
Tatum: (English): joyful, spirited
Taura: (Latin): bull
Tavi: (Aramaic): well-behaved
Tawny/Tawnee: (Gypsy): little one: (English): brownish yellow, tan
Tayanita: (Cherokee): beaver

Taylor: (English & French): a tailor
Teagan: (Gaelic): handsome, attractive
Temperance: (English): temperate, moderate
Tempest/Tempestt: (French): stormy
Terelle: (German): thunder ruler
Teresa/Theresa: (Finnish): summer, harvester; (Greek): reaper
Terrene: (Latin): smooth
Terrwyn: (Welsh): valiant
Tertia: (Latin): third
Tess/Tessa: (English): harvester
Thalia: (Greek): plentiful, blooming
Thea: (Greek): gift of God
Thelma: (English): ambitious, nurturing
Thema: (African): queen
Theodora: (English): gift of God
Theora: (Greek): a watcher
Theta: (Greek): eighth letter of the alphabet
Thomasina: (Hebrew): a twin
Thora: (Scandinavian): thunder
Tia: (Greek); princess; (Spanish): princess, aunt; (African American): aunt
Tiana: (Greek): princess
Tiara: (Latin): crowned
Tiegen: (Aztec) : princess
Tierney: (Gaelic): regal, lordly
Tiffany: (Greek): lasting love
Tijuana: (Spanish): border town in Mexico
Tilda: (English): strength in battle
Timothea: (English): honoring God
Tina: (English): river
Ting: (Chinese): graceful and slim
Tipper: (Irish): water pourer
Tira: (Hindi): arrow
Tirranna: (Australian): stream of water
Tirza: (Hebrew): pleasant
Tisa: (Swahili): ninth-born
Tisha/Tish: (Latin): joy
Tobi/Toby: (Hebrew): God is good
Toki: (Japanese & Korean): one who grabs opportunity
Tola: (Polish): praiseworthy
Tomiko: (Japanese): wealthy
Tomo: (Japanese): intelligent
Tomoko: (Japanese): two friends
Toni: (Greek): flourishing; (Latin): praise-worthy
Tonia/Tonya: (Slavic): fairy queen
Topagna: (Native American): from above
Topaz/Topaza: (Mexican): golden gem
Tory/Tori: (American): victorious
Toshi: (Japanese): mirror image
Tova/Tovah: (Hebrew): well-behaved
Tracy/Tracey: (English): brave
Trang: (Vietnamese): intelligent
Treasa: (Irish): great strength
Trevina: (Irish): prudent; (Welsh): homestead
Trina: (Greek): pure
Trinity: (Latin): the holy three
Trish/Trisha: (English & Latin): noble

Trixie: (American): a form of Beatrice, which means blessed
Trudy: (German): adored warrior
Tryna: (Greek): third-born child
Tula: (Hindi): balance
Tully: (Irish): at peace with God
Twila/Twyla: (English): woven of double thread
Tyne: (English): of the river Tyne
Tyra: (Scandinavian): God of battle; (Scottish): land

Ualani: (Hawaiian): rain from heaven
Udele: (English): prosperous
Ugolina: (German): bright mind and spirit
Ula: (Irish): sea jewel
Ulima: (Arabic): wise, astute
Ulrica: (German): wolf ruler
Ultima: (Latin): last
Ulva: (German): wolf
Uma: (Hindi): mother
Umiko: (Japanese): child of the sea
Una: (Welsh & Celtic): white wave; (Irish): unity: (Native American): remember; (English): one
Unique/Unika/Uniqua: (Latin): only one; (American): unlike others
Unity: (American): unity, togetherness
Urbana: (Latin): from the city
Uriana: (Greek): heaven, the unknown
Uriel: (Hebrew): light of God
Urika: (Omaha): useful
Ursula: (Danish & Scandinavian): female bear
Uta: (German): rich; (Japanese): poem
Utina: (Native American): woman of my country
Uzzia: (Hebrew): God is my strength

Vail: (English): valley
Vala: (German): chosen one
Valencia/Valentina/Valene: (Spanish & Italian): brave; (Latin America): health or love
Valeria/Valerie/Valery: (French): brave, fierce one; (English): strong, valiant
Vanessa: (Greek): resembling a butterfly
Vanity: (English): excessive pride
Vanna: (Cambodian): golden
Vanora: (Welsh): white wave:
Vara: (Scandinavian): careful
Veda: (Sanskrit): sacred lore
Vega: (Arabic): falling star
Venecia/Venetia: (Italian): from Venice
Venus: (Greek): love goddess, little bird
Vera: (Russian): verity, truth
Verda: (Latin): young and fresh
Verna: (English): alder tree
Verena/Verity: (Latin): truthful
Veronica: (Latin): displaying a true image
Vespera: (Latin): evening star
Vesta: (Latin): keeper of the house
Victoria/Vicki/Vicky/Vickie: (Latin America): winner
Victory: (Latin): victory
Vienna: (Latin America): from wine country
Vignette: (French): from the little vine
Villette: (French): small town

Vina: (Hindi): musical instrument; (Spanish): vineyard
Viola: (Italian): violet flower
Violet: (French): resembling the flower
Violeta: (Bulgarian): violet
Virgilia: (Latin): staff bearer
Virginia: (English, Spanish, Italian & Latin America): pure
Vita: (Latin): life
Viv: (Latin America): alive
Viveka/Viveca: (German): little woman of the strong fortress
Vivian: (Latin): lively
Vivianne/Vivienne/Vivian/Vivien: (English): the lady of the lake
Vixen: (American): flirtatious
Vonna: (French): young archer; (Latin): true image

Wallis: (English): from Wales
Wanda: (German): wanderer
Waneta: (Native American): charger
Wanetta: (English): pale face
Waynette: (English): wagon maker
Wednesday: (American): born on a Wednesday
Wen: (Chinese): refinement
Wendy: (English): white-skinned, literary
Wesley: (English): western meadow
Whisper: (English): soft-spoken
Whitley: (English): from the white meadow
Whitney: (English & African American): white island
Wilhelmina/Wilma: (German): resolute protector
Willa: (English): protector
Willow: (English): willow tree
Winetta: (American): peaceful
Wing: (Chinese): glory
Winifred: (Irish): friend of peace; (Welsh): reconciled, blessed
Winnie: (Irish & Celtic): white, fair
Winola: (German): gracious and charming
Wren: (Welsh): ruler; (English): small bird
Wynonna/Winona: (American): oldest daughter

Xanadu: (African): from the exotic paradise
Xantara: (American): protector of the earth
Xanthe: (Greek): yellow, blond
Xaviera: (Arabic): bright
Xema: (Latin): precious
Xena/Xenia: (Greek): hospitable
Xenosa: (Greek): stranger
Xerena: (Latin): peaceful disposition
Xiang: (Chinese): pleasant fragrance
Ximena: (Greek): heroine
Xiu: (Chinese): grace
Xoana: (Hebrew): God is compassionate and merciful
Xuan: (Vietnamese): spring
Xyleena: (Greek): forest dweller

Yadira: (Hebrew): friend
Yadra: (Spanish): mother
Yael: (Hebrew): strength of God
Yaffa: (Hebrew): beautiful

Yalena: (Greek): shining light
Yama: (Japanese): from the mountain
Yaminta: (Native American): minty
Yamka: (Hopi): blossom
Yamuna: (Hindi): sacred river
Yana: (Hebrew): he answers
Yanaba: (Navajo): brave
Yang: (Chinese): sun
Yanessa: (American): resembling a butterfly
Yara: (Brazilian): goddess of the river; (Iranian): courage
Yashira: (Japanese): blessed with God's grace; (Afghan): humble
Yasmine/Yasmeen: (Persian): resembling the jasmine flower
Yei: (Japanese): flourishing
Yeira: (Hebrew): light
Yelena: (Russian): a form of Helen, which means light
Yen: (Chinese): yearning
Yenay: (Chinese): she who loves
Yeo: (Korean): mild
Yepa: (Native American): snow girl
Yesenia: (Arabic): flower
Yessica: (Hebrew): the Lord sees all
Yetta: (English): ruler of the house
Yin: (Chinese): silver
Yitta: (Hebrew): one who emanates light
Yoki: (Native American): of the rain, bluebird
Yoko: (Japanese): good girl
Yolanda: (Greek): resembling the violet flower
Yon: (Korean): lotus blossom
Yori: (Japanese): reliable
Yoshi: (Japanese): respectful and good
Yu: (Chinese): universe
Yuki: (Japanese): snow
Yukiko: (Japanese): happy child
Yumiko: (Japanese): beautiful and helpful child
Yuna: (African): gorgeous
Yuri: (Japanese): lily
Yvette/Ivette: (French): a form of Yvonne, which means young archer
Yvonne: (French): young archer

Zaba: (Hebrew): she who offers a sacrifice to God
Zada: (Arabic): prosperous
Zahara: (Arabic): shining, luminous, the bright dawn
Zaidee: (Arabic): rich
Zakia: (Swahili): smart; (Arabic): chaste
Zakila: (Swahili): born to royalty
Zakiyyah: (Muslim): sharp, intellectual, pious, pure
Zaltana: (Native American): high mountain
Zana: (Romanian): the three graces
Zara: (Hebrew & Israel): princess
Zaynah: (Arabic): beautiful
Zelda: (Yiddish): gray-haired
Zelene: (Greek): sunshine
Zelia: (Greek): having zeal; (Spanish): of the sunshine
Zelmira: (Arabic): brilliant
Zemira: (Hebrew & Israel): praised
Zena: (African): famous; (Greek): hospitable; (Persian): woman; (Ethiopian): news

Zenda: (Persian): sacred, feminine
Zenia: (Greek): hospitable
Zenobia: (Greek): child of Zeus
Zephrine: (English): breeze
Zephyr: (Greek): of the west wind
Zera: (Hebrew): seeds
Zerlina: (Latin & Spanish): beautiful dawn
Zesta: (American): with zest or gusto
Zeta: (English): rose
Zetta: (Portuguese): rose
Zi: (Chinese): flourishing, beautiful, with grace
Zia: (Arabic): one who emanates light
Zila: (Hebrew): shadow, shade
Zilla/Zillah: (Hebrew): shadows, shade
Zina: (African): secret spirit; (English): hospitable, welcoming
Zinnia: (English): the flower: (Latin America): beautiful
Zipporah: (Hebrew & Israel): bird
Zita: (Spanish): little rose
Ziva: (Hebrew): bright, radiant
Zoe/Zoey/Zooey: (Greek): life, alive
Zola: (Mexican): Earth; (French): famous bearer
Zora: (Slavic): sunrise
Zoya: (Greek): life
Zudora: (Sanskrit): laborer
Zula: (African): brilliant
Zuri: (French): lovely and white

9 781933 819747